Praise for *Au Contraire!*

"*Au Contraire!* takes you on a journey of not only uncovering cultural differences but understanding and appreciating these differences in practically every aspect of life—whether it is business, public, or private. . . . A must-read for anyone seeking to gain better insight into French culture."

—**Michael O. Davenport, Director, Human Resources,
UniStar Nuclear Energy**

"Mastron and Asselin have truly grasped the complex interfacing with French culture. And nobody's right or wrong, just different! I find *Au Contraire!* delight-fully validating—a great piece of work."

—**Nancy Bragard, Franco-American interculturalist, trainer, and coach**

"This new edition rightly underlines the regional and cultural diversity that contributes to the charm of France. The authors have moved France far from the clichés of an old-fashioned country. *Vive le dialogue interculturel!*"

—**Olivier Brunet, European Commission's Regions
of Knowledge Programme**

"Chock-full of practical examples, humor, and just the right amount of historical context, *Au Contraire!* is a valuable book for anyone working or living with the French. Even better than the first edition!"

—**Natalie Lutz, intercultural trainer**

"Give it three Michelin stars for both nourishing the mind and charming the heart."

—**George Simons, Associate Director, Diversophy France**

AU CONTRAIRE!

FIGURING OUT THE FRENCH

GILLES ASSELIN
AND RUTH MASTRON

NICHOLAS BREALEY
PUBLISHING

BOSTON • LONDON

First published by Intercultural Press, an imprint of Nicholas Brealey
Publishing, in 2010.

20 Park Plaza, Suite 1115A
Boston, MA 02116, USA
Tel: + 617-523-3801
Fax: + 617-523-3708
www.interculturalpress.com

3-5 Spafield Street, Clerkenwell
London, EC1R 4QB, UK
Tel: +44-(0)-207-239-0360
Fax: +44-(0)-207-239-0370
www.nicholasbrealey.com

© 2010 by Gilles Asselin and Ruth Mastron

Printed in the United States of America

14 13 12 11 10   1 2 3 4 5

ISBN: 978-1-931930-92-5

Library of Congress Cataloging-in-Publication Data
Asselin, Gilles.
    Au contraire! : figuring out the French / Gilles Asselin and Ruth Mastron.
        p. cm.
    Includes bibliographical references and index.
    ISBN 978-1-931930-92-5
    1. National characteristics, French.   2. France—Social life and customs.
I. Mastron, Ruth.   II. Title.
    DC34.A77 2010
    944—dc22

                                                    2010016897

DEDICATION

To Mom and Dad for the American bits and to Pierre for the French bits

—Ruth Mastron

*To my parents, Pierre and Denise, who opened up "international curiosity"
in me, my wife Chern, and all those involved in furthering intercultural
understanding and peace*

—Gilles Asselin

CONTENTS

vii

Contents

Contents

ACKNOWLEDGMENTS

No book is entirely the work of those whose names appear on the cover. All along the way of writing the first edition we were helped and encouraged by a number of generous people without whom we could never have completed the journey. We are particularly grateful to the editorial team at Intercultural Press—David Hoopes, Judy Carl-Hendrick, and Toby Frank—for their guidance and suggestions, which were always insightful even when we disagreed with them!

Special thanks are due to Paul Orleman, who opened doors for us at Rhône-Poulenc Rorer, and to all employees from RPR and other international companies who kindly took time from their busy schedules to participate in our interviews.

Other friends and colleagues who played an important role in making this book possible and to whom we wish to express our thanks are Nancy Babcock, Geneviève Brame, Christy Le Coz, Sarah Manire, Pierre Morel, Peggy Pusch, Joseph Rachel, Michel de Rosen, Jo Ann Ross, George Simons, Denise Starrett, Annette Stevenson, Severin Swanson, and Pierre Verdaguer.

We are also very grateful for the feedback we received since the publication of the first edition, which allowed us to make updates and improvements, and emphasize areas that we hadn't addressed. People who have helped us in this second adventure are Olivier Brunet, Roisin Donohoe, Alan King, Natalie Lutz, Vincent Merk, and many readers who contacted us to discuss particular points that caught their interest.

To all those mentioned and unmentioned, *merci beaucoup*!

comment décrire?
comment raconter?
comment regarder? . . .
comment aller au-delà,
aller derrière
ne pas nous arrêter
à ce qui nous est donné à voir
ne pas voir seulement ce que l'on savait d'avance que l'on verrait?
Comment saisir ce qui n'est pas montré, ce qui n'a pas été photographié,
archivé, restauré, mis en scène?

—Georges Pérec and Robert Bober

how to describe?
how to tell?
how to look? . . .
how to go beyond,
to go behind
not to stop at what we are given to see
not to see only what we already knew we would see?
How to comprehend what is not shown to us, what has not been
photographed, archived, restored, displayed?

—Translation by the authors

FOREWORD

CULTURE AND ITS EFFECTS

Culture encompasses many things. In fact, in a very real sense, culture encompasses everything. It can be defined broadly as the sum total of the way people live, including elements such as the environment, economy, politics, ecology, adaptation to climate, level of technology, concepts of health and illness, work, leisure time, family, religion, class, values, and beliefs.

Interculturalists often use the iceberg metaphor to describe culture. In this metaphor, as in reality, only 10 percent of the iceberg is visible above the waterline, while 90 percent remains hidden. The visible part of culture (also called "big C culture") includes obvious elements such as art, literature, music, dance, traditional dress, and cuisine—all the things that make a visit to a foreign culture different and interesting.

The invisible part of the iceberg ("small c culture") becomes apparent only after an extended period of living or working in another culture. In fact, the part we can't see is where we are most likely to founder. Here is where we run headlong into different values, beliefs, assumptions, notions of morality, and, in general, rules about what is and is not done, what is and is not appropriate. Spending substantial time abroad also allows us to understand the hidden elements of our own culture.

We are in essence cultural beings, and yet we do not realize the deep and important role culture plays in the ways we act and react to our environment. We are simply doing things in the normal, natural, and proper manner. Only when we are confronted with someone doing things differently—which we often perceive as abnormal, unnatural, and improper—can we begin to understand to what degree we are products of our own culture and to what extent our actions and reactions are culture-bound. Particularly in cultures that emphasize individual freedom and personal responsibility (e.g., the United States), people may be completely unaware of culture's effects in shaping their convictions and behaviors. Such people tend to see their actions as their own individual choices rather than as the result of cultural norms and attitudes.

We have time-honored traditional observances, while *they* have quaint folkloric festivals. In the same way, a Hispanic poet writes of a *curandera*, a healer:

> *They call her superstitious*
> *We know what the facts are.*

> —Gina Montoya

Our culture also determines to a large extent what we believe to be good and bad, right and wrong. If our culture tells us that a good person is someone who is autonomous, competitive, independent, and out for him- or herself, then actions that lead to this goal are good. If instead our culture evaluates the goodness of people by how much respect they show toward parents and elders, and how well they look after them, different actions will then become desirable. Some of the actions that were good because they led to autonomy will now be considered bad because they interfere with close family relationships, obligations, and duties.

The challenge, then, is to imagine a place in which things that seem odd or even wrong to us could be normal and proper. In other words, we must try to enter the assumptive world of the other culture to understand how it works and makes sense. In order to do this, we have to look beyond what we are given to see, to look for the subtle, invisible connections. What we note as only peripherally interesting—or not interesting at all—may be the key to a cultural characteristic. What is not obvious or is even unsaid or invisible to us may actually unlock a door to another culture's reality. And our awareness of obvious and not so obvious connections, of what "naturally" goes together, and of what constitutes cause and effect is the way we begin to learn another culture.

A COMMON FRAME OF REFERENCE
FOR MUTUAL RECOGNITION

Culture begins as soon as we are born. It is so much a part of us that it is difficult to understand, much less express, its essence. Sanche de Gramont, a Frenchman who settled in the United States and Americanized his name to Ted Morgan, constructs an evocative French cultural collage.

The French occupy an area colored in green in my atlas, with borders and terrain features. They speak a language distinguishable from other languages, which French writers have used to compose a literature. They obey (or disobey) the same laws, and are ruled by and overthrow the same governments. They recognize certain events as forming their history, and some of these events are reinterpreted to contribute to a sense of national kinship. The past is a lesson to be learned and a legacy to draw from.

Finally, there is a common frame of reference by which the nation's inhabitants know one another to be French. It is not revealed by the study of physical appearance or personality traits, for there again one falls into the stereotypes such as the *bon vivant* anarchist or the rationalist-libertine. It is a fund of data acquired by being raised in a country, knowledge less learned than absorbed through the pores as well as the mind: a mixture of proverbs like "Long as a day without bread" and trademarks like the Michelin-tire man, sermons and travelogues, prohibitions and platitudes, menus and metro tickets, the inbred notion of a certain way things are done and said (1969, x–xi).

Roger Rosenblatt creates a similar American collage:

We celebrate ourselves and sing ourselves. We've sung ourselves so often we may have forgotten the reasons why. Open your eyes and take it in. The quiet little towns sit like drowsy dogs at the sides of the rivers. The city office buildings mirror one another in walls of blackened glass. Sing airport noises, freeway noises and broad smiles and arm-wrestling matches in a Minnesota diner with the President watching *Rocky* on TV and Bix Beiderbecke tooting blues in the corner. How about them Mets? O Kissinger. O Cher. The bellowing variety, the great mixed bag of nations. Of course we celebrate ourselves. The fact of our existence is reason enough to shout.

But can you pin it down precisely? In a week or two, a hundred million citizens will be cooing at the Statue of Liberty and popping Chinese firecrackers like machine guns far away. Another Fourth. Can anyone say why, exactly, we think we're something special? After all, the Chinese made more than firecrackers, and the Greeks and the Romans ran the world once too (not that we really do). In a heavenly accounting, those civilizations could provide a hefty list of what they offered to the world. If St. Peter asked Americans what they have offered, what would you say? Do car phones count?

... And still, can you pin it down? Sitting cross-legged on the green, sucking on your McDonald's vanilla shake, listening to the American

Legion band play Dolly Parton songs on tubas, can you say what makes you feel different, special, pleased? Maybe it's because you are in a place where the self came to discover what it could do on its own. Because of an unspoken awareness that all people everywhere are alone with their possibilities and that you live where that fact, both the menace and the dream of it, is the message of the land. Because the country is inside you: better or worse as you are better or worse; fairer, saner, kinder as you are any of those things. At night lie still and feel the struggles of your countrymen to make the progress of the nation fit the progress of their souls. They celebrate themselves and sing themselves. (1986, 24–25)

What is remarkable about these two accounts is that, in their specificity, they are both intensely personal and collective. A particular French or American person reading the description of his or her own culture might not assign the same importance to each element as the authors do, but he or she will recognize virtually all of them, and they will resonate internally in a way that the other culture's description cannot. As de Gramont notes, knowledge of these things is acquired through osmosis. It is "less learned than absorbed through the pores as well as the mind" (1969, xi).

These elements are part of our internal landscape, like the trees in a favorite park. They were in the park the first time we visited it, and, as far as we can tell, they have always been there, although cognitively we know that they were planted at some specific time. If you grew up in a Western culture, try to remember the very first time you saw a picture of, say, the *Mona Lisa* or the first time you heard Beethoven's Ninth. Most of us are unable to recall at what point such things first entered our consciousness, and yet we can all recognize them instantly.

Not Another Book about France!

The French have been observed, analyzed, dissected, praised, and denounced by thousands of commentators from the moment they became an identifiable tribe. Julius Caesar did it, as did Heinrich Heine, Thomas Jefferson, and many others. More recently, Raymonde Carroll, Laurence Wylie, Richard Bernstein, Ted Stanger, Jean-Benoît Nadeau, and Julie Barlow have taken up the challenge. So what's different about *this* book?

Like the impressive list of people above, we, the authors of this book, deal with French and American beliefs, assumptions, and patterns of living. In addition, and unlike most of the writers above, we specifically address the cultural interactions of French and Americans in the various contexts where people come together. An understanding of hidden and often unconscious cultural patterns is essential for achieving pleasant, beneficial, and lasting relationships with each other. We believe that with this understanding, you will have the resources needed to deal with unfamiliar situations that a simplistic list of dos and don'ts cannot provide. Therefore, we offer practical information that can be of immediate use.

Our approach is to bring into awareness the invisible cultural forces that inform or govern French and American behaviors. We provide some suggestions and guidelines throughout the book that will facilitate interaction, but more importantly, we explore what lies behind observable behavior: assumptions, attitudes, patterns of thought and belief, and so on. The guidelines we offer are not checklists or techniques for avoiding faux pas or getting French or American people to do what you want them to. Instead, we provide the tools that will help you think through a given situation or deal with a relationship based on your own knowledge of French and American cultures, thus enabling you to develop your own creative and appropriate response.

Through our own life experiences, each of us has already developed a sophisticated set of intercultural communication skills, but we may never have thought of them in such a framework. Imagine for a moment that you have an elderly relative who is very ill in the hospital and the prognosis is not good. You have to convey this message to three other people in your family: a small child (about three or four years old), a young adult (about 25), and an older person (about the same age as the sick person).

Take a moment to think about adapting the message to the characteristics of each of these people. What elements will you take into account? How will you decide what to say and what not to say? How will you determine exactly how the message will be delivered? When and where will you deliver the message? What about body language, tone of voice, facial expression?

You probably determined that many elements of this communication would need to be adapted in order for your message to be delivered effectively. You may even have had to think about what "effective" would mean in this context, considering each person's emotional state as well as his or her need for information.

For the small child, you may have decided that a simplified vocabulary would be appropriate, so you would avoid medical terminology he or she might not understand. You might want to reassure the child physically by sitting or squatting at a lower height or by taking him or her on your lap. You might consider the child's relationship to the sick relative—is it Grandma or Grandpa or a more distant relation? What is the child's relationship to you?

The young adult might be able to absorb more complex medical information, but might also need to be reassured. This person might want to take a more active role and ask what he or she could do to help either the sick person or other family members, and might look to you to provide this information. Again, the relationships among the young adult, the sick relative, and you will need to be considered.

The older adult might need even more emotional support, particularly if the sick person is a spouse or sibling. Depending on his or her own health, the news could be extremely distressing and you would need to be ready for such a reaction.

This example illustrates the central skill of intercultural communication: considering and adapting all elements of communication so that the person you are dealing with can take in, understand, and use what you have to say. You already know how to do this for family members of different ages, even when you have a difficult message to deliver. In fact, it's so natural to do this that it may seem odd or difficult to describe how you thought about the question. Once you understand the frame of reference of your intercultural colleagues, you will be able to do the same thing for them.

Regardless of how you adapt your communication style, you can remain authentic and true to yourself and your own values. You are not changing who you are, only how you present yourself and your message. Just as you would not wear grubby jeans to a four-star restaurant or evening clothes to paint a closet, you choose how to present yourself appropriately in intercultural communication.

As a bilingual, bicultural team, we bring to this work our complementary backgrounds and experiences of living across cultures as well as our expertise as trainers and consultants in the French-American intercultural arena. Born and raised in Paris (Gilles Asselin) and the United States (Ruth Mastron), we each struck out early on toward new horizons. Gilles' first experience of living in a different culture was three years as a technical assistant in Africa (Cameroon and Congo). Later, he headed for the United States, where he studied for several years and is now working. Ruth's first intercultural experience was attending secondary school in London. She also studied and worked in southwestern France for many years.

Our research and the intercultural seminars we have conducted with French and American participants have helped us to analyze the kinds of issues that cause misunderstandings between members of these cultures. We have distilled in this book the best and most useful analysis of and advice on French-American intercultural relations that have emerged from our work. It is a practical response to questions we commonly encounter "on the front lines."

Our intended audience comprises people involved in intercultural interactions in a variety of contexts and places: businesspeople, expatriates and their families, government and nongovernmental organization (NGO) officials, students, teachers, counselors, travelers, and anyone open to learning more about the culture of the people they are dealing with. While our primary focus is on Americans interacting with the French, it is likely that French people dealing with Americans will also find much useful information here. Readers from many other countries will also gain insight into their own cultures as well as how they are perceived by others.

The French part of our minds told us we had to have a structural framework for the book before diving in. Since our initial discussion took place over deli sandwiches in New York City, we came up with the analogy of a French meal, in which the proper order is an essential element. In fact, a penchant for classification and the proper order is an aspect of the French mindset. An example is the complex system of classification of wines and other alcohols, a government policy so stringent that it prohibited a perfume company from calling its new fragrance "Champagne." Things must be called by their proper names and must occur in the proper sequence and the proper fashion. This book, therefore, unfolds like a fine French meal: in the proper order and at the proper time, with the courses and the wines contrasting with and complementing each other.

Bon appétit!

PART I

From Far Away

ONE

Welcome to France

French cultural values, behaviors, and attitudes differ markedly from those in the United States. Perhaps what makes this discovery startling is that we look a lot alike. We've seen each other's movies, read each other's books, tried each other's food. We feel that we already know each other. A Frenchwoman observed,

> We think that we know everything about [the United States]: the derricks, the bayou and the skyscrapers, the rotating lights of the police, rock from Memphis, Tennessee. You can tell a Texan by his Stetson, a Californian by his biceps: seen from France, America is familiar to us.
>
> But as soon as you arrive, the signs get fuzzy . . . the contrasts cannot be avoided, day-to-day American life is filled with facts and values that disrupt the myth. (Vitiello-Yewell and Nacher 1991, 11; translation by the authors[1])

From the American perspective, too, the surface familiarity is deceptive.

Outsiders go wrong by looking at France through their own optics. It is always a jolt for veteran travelers to find that culture shock in France is more severe than in Saudi Arabia or Bolivia. Elsewhere, things look and sound different, so

---

[1] Unless otherwise specified, all French translations to English are by the authors.

you expect them to be different. France looks like home, or at least like familiar old postcards and paintings. Surprise. (Rosenblum 1988, 25)

Because of these surface similarities and hidden differences, French and Americans dealing with the other culture can find themselves in situations that are uncomfortable, confusing, comic, or catastrophic. It's as if, when an apple falls from a tree, it could just as easily fall *up* as down. People might react as you expect them to—but then again, they might not, as the following examples demonstrate.

An American walking his dog on the Champs-Elysées in Paris behaved as any good (American) citizen would; equipped with plastic bags especially for the purpose, he carefully cleaned up after his canine companion. A French-man who had observed the performance smiled and remarked in English, "*Monsieur*, you must be American!" Startled, the American answered, "Yes, how did you know?" The Frenchman explained that in Paris, the law requires dog owners to curb or clean up after their pets. But as anyone who has walked more than two meters in the City of Light can attest, nobody pays the least bit of attention—except, of course, newly arrived Americans.

One [American] traveler took a trip to Normandy and stopped in a shop in Bayeux, a town not far from the D-Day beaches, to buy a bottle of mineral water. When the shop lady determined that the traveler was American, she took the American's hand and said, "Thank you." "For what?" the traveler responded, not thinking that a 30¢ bottle of mineral water could have produced such gratitude. "For saving us," the shop lady replied. (Axtell 1994)

In the late 1980s, Coca-Cola ran headlong into French culture when an aggressive American manager was sent to Paris to "conquer the French soft-drink market." Though he achieved large increases in volume and per capita consumption of "The Real Thing," his go-getting, bottom-line management style rubbed French distributors the wrong way.

At one point, cafés in Bordeaux boycotted Coke to protest the rapid installation of curbside vending machines, which they considered unfair competition. Coke had to promise to withdraw the machines.
[The American manager's] emphasis on American-style sales gimmicks, such as huge promotional displays, also annoyed some French supermarket owners. So did his repeated insistence that they should stop worrying so much about profit margin, and instead focus, like U.S. store

managers, on volume. Some businessmen complained that he was too much of a "steamroller." (Browning and McCarthy 1991, 43)

Before the opening of the park in 1991, employees at Disneyland Paris (or Euro Disney as it was then called) were already upset about the dress code the company tried to impose. Everything from beards to women's underwear was specified in detail, and any deviation from the rules was cause for disciplinary action.

Labor unions protested that Disney's regulations about appearance were "an attack on human dignity." One spokesperson from the Communist-controlled union complained that the government, by allowing the company to impose such discipline, had awarded Disney extraterritorial rights and that the region was becoming "the fifty-first American state." (Kuisel 1993, 227)

On the other hand, once you have successfully negotiated the obstacle course, and after a few years (or decades), you may almost become part of the family—or at least a good neighbor. McDonald's hamburgers have been a huge commercial success in the land of *haute-cuisine*, despite the reservations of gourmets. In 2007, the chain's French revenues increased by 11 percent to €3 billion, and in terms of profit, France is second only to the U.S. itself. Cheeseburgers are served with local cheeses, and other menu adaptations have tempted more French people to "the dark side." "Le Big Mac" is offered in an exclusive whole wheat version in France to appeal to French consumers' love of bread (Valente 1994, A1). McDonald's European design studio outside Paris is developing new "upmarket" design environments.[2] Nonetheless, the leader of *basse-cuisine* ran into problems with its French employees and was accused of violating French labor laws. The chain also met with criticism from other quarters.

Perhaps the most galling aspect of the invasion of "McDo," as French children and adolescents affectionately refer to it, is its success in conquering the tastebuds of the younger generations. The Ministry of Education, working with a curriculum developed by the French National Council of Culinary Arts, has fought back with "taste education" programs in elementary grades designed to train children's palates to appreciate finer fare than their favorite Le Big Mac. Since its inception in 1990, the annual "La Semaine du Goût"(Taste Week) has evolved into a nationwide celebration of taste, French culinary heritage, and food-related careers. Schools, restaurants, local governments, and many other

---

[2] *www.timesonline.co.uk/tol/life_and_style/food_and_drink/article4560082.ece*

associations put together tastings, cooking classes, special menus, debates, festivals, and other events designed to highlight the pleasures of the palate, crowned with a prestigious competition in Paris.[3]

Starbucks Coffee launched its French business in 2003 via a joint venture with the Spanish restaurant organization Grupo Vips. Despite skepticism and resistance from traditional French café culture, Starbucks has imported its friendly U.S.-style customer service along with its coffees at more than 45 shops in the Paris and Lyon regions, and plans for expansion. "I could hardly believe it when the barista asked me for my first name when I placed my order," one woman reports of her first encounter with Starbucks Opéra, "but it was actually a very pleasant experience overall."

Success can go in both directions—once the French learn to navigate U.S. culture effectively as well.

> While yogurt has long been a familiar dessert, snack, or breakfast in France, it was seen as exotic or odd in the U.S. only 30 years ago. Thanks to a licensing agreement with U.S. food giant General Mills, the French company Yoplait was able to play on its French origin by featuring U.S. celebrities speaking a few words of French followed by the tagline, "Get a little taste of French culture." At the same time, the product line was gradually adapted to American tastes and U.S.-style marketing techniques were adopted, such as supporting the fight against breast cancer. Using General Mills as a cultural translator has helped Yoplait attain the No. 2 spot worldwide in its industry. (Croze and Croze 2008, 51)

Several young French designers have found success in the U.S. by combining the "culture of couture" of their French heritage with the American way of doing business, especially aspects like willingness to take risks, networking, and financing. Gilles Mendel recalls, "I remember going to a French bank in 1982 that had been working with my family's company for 35 years. I asked them for a loan and they never got back to me . . . In New York, I got my first loan of $200,000 from Manufacturers Hanover on the spot. You still cannot find that in Europe today" (Weisman, 2006, 2). Another French designer credits the work ethic of her American team: "Their capacity to work, the enthusiasm and their choice not to stop for lunch."[4]

By reading between the lines of these examples, you may already have a good idea of what hidden differences between the two cultures might account

---

[3] See *www.legout.com/* for details and events scheduled during La Semaine du Goût
[4] *www.iht.com/articles/2006/10/05/reports/rusa.php?page=1*

for problems or successes. Sometimes things go well, sometimes they don't, but it's not just a matter of the luck of the draw. Once you understand what's happening beneath the surface, you will be in a better position to react appropriately and choose effective strategies.

Interestingly, one of the classic areas of friction between French and Americans is a result not of their differences but of their similarities. Both cultures tend to see their own social model not just as the best for them, but as a model that others would do well to adopt. And in this, they differ from most other cultures! Many cultures see their own way of life as preferable or even superior, but the United States and France have sought to bring the benefits of their systems to the rest of the world, and in many ways (some subtle, some less so) continue to do so.

Americans often see their model of democracy, freedom, and economic opportunity as a beacon that can inspire the progress of other nations. The French tend to see their social model as the one other countries should adopt in order to protect human dignity, human rights, and quality of life. No wonder the two cultures often butt heads!

In subsequent chapters, we analyze the intercultural dimensions of why the French think and react the way they do, and we provide suggestions and guidelines for more mutually satisfying relationships. To begin, we will look at *what makes the French so French* by examining unique elements of French culture and how they affect French attitudes and behavior.

TWO

What Makes the French So French?

FRENCH ICONS: MARIANNE, ASTÉRIX, AND THE ROOSTER

Marianne is the feminine symbol of the French Republic and represents the daring bravery of Frenchwomen fighting for the Revolution, for freedom. She wears a red Phrygian cap, similar to one worn by emancipated Roman slaves, as a symbol of liberty and the republic. The very words *republic*, *revolution*, and *freedom* are feminine in French. Marianne continues to represent France in the European Union, appearing on French-minted Euro coins.

Marianne also appears on French postage stamps of various denominations and as a statue in every town hall in the country. Famous entertainers such as Brigitte Bardot, Mireille Mathieu, and Catherine Deneuve have served as models for these statues. In 2000 fashion model Laetitia Casta was chosen by the mayors of French towns to embody a new Marianne. Evelyne Thomas, a talk show host, was selected in 2003.

In late 2009, the mayors' association of France voted for actress Florence Foresti to become France's next Marianne. This vote has yet to be ratified by the State. Other candidates were Carla Bruni-Sarkozy, Laure Manaudou (a swimming champion), and Rama Yade (Secretary of State for Sport, originally from Senegal).

Marianne has undergone a more radical "relooking"—a popular "Frenglish" term, like "le footing" (jogging), that's based on an English word but relatively opaque to an English speaker—to reflect the multicultural reality of France today. For Bastille Day in 2003, the French National Assembly organized a special event in collaboration with a women's organization called "Ni Putes Ni Soumises" ("Neither Sluts nor Doormats"). In public recognition of the multicultural reality of France, fourteen women were selected to pose as "new" Mariannes: black women, Arab women, white women, women from France's poorest urban neighborhoods. They were photographed as Marianne, symbolizing strength, wisdom, intelligence, and freedom, and their enormous portraits graced the façade of the National Assembly in Paris for about two months.

The core concept was this:

> Au moment où l'intégration est parfois remise en question, où les droits des femmes—leur liberté, leur dignité, leur intégrité physique ou même leur vie . . . sont menacés, elles ont redit patiemment mais farouchement qu'elles étaient pleinement françaises, et que la République était leur meilleure protection quelles que soient leurs origines, ainsi que leur plus bel espoir et leur combat quotidien.[5]

> At a time when integration is sometimes called into question, where women's rights—their freedom, their dignity, their physical safety and even their lives . . . are threatened, they have repeated patiently but fiercely that they are completely French, and that the Republic is their best protection whatever their origins, as well as their brightest hope and their daily struggle.

In other words, whatever a woman's origins may be, she is first and foremost a citizen of the Republic—this is her primary identity and characterizes what is shared among all French people.

Astérix, the inseparable companion of Obélix in the famous French comic book series of the same name, is loved by European children and adults alike. He and his friends are symbols of the French inclination toward resistance and rebellion. Fighting for the survival of Gaul—later to become France—under the Roman occupation, Astérix represents the clever fellow who uses his brain more than his biceps, even after gaining strength from the magical potion of the Druid Panoramix. One Frenchwoman sees the inhabitants of Astérix's village as mirroring her modern-day descendants: "They're like us, exasperating but endearing. Astérix is our ego." Unlike his real-life inspiration, Vercingétorix (82–46 BCE), Astérix and his plucky friends beat the Romans soundly in every episode.

---

[5] *www.assemblee-nationale.fr/evenements/mariannes.asp*

Astérix fête ses 40 ans
(27-9 Astérix le gaulois a 40 ans !)

Astérix and his adventures have been translated into dozens of languages since his creation in 1959. But he remains firmly and identifiably French, even when he is speaking Basque or Swäbisch. In early 1999 a film was released with French actors Gérard Depardieu and Christian Clavier appearing as Obélix and Astérix. It was extremely successful and others films followed. Astérix and his friends even have their own website, *www.asterix.com.* An Astérix theme park is located north of Paris; valiant Astérix may well be fighting against the invasion of another "threat" to France and its culture: Disneyland Paris.

The rooster is to the French what the bald eagle is to Americans. Yet a rooster does not fly high in the sky, and it does not soar to reach high peaks and discover new horizons. Rather, a rooster wakes up the entire village at dawn, attracts attention from others, and never retreats from his defiant and domineering attitude toward the rest of the coop. Nowadays, French influence is certainly not as far-reaching as it used to be, and the world is much larger and more complex than a single coop. Still, some French roosters like to remind everyone that France has awakened the entire world to the beauty and grace of its civilization, culture, and language.

Coq Français (circa 1875), a sand-cast bronze by French sculptor Prosper Le Courtier (1851–1924); 15 ¾" (40 cm) tall.

An Italian observer notes that the rooster is a most appropriate French symbol:

> The choice is fortuitous, of course, because of a Latin pun, Gallus, meaning both the courtyard animal and the inhabitant of Gaul. The English pun could probably be considered even more apt. The brilliantly plumed cock is the first to announce the dawn of a new day to everybody, dominates his immediate world, seduces and fecundates all the unresisting hens, destroys his rivals, and crows triumphantly from the top of the dungheap. (Barzini 1983, 120)

FRENCH CULTURAL ELEMENTS

When trying to examine the "real" France, we need to be aware that there are, in fact, several Frances, all equally real. The nation and its culture are changing rapidly. External influences and the younger generations are making the country a different place, though not necessarily less French.

The France of the chambers of commerce and industry, of *l'Administration*, and of its official institutions could easily take up a scepter and crown and step into a monarchist regime—certainly in style, if not literally. An example of "old France" proves that it is still very much alive and kicking: if you meet with a French *notaire* (a certifier of legal documents who provides many more legal services than a U.S. notary), you refer to him or her as *Maître* (master). "Bonjour Maître Dupont. Thank you for taking the time to meet with us, Maître."

On the other hand, *la France branchée* (plugged in, hip, and with-it) of international companies, the Internet, and younger generations does not fit the stereotypes of tourist brochures. French teens are as tech-savvy as their counterparts anywhere, and French SMS language (or textese) continues to develop and to puzzle older generations. It is important to keep this contrast in mind as we discuss French particularities.

Deeply conservative yet avant-garde, dispassionately rational yet given to wildly dramatic outbursts of anger or affection, reserved with strangers yet passionate romantics: the French take in rationalism and logic with their mother's milk, and yet France presents paradox upon paradox. Quite simply, the French defy classification—even their own. Robert Moran and his colleagues observe, "the French seem to abound in contradictions and are not overly disturbed by them" (Moran, Harris, and Moran 2007, 531).

This being said, there are some elements that set France and the French apart from other nations. We can think of these elements as threads that, woven together, form the backdrop of French culture and society.

The Hexagon and French Rationality. If you look at a map of France, you will see that the country has a vaguely hexagonal shape. There is nothing vague about the notion of the hexagon in the French mentality, however, where it not only sums up the physical shape of the land but also shapes French culture. In official documents and tourist information pamphlets, an actual geometric hexagon often serves as a visual shorthand for France, and summaries of domestic news in the media are headlined simply *L'Hexagone*. The clarity and precision of geometric borders are reassuring for the French, giving them a firm sense of where they stand, figuratively as well as literally. Perhaps the dramatic shifts in France's borders over the centuries account for this need for security.

Laurence Wylie, an American professor of French civilization and culture with decades of experience in France, notes,

> It is difficult for Americans to realize how important [the hexagonal shape of France] is to the French. Not consciously, but at some level, I believe French people have the impression that it is good to have this geometric shape. As a matter of fact, it is rather difficult to persuade a French person that Americans may doubt that France actually does have this shape, since it requires so much filling in and cutting off. I think France is the only country in the world that thinks of itself as a geometric figure. And it is important to be a geometric figure. (1981, 31)

The French think of themselves as supremely rational beings—logical and intellectual. They have a high regard for reasoning, and their schooling, particularly secondary education, places a premium on philosophy regardless of the student's area of specialization. Unlike in the United States, where intellectualism is vaguely suspect, it is a high compliment to refer to a French person as an intellectual, and the realm of ideas for their own sake is valued and respected.

The vision of their country as a geometric structure—neat, tidy, organized, and clear—confirms for the French their prowess and pride in matters of the mind, Cartesians to their fingertips. Cartesianism, or Cartesian thinking, refers to the typically French way of reasoning or working through a problem. It is characterized by an emphasis on the proper approach, the right method for addressing the situation, rather than on practical applications. Cartesian logic will be explained in greater detail in chapter 15, "Dialogue between Two Worlds."

The Republic. Liberté, Egalité, Fraternité!—the clarion call of the Revolution— still resounds in the soul of every French citizen. Attached to these republican values are notions of unity, solidarity, and universalism. Unlike the United States, Germany, and other federations of semiautonomous states, France is one united country and one indivisible republic. This has not always been the case, of course, and the importance attached to republican values may reflect France's checkered political past: monarchies, revolution, restoration of the monarchy, two empires, assorted popular uprisings, occupation governments, and five republics. Whether or not republican ideals have been or even can be achieved, most French people believe in them deeply. With the exception of Corsica, even regions with a strongly marked local identity such as Brittany, Alsace, and the Basque country make their point with particular customs, languages, and traditions rather than with calls for self-determination or political autonomy. (See chapter 13 for more information on French regions.)

France has been divided since the Napoleonic era into administrative units called *départements*, which are grouped into regions. For the most part regional power has been minimal, but in the last thirty years there has been a serious effort to decentralize. Regions now have their own assemblies and their own budgets. Other powers traditionally held by the central government have been transferred to the European level. Both are a dramatic contrast to the centralization tendencies that have marked French history. Despite these changes, France is still quite centralized compared with the United States. In the Declaration of the Rights of Man and Citizen, dated 1789, the Revolution's founders affirmed that human rights are universal, superseding an individual's nationality, ethnicity, religion, or other particularities. Accordingly, a single system treating everyone the same is seen as most fair and equitable, as opposed to the U.S. model, which sees taking into account particular circumstances—gender and ethnicity, for example—as the best and fairest way to compensate for past discrimination and create a "level playing field." This universalist principle is still strongly reflected in French society and social legislation. For example, the health-care system covers all French residents equally.

Centralization and Authority. Centralization of power can be seen as the practical side of the republican values described above. In fact, centralization in the form of a centralized administration and bureaucracy has been the one stable feature in all of France's political landscapes. Louis XIV was not speaking meta-phorically when he said, *"L'état, c'est moi!"* ("I am the state!"). Strong leaders from Napoléon to de Gaulle have personified and ruled the French state, but even when not wielded by a single individual, power in France has always been concentrated. French ministers of education, for example, used to boast that at any particular time on any given day, they could tell you precisely what was being studied in every school in France and her possessions. Nicolas Sarkozy, sometimes called the "omnipresent president," is a twenty-first century example of centralization and power—keeping several fingers in every pie.

Paris is not just the capital but virtually the center of the French universe. It is the nation's political, literary, historic, economic, artistic, financial, and cul-tural heart in a way that no single U.S. city can approach. Look again at a map of *l'Hexagone* and you can see that all roads—and railways, for that matter—lead to Paris. The country's system of transport is built on the assumption that everyone wants to, or has to, get to Paris. In some cases, it is difficult or impossible to get directly from one major provincial city to another; you must first go to Paris.

Another example of the French centralizing tendency is the change in automobile license plates as of 2009. Previously, a car's number ended with the two digits that identified the *département* in which it was registered. New plates are issued with uniform national numbers; however, a regional logo and *département* number appear on the right side. This also brought the French in line with the European system.

Education. Public education—*"l'éducation gratuite, laïque et obligatoire"* ("free, secular and mandatory") in the words of the great nineteenth-century educa-tional reformer Jules Ferry—is the key to advancement and acculturation in French society and the keystone in the edifice of French culture. French pupils are reminded that the basic notion of sending children to school was developed by Charlemagne, the famous eighth-century king of the Franks.

Some of those children may not be overwhelmed with gratitude, as the French school system is notorious for its rigor, inflexibility, and competitiveness, particularly from the sixth grade to *le baccalauréat,* or *le bac* (secondary school degree). In fact, one's academic results and grades in secondary school virtu-ally determine one's options in higher education and career; doors that remain open in the U.S. system are slammed shut early on in France. School reforms and anxiety about falling standards are perennial themes in French life, and the fact that the entire nation is concerned about the rate of success of *le bac,* for example, indicates the level of interest in education.

Conscience and Practicality. In France, rules for good behavior tend to be defined by the individual as he or she matures. Precepts from parents and school are integrated from an early age, and each person develops an internal guide with a great deal of built-in flexibility. This internal guide is the standard against which a person judges his or her own acts.

Compared with the United States, French ethics are not set in stone and tend to be applied in a very contextual manner, taking into account all variables involved. This is paradoxical in light of the emphasis placed on universalism as a republican value, but the French easily distinguish between what is true in theory and what is true in practice. Everything in France happens at least twice: once *en théorie* (or *en principe*) and once *en pratique* (or *en réalité*). The two may be identical or may not bear the slightest resemblance.

In the contextual ethics of the French, practical self-interest is important, and they tend to admire someone who can gain an advantage in a situation. The American notion of the level playing field is not particularly meaningful to the French, who tend to adapt their approach to the context in an effort to give themselves an edge. Self-interest must be served, of course, but this should be done subtly, almost indirectly. Nike's "in your face" promotion style, which enjoyed huge success in the United States, was not appreciated in France, where blatant self-interest and greed are seen as tactless, unsophisticated, and brash. Hypocrisy in itself is not necessarily negative, but it mustn't be too obvious. Style counts; the way the result is obtained may be more important than the result itself, particularly if an individual displays a great deal of cleverness and panache in the process.

Telling the French that something is not allowed is a direct challenge to their ability to do it gracefully, finding an elegant way of bypassing the rules and not getting caught. Being able to do this well is a source of personal pride and satisfaction. It is a way of distinguishing oneself and standing out discreetly—or not so discreetly—from the crowd.

Aesthetic Sense. Many Americans are struck by how well the French dress them-selves and their children. They admire the elegance of French adults and the elaborate fashions worn by French children. Even popping out for a baguette at the *boulangerie* (bakery) around the corner may require proper dress, hairstyle, and makeup—a source of irritation for expat American women used to running errands in comfortable sweats, sneakers, and baseball caps. Although the French often dress more casually than they have in the past, in most cases style still counts, and good presentation is more important than comfort and convenience. The French are willing to put up with a considerable amount of physical discomfort to maintain their appearance. A Frenchwoman, for example, would sooner die than change into a pair of comfortable athletic shoes for the long *métro* ride home. French children's clothes are adorable and not particularly practical from an American viewpoint. They often require ironing or other meticulous care, and outfits for small babies may not have snap openings for diaper changes. These things are simply accepted as a part of daily life.

Esprit Critique. French conversations sometimes look borderline homicidal to someone who does not understand the language. Even in the family circle, voluble arguments and intense cross fire are fairly common modes of communication. For the French, even violent confrontation is not necessarily a loss of harmony in a group; rather, argument serves to move things along and prevent boredom and stagnation.

Consensus may or may not be achieved, but it is rarely an important goal. In the United States, groups normally aim for harmony and agreement as a way to reinforce group unity and dynamics. This can look bland and unnaturally detached to the French, who prefer to hash out ideas together and disagree with an idea rather than with a person—even when the disagreement is couched in quite personal terms.

What interests the French is not what people have in common, but their differences—*vive la différence!* Uniformity is dull; difference, exciting. Standardization is seen as stifling to individuality, an unacceptable attempt to impose mindless conformity. It may seem paradoxical that the French are simultaneously universalist and nonconformist. In fact, we can say that the French are universalist *en théorie* and nonconformist *en pratique.* On an intellectual level, virtually everyone agrees with universalist principles. However, because of their strong feelings about individuality, the French tend to resist rigid procedures and look for a more personalized way of doing things. This is a way of establishing their unique character, not knuckling under to an anonymous system.

National Solidarity and French Individualism. The French political and social system reflects a concern with national solidarity. Citizens in essence agree that the unemployed, the homeless, the poor, and the sick must be protected and cannot simply be left to their fate—at the mercy of economic forces. They accept a system of taxation and social contributions to make this possible. Despite calls for reforms and the French national indoor sport of griping about high taxes, the existence and goals of the social welfare system are not seriously called into question.

The concept of solidarity can be seen in support for striking workers, despite the huge problems caused by a strike. A farmers' demonstration that involved planting a wheat field down the Champs-Elysées snarled traffic for hours, but frustrated drivers nevertheless expressed support for the demonstrators' goals—and admiration for their style. Similarly, many French citizens show broad support for undocumented immigrants threatened with deportation.

Solidarity also involves the concept of sharing equally what is available rather than letting the strongest or most powerful get more than they need. Contrast American and French plans for increasing employment opportunities and the different assumptions on which they are based. American politicians and economists see business growth as the key element in job creation, but the French Parliament approved a Socialist-sponsored program (*les 35 heures*) in 1998 and 2000 to reduce the workweek from 39 to 35 hours in order to decrease unemployment by sharing available work among more people. There is considerable debate over whether or not the 35-hour week has been effective in reducing unemployment or encouraging companies to hire more workers. Unemployment and underemployment continue to be major concerns, particularly in a difficult world economy. Regardless of its success in meeting its original goal, the reduction of hours has become part of "*les acquis sociaux,*" workers' benefits or entitlements. Although right-wing governments since 2002 have simplified regulations and made it easier to work overtime, it is hard to imagine that such an important element of "French social progress"—what the French call, *la réduction du temps de travail* or reducing the workweek—would ever be called into question. If it were, it would probably lead to a modern version of the 1789 Bastille Day.

At the same time, the French may display complete disregard for the welfare of those around them—smoking in nonsmoking areas, for example. In public and even university libraries in France, books disappear and articles are torn out of magazines. That others might want to use these public resources seems not to matter; there is little sense of civic responsibility in relation to common property. In some cases, the need to *défendre son bifteck* (defend one's own steak) can be more important than high-flown notions of solidarity and unity.

Mission to Civilize. La Semeuse, the woman sowing grain who appears on French coins and stamps, represents the importance of agriculture in nourishing the people. By extension, in some contexts, she might also be a symbol of the dissemination of French culture. A slightly modified *semeuse* appears in the logo of French publishing giant Larousse, blowing dandelion seeds that symbolize knowledge. The words *Je sème à tout vent* (I scatter to the four winds) were dropped from the logo in an internationalization effort, but the goal of the company's founder, educator Pierre Larousse, remains intact: "To instruct everyone about everything." Even in a united Europe, *la Semeuse* has a symbolic role to play, for like Marianne, she appears on Euro coins minted in France.

From the sixteenth to the mid-nineteenth century, France was a center of power, culture, and influence. Despite dramatic changes in France's political structure and importance in world affairs, the *mission civilisatrice* (mission to civilize) has remained a fixed point in the French collective unconscious. It was a vital element of the French colonial enterprise and continues to inform French foreign policy. This attitude can come across as cultural superiority due to its implicit assumption that members of other societies will be improved by their exposure to and adoption of French culture. The French language is a primary means by which to spread its culture. Over the centuries, the upper classes of many nations have provided a French education for their children in hopes of improving their chances for advancement. French governesses ensured that generations of European aristocrats could express themselves in the language of Voltaire. Pages and pages of the great Russian novel *War and Peace* are in French in the original text, including the opening words: *"Eh bien, mon prince. Gênes et Lucques ne sont plus que des apanages de la famille Buonaparte"* ("Well, my Prince, so Genoa and Lucca are now just family estates of the Buonapartes"). The French have not accepted gracefully the decline in importance of French as a world language and have looked darkly at the progress of English as the international lingua franca. They have enacted legislation to protect the purity of French, prohibiting the use of foreign (read, English) words in advertising and in public places—although even a quick look through the French press demonstrates that the laws are toothless and rarely obeyed. At the same time, there still seems to be a real resistance to learning and speaking English. We will address this in more detail in chapter 4.

Social Classes and Democracy. Despite the French Revolution and its demands for *liberté, égalité, fraternité*, neither the entire aristocratic class nor its attendant mentalities were finished off by the guillotine. Status and rank still count in this hierarchical culture, and money alone is not enough to buy one's way into the inner circle. Nor is money a requirement for membership if one's family background is distinguished enough. Some modern-day aristocrats live quite modestly and work for a living.

The key to the upper reaches of French society is education. The French Revolution essentially replaced an aristocratic class based on bloodlines with an aristocracy of educational degrees. The French system is unapologetically elitist, despite efforts to reduce the pressure on primary and secondary schoolchildren. The brightest and the best are noted early on and encouraged by their teachers and parents. The goal is acceptance and success at one of the *grandes écoles*—a group of institutions of higher learning that virtually guarantees access to the highest levels of power, prestige, and wealth. Major French corporations often recruit directly from particular grandes écoles, reinforcing an old-boy (and girl) network of enormous influence.

Formality and Reserve. French people may be less formal than some other Europeans, but they are definitely more formal than Americans, and rules of proper behavior should be observed. The American habit of being instantly on first-name terms with total strangers strikes the French as invasive and presumptuous. They reserve first-name terms for more intimate relationships. As in many other languages, there are two ways to say *you* in French. *Vous* is formal and distant, while *tu* marks a closer relationship. The latter can also signify a power differential, as in the case of the mistress of the household calling the maid *tu* and being called *vous* in return.

Even body language reveals cultural attitudes. French people claim that they can spot an American instantly by the way he or she walks: arms swinging loosely, a bouncing stride, and an open, cheerful expression. French mothers remind their children, *"Tiens-toi droit!"* ("Stand up straight!"), and walk properly: arms held to the sides, feet straight, and a reserved facial expression.

French people are experts at creating islands of psychological privacy in crowded public areas as well as in small apartments. This desire to keep one's personal affairs private means that two people carrying on a conversation in the métro, for example, can barely be overheard by someone strap-hanging above them. Americans in the same situation see nothing unusual about carrying on a conversation at a greater volume or even from some distance apart.

THREE

The Weight of the Past

PAST, PRESENT, FUTURE

In the United States history is a source of pride, but it tends to be conceived of as a preface: events that happened in order to make possible the present and, above all, the future. Moving toward the future in the U.S. context may imply a rejection of or break with the past. This is due in part to the profound belief Americans have in personal and social progress. Things are better now than they used to be and will be even more improved in the future. From its beginnings as a nation, the United States has turned its face away from its past and has focused on the new day dawning. Physically and mentally, Americans discard what is old and eagerly embrace the new. History is yesterday's news. It may be interesting and even inspiring, but it has little bearing on everyday life.

It is difficult to overemphasize the importance of history to the average French person, and perhaps just as difficult for the average American to understand it. A French PDG (*Président Directeur Général*—equivalent to a chief executive officer, or CEO) making a presentation on his company's plans to open a new, high-tech manufacturing facility began by showing slides of the site and describing the pivotal battle that was fought there in the Hundred Years War (fourteenth and fifteenth centuries). The past in France is immediate and important. The French employees attending the presentation found nothing odd about it. In fact, by filling in the historical background of the site, the PDG was not just giving them an interesting footnote; he was providing them with a framework within which they could fit all the information they were given about the new facility.

Similarly, a French international marketing manager gave a one-hour presentation at a college conference on the topic of "Doing Business in the Middle East" for students and business consultants. He began by showing a series of regional maps from the Neolithic period (ca. 10000–4000 BCE) to the early nineteenth century. He described important developments in the region during the period (e.g., Code of Hammurabi, 2500 BCE) and religious figures such as Moses (Judaism), Jesus (Christianity), and Mohammed (Islam). In the last ten minutes of his presentation, he showed photos of the company's office staff in various Middle Eastern countries, pointing out that in some countries people were wearing traditional Arab clothing while in others they were dressed in Western business suits. Finally, he showed photos of the company's product line, which was electrical generators.

Was this a good, useful presentation? The French attendees thought so and took careful notes. The Anglo-Saxon participants were not so sure!

In France, the present is seen as the link between the past and the future; the future is the continuation of the past, so all three are inextricably interwoven. The past often represents the roots of a successful future and gives stability to the foundations of decades to come. Ample historical background also demonstrates that the presenter is competent and credible, that he or she *maîtrise son sujet* (masters his subject)—in other words, "knows his stuff" and should be taken seriously.

An American journalist analyzing the strategy of a very traditional knife-making factory in the middle of France put it in a nutshell: "In the midst of economic decline, Laguiole looked to its past to carve out its future" (Carter 1996, 34); the past in this case dates back to 1829. Most French people would agree with Southern American writer William Faulkner, who said, "The past is never dead. It's not even past" (1994, 535).

To the French, history, continuity, and tradition are critical to their conception of themselves and their culture. These things are not to be taken lightly or discarded easily. Change is not seen as intrinsically good, as it tends to be viewed in the United States. The French are willing to change, but only if they can see a logical reason to do so; the benefits of the change must clearly outweigh the loss of security and continuity.

In a way that may seem paradoxical, traditional French have a weakness for the avant-garde, although many of them prefer that it not appear in their living rooms. It is no accident that the very term *avant-garde* is French. In fact, once one understands how the French see past, present, and future as a continuum, it becomes obvious that there is no internal contradiction in being at the same time a traditionalist and a modernist. They are attracted to modern technology and gadgetry, and their infrastructure, particularly in communications and transportation, has moved in living memory from being worthy of display in a museum of obsolete technology to being one of the most up-to-date and efficient in the world.

PAST SUBJECTIVE

Here are thumbnail sketches of a few pivotal French historical figures of mythic proportions who resonate strongly in the French soul and psyche and whose influence can still be felt today. The intent is not to provide a history course, but to give non-French readers some key names and dates that they should know to show that they are serious, credible partners. Asking questions about French history is always appreciated, and many French people are both very knowledgeable and very pleased to share.

Vercingétorix (82–46 BCE). Chief of the Gauls during the revolt against Roman occupation in 52 BCE., Vercingétorix was forced to surrender to Caesar when he was cut off from forces trying to rescue him. He was paraded in Rome as part of a triumphal display and executed there after six years of captivity. Only the French could admire a leader who actually lost, albeit with courage and honor, but plucky little Astérix inevitably avenges his real-life counterpart against the Roman invaders.

Clovis (ca. 466–511 CE). Clovis was the first king of the Franks to reign over all of Gaul. He is considered by many historians to be the founder of the French nation. To this day, France commemorates his conversion to Catholicism and his baptism in 496. He was instrumental in spreading the Catholic religion in a barbarian Europe.

Jeanne d'Arc (1412–1431). This young woman was the mystical, religious liberator of France from the English. Her actions also began a consolidation of French power, since, at the time, the area that is now France was divided into multiple fiefdoms. She was burnt alive as a heretic, something for which the French have still not quite forgiven the English, and canonized as a saint in 1920. Revered as the patron saint of France, she has been used by the extreme right-wing *Front National* (National Front) party as a rallying symbol.

Louis XIV (1638–1715). Louis XIV, the Sun King, was largely responsible for the centralization of power and influence in France at a national level. He reigned as absolute monarch and was preoccupied with glory and etiquette. The castle of Versailles is proof of the extravagance and splendor that characterized his leadership of the country. His elegant court was the backdrop for many political intrigues, a tradition continued in the courts of his successors. Under his reign, France experienced her most glorious and frivolous decades and her *mission civilisatrice* to the world was launched.

Revolutionary Figures (1789–1799). Several important figures emerged during this period: Danton, Robespierre, Marat, and Louis XVI and his wife, Marie-Antoinette. The Revolution crystallized and legitimized public protest and insurrection as a means of taking power. It is still echoed in massive protests and national strikes, such as the particularly significant ones of May 1968. It took its inspiration from the Enlightenment philosophy that had also shaped the American Revolution thirteen years earlier. The French were not, however, gaining independence from a colonial power. They actually brought down the entire political structure and ultimately replaced a hereditary monarchy with a representative democracy. It was a true transfer of power from one class to another. The Revolution promoted the abolition of the class system represented by *la Noblesse, le Clergé*, and *le Tiers-Etat* (the nobility, the clergy, and the common people). It also hastened the decline of the Catholic Church both spiritually and politically. The bicentennial of the Revolution in 1989 was marked by parades, festivals, conferences, films, television programs, debates, and an avalanche of books and articles. Fascination with and debate around the Revolution continue to this day.

Napoléon (1769–1821). Perhaps more than any other single person, Napoléon, emperor of the French, left his mark on France and determined to no small extent what it is today. He changed the face and destiny not only of France but of much of the world as well. His original goal was the *rayonnement* (shining the light) of French culture as expressed in the ideals of the Revolution and the Declaration of the Rights of Man and Citizen—the *mission civilisatrice* in political form. He reorganized the French administrative and legal system (the Napoleonic Code) and consolidated and centralized the government and the economy. He shaped French culture to this day by founding or reorganizing some of its most important institutions, including the Banque de France (equivalent to the Federal Reserve Bank), the Légion d'Honneur (France's highest award for military or civilian achievement), and the grandes écoles that established the importance of engineering in the French educational system.

He also supported fine and performing arts as well as scientific and historical research. Archaeological finds made in Egypt during one of Napoléon's expeditions allowed Champollion to discover the key to hieroglyphics. He founded the Institut de France by regrouping and reorganizing five existing *académies*, including the famous and influential Académie Française, which oversees the content and purity of the French language.

Jules Ferry (1832–1893). Lawyer, politician, deputy and mayor of Paris, Minister of Public Instruction, and Prime Minister. Jules Ferry was the education reformer responsible for a set of laws bearing his name that made public education in France "*gratuite, laïque et obligatoire*" (free, secular and mandatory). His goal was to abolish clerical (read, Catholic) influence on the nation's public schools. He also extended public secondary education to girls and enforced the use of French as the national language of education.

Jean Jaurès (1859–1914). Jean Jaurès was a journalist and elected official, an intellectual champion of early Socialism, and the leader of the French Section of the Workers' International (Section Française de l'Internationale Ouvrière, SFIO), which later became the Socialist Party. He is seen as a hero for his defense of workers' rights and benefits, as well as for his pacifism and support for such unpopular causes as the defense of Alfred Dreyfus. Jaurès was the founder of *L'Humanité*, the newspaper once linked to the Communist Party; the paper is now independent, though it still presents a broadly leftist perspective.

Charles de Gaulle (1890–1970). Charles de Gaulle was president of the French Republic from 1958 to 1969. General de Gaulle was the quintessential hero who restored France's honor and her national soul after the defeat by Germany. He led the Free French forces from London during World War II and is seen as the liberator of the French nation. He led the postwar government from 1944 to 1946 and was called back to power in 1958 during the Algerian crisis. He founded the Fifth Republic (a new political regime), reinforced presidential authority by implementing universal suffrage (1962), and resigned in April 1969 following nationwide strikes and protests by workers and high school and university students (May 1968). He went on to attain a truly mythic stature in the eyes of many of his generation.

François Mitterrand (1916–1996). François Mitterrand was president of the French Republic from 1981 to 1995, the longest serving twentieth-century president and the first socialist president of the Fifth Republic. He implemented the first decentralization efforts in French history and was a strong promoter of the European Union. He was instrumental in abolishing the death penalty in France and in expanding the role of French diplomacy and military forces in world affairs, for instance, in the Gulf War and in Bosnia. He will be remembered for his efforts toward social progress and a better quality of life. One of his governments reduced the workweek to thirty-nine hours and added a fifth week of mandatory paid vacation. Through a series of ambitious and controversial construction projects known as *Les Grands Travaux* (The Great Works)—the Pyramide du Louvre, the Arche de la Défense, the new Bibliothèque Nationale, and others—he left his signature on the Paris skyline. During the final years of his life, several major controversies came to light, tarnishing to some degree the reputation he had built during his ascent to power and tenure at the Elysée Palace (equivalent to the White House).

LESSONS FROM THE PAST

The importance of history and its connection to the present and the future can be a sticking point in French-American interactions, both in politics and in business. Incidents in the closing days of World War II have had a profound influence on French foreign policy decisions. In 1940, after the fall of France, de Gaulle moved to London and formed the *France Libre* (Free France) government in exile. Churchill helped in this effort, albeit reluctantly at times. Meanwhile, Franklin Roosevelt recognized the Pétain puppet government of France in Vichy, which was in fact controlled by Germany and had sentenced de Gaulle to death; furthermore, Roosevelt's friend Admiral Leahy served as U.S. ambassador to Vichy from December 1940 to April 1941. These actions account for de Gaulle's initial mistrust of Roosevelt and the United States.

The relationship between the French and American leaders became more strained after the United States entered the war in 1941. Roosevelt, who in return did not trust de Gaulle, perceived himself as a political and military leader in a global conflict. France was a minor player in the worldwide struggle. De Gaulle, on the other hand, was determined to put France back into the war and to restore its independence. Their differing goals led them to take actions that were sometimes at odds with each other. Roosevelt planned for an Allied occupation force and military government to be installed in France after D-Day, as if it were a defeated enemy nation. De Gaulle instead sent his own followers in quickly to take over positions occupied by the Vichy government and set about reconstructing the French army and restoring republican order. In a strongly symbolic move, he ordered General Leclerc to march the French army into Paris, in direct defiance of Eisenhower's plan to arrive first with the Americans.

Such events form a backdrop of mistrust and some resentment in French dealings with Americans. Their history tells them to be wary, and though they may recognize a bit grudgingly the role of the United States as leader of the world, the French prefer to go their own way when they can rather than be seen as blindly following the American lead. This was clearly illustrated—by de Gaulle once again—during the NATO (North Atlantic Treaty Organization) crisis in 1966, when France withdrew from the military command and closed NATO bases in the country. The desire to show France's independence from U.S. influence in thought and action did not die with de Gaulle and is almost a reflex in most French politicians: France's refusal to allow American military planes to use French air space on their way to bomb Libya; Mitterrand's official invitation and reception of Fidel Castro for a state visit; and former President Jacques Chirac's involvement in the Middle East peace process. France also maintained a very vocal position against the U.S.-led war in Iraq, and formed a coalition with Germany and Russia to attempt to oppose and counterbalance the United States' actions. The pattern suggested by these events indicates that the French may be wary of American initiatives simply because they are American. The actual merits of the initiative may not be the issue.

At the same time, President Nicolas Sarkozy has expressed open admiration for many aspects of U.S. life and policy. In concrete terms, he has also sought a rapprochement and stronger cooperation with the U.S. and U.S.-led initiatives. Under his lead, France rejoined NATO's military command—to the point that a French Air Force general was appointed in 2009 to the position of Supreme Allied Commander Transformation in Norfolk, Virginia.

Despite the success of American pop culture, the French tend to be suspicious of the tidal wave of worldwide Americanization and standardization. They worry that it may sweep away their uniqueness and identity as French people. Their concerns are not only political and economic; they reverberate in the cultural area as well, as the French see their youth being caught up in the dehumanization of mass consumption.

Americans doing business in France need to take this touchiness into account. They may be seen as purveyors of American cultural uniformity first, regardless of their personal beliefs or the merits of their product, proposal, or management practices. Some Americans may be aware of this perception, but in any case, the weight of the past and the history of French-American tensions will not make their task an easy one. Bringing the best the United States has to offer may not necessarily be the advantage American businesspeople might believe it to be.

The past should also be taken into account in French-American business relations if the parties involved want to build a better future together. This means that Americans need to show an interest in the history of the company they are dealing with or acquiring and acknowledge the company's heritage and traditions that give its employees a sense of identity and security.

Implementing change simply to stamp the new management's mark on the organization, or because change and the future are more valued in the United States, would clearly devalue this heritage and what the company has accomplished. Taking a company in a completely new organizational direction without consulting or involving anyone *from the past* would cut the organization off from its roots and send the message that the company's past is valueless. The wisest decision might be to rely on cultural and historical informants, people who have been with the company for a long time, have witnessed its progress and difficulties, and are aware of its traditions, rituals, and symbols. By involving experienced and company-seasoned people in the process of defining a new direction and future, the new management shows both respect and appreciation for what has been achieved thus far.

FOUR

They Drive Me Crazy!
Ils Me Rendent Dingue!

DEFAULT MODE

Any description of a culture (The French are . . . ; Americans tend to be . . .) invokes an implicit comparison or contrast: The French are . . . compared with whom? Americans tend to be . . . compared with whom? Just as the mistakes of a nonnative English speaker tell you a great deal about the grammar and vocabulary of his or her native tongue, descriptions and stereotypes reveal at least as much about the describing culture as they do about the culture being described.

When speaking about cultures in a general way, it is important to remember the phrase *tend to*. What can you possibly say, for example, about over 300 million Americans that is 100 percent true of 100 percent of the people 100 percent of the time? It's better to express cultural values and behaviors as tendencies, since that is exactly what they are.

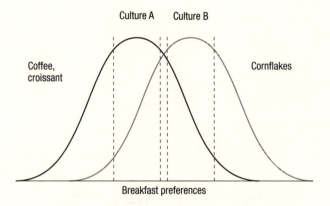

Referring to the chart about breakfast preferences, for example, we can say that people in Culture A tend to have coffee and a croissant for breakfast, while people in Culture B tend to have cornflakes or some other cereal. By phrasing the comparison in this way, we are trying to compare what is normal, accepted, and expected in one culture to what is normal, accepted, and expected in another—knowing full well that some people in Culture A have cornflakes while some in Culture B have a croissant, some have nothing at all, and some have an entirely different breakfast menu!

Computer programmers use the term "default mode" to describe what a computer does if it is not given specific instructions. Using this as a metaphor, we can think of our own culture as our default mode. When we look at another culture's values and behaviors, we are unconsciously comparing them to our own default mode and judging them accordingly.

For example, many Americans believe that French people, and particularly French shop and restaurant owners, are not friendly. French default mode for a shopkeeper selling a croissant would involve a polite smile or a more neutral expression and the following interaction with the customer: "*Bonjour, Madame.* What would you like? Plain or butter? Anything else? That will be €3. Thank you and good-bye."

This is an example of French default mode—what the French feel is normal, correct, proper, the right way to do things, the way things should be done. From an American customer's perspective, it might be described as polite but aloof, distant, and not friendly or personal—compared with the American default mode.

The notion that salesclerks should be friendly and personal is an important element in American culture, an example of which is the bagger in the supermarket—a position which rarely exists in Europe—who wears a name tag and usually addresses the customer with a friendly smile: "Hi. Would you like paper or plastic? Would you like some help loading this in your car? Thanks for shopping at Johnson Foods and have a great day!"

Compared with the French mode just described, this U.S. mode—what Americans consider normal, correct, proper, the right way to do things, the way things should be done—might appear forced, artificial, insincere, and even a little invasive to the average French person.

In Southern California, and increasingly elsewhere in the United States, the assumption is that waiters and waitresses should be very friendly and person-able. "Hi, I'm Heather, and it's my pleasure to be your waitress tonight. We have some really great specials I'd like to tell you about. They're all delicious, but my personal favorite is the shrimp fajitas seasoned with cilantro and epazote; they are just fabulous!"

To Americans not yet used to it, Southern California default mode might seem just a bit over the top. To the French, friendly and personable servers are probably going to seem manic and almost offensively personal. What we need to remember, then, is that we don't have to change or give up our default mode; we just have to be aware that it is *our* mode and not *the* mode.

PERCEPTIONS AND STEREOTYPES

Before we delve into reciprocal perceptions and stereotypes, we would like to share the "American impressions" of Julie, a 17-year old French woman who spent a month visiting the East Coast of the U.S. in the summer of 2007. Julie's account is written in the form of a telegram addressed to an American friend visiting her home in France. In order to put things into perspective, it is necessary to mention that Julie's father is a professional cook who prepares lunch and dinner for his family every day.

> Hello friend—STOP—Exchanging houses and home countries is very educational—STOP—France and the U.S. are definitely two very different countries—STOP—I met Americans who were ready to invite me into their homes the first time we set eyes on each other—STOP—Should I be suspicious?—STOP—Traveling along the East Coast of your country, I discovered many different kinds of landscapes—STOP—This makes for a real change of scenery as you cross the kilometers (more than six thousand) which contrasts with the sameness of the towns—STOP—Big difference in food—STOP—Too many burgers, too much sugar, not enough proper table settings—STOP—Your country is very big, but hasn't got the charm you can find in small French towns—STOP—Certainly a matter of History—

STOP—But it's still very enriching to discover this country and its customs which are so different from ours, even though the conditions of life are similar—STOP—I hope that France gives you this feeling and this impression of discovery—STOP—For example, you must have noticed that, contrary to what you thought, we have electricity in France!—STOP—I wish you all the best for the rest of your trip—STOP—See you soon—STOP—

PS: Don't forget to feed Médor the puppy—STOP—He eats salmon croquettes—STOP—

PPS: Don't worry if the card gets damaged on the way, you can't always trust carrier pigeons these days . . .—STOP—

While each person's experience is different, it is interesting to note that this young woman echoes the impressions of many of her countrymen and women who have explored the U.S. in previous generations. This suggests that, despite surface similarities in fashion and musical tastes, and modern communication technologies that are making the world smaller and more homogeneous, cultural differences are not going to disappear anytime soon!

French and American people know quite a lot about one another—or at least they think they do. Ask the average French person to tell you about Americans, and he or she will probably go on for quite some time about life in the United States—based primarily on exposure to TV's *Desperate Housewives* and *Without a Trace*.

Similarly, if you were born in the United States after about 1950, your first knowledge of France and French culture probably came from a romantic little cartoon skunk from Warner Brothers named Pépé Le Pew. Before you had ever heard of France, before you had ever met a single French person, if you had met Pépé, you already knew that the French are wildly romantic. And that they smell awful.

While Pépé teaches little Americans about the French, a cartoon cowboy called Lucky Luke teaches French children about Americans. "The man who shoots faster than his own shadow" teaches the French early on that Americans go for the "ready, fire, aim" approach as they shoot from the hip on their way across the wide-open spaces.

We all have images or stereotypes that come to mind when we think about other cultures. These images may be based on personal experiences, what we have seen and heard from other people, or from books, films, and television. Stereotypes are inevitable because they help us classify quickly and efficiently the world we experience, but they are nevertheless distortions of reality and need to be examined carefully and challenged—preferably with thoughtful intercultural analysis. We should also keep in mind that our images of other people say as much about us as they do about them.

At one international company, managers from several countries who were participating in an in-house leadership seminar were asked to give their opinions about people from other cultures. Here are some of their responses concerning French and Americans.

Stereotypes and Generalizations about the French. The French

- believe that if God lived on earth, he would live in France.
- have a different idea of personal hygiene.
- are culture and language elitists; are arrogant.
- engage in endless discussions without coming to a decision.
- seek perfection before taking action.
- are aloof and unfriendly.
- openly show emotion and are temperamental.
- are formal and class- and status-conscious.
- are reluctant to change.
- show no respect for rules, procedures, and deadlines.

Stereotypes and Generalizations about Americans. Americans

- are loud, vulgar, unsophisticated, and uncultured.
- are slaves to a money culture that is no culture.
- believe that the American way is the only way.
- act first, then think; shoot from the hip.
- are superficial.
- need to be the first everywhere and are cultural imperialists.
- believe in the "change is best" policy.
- are extravagant and exaggerate grossly.
- give more importance to glitter and hype than to substance.
- are obsessed with time.

Some of these stereotypes are obviously mirror images. For the French, Americans are too time-conscious, while Americans find that the French are not time-conscious enough. While stereotypes are generally negative, they can also be positive. Some of these above indicate potential for sharing, for taking the best from both cultures, or at least for finding something to appreciate. For example, Americans admire French people's romantic flair, their ability to balance work and private life, and their joie de vivre, while the French are impressed by American efficiency and organization, customer orientation, and ability to get things done quickly. Before going into further analysis, we will discuss some basic cultural characteristics that are not shared across cultures and that account for some of these stereotypes and misunderstandings.

Style, Form, and Substance. Style—in dress, manners, conversation, and in presenting oneself—is an important point of divergence. The French prefer a certain restraint, while Americans are more informal. The French dress with understated elegance; Americans like bright, even flashy, colors and comfortable lines.

In conversation French people prefer to make their points quite directly but in well-phrased, articulate arguments. The linguistic subtleties may be lost on Americans, who hear only the brutally frank (for them) opinions. American conversations and presentations, on the other hand, are designed to impress. The listeners become an audience, and fancy binders, graphics, and hyperbole are used to make a strong case.

The French generally feel that the "meat" of a discussion or presentation (*la substance*) should speak for itself. An American receiving a stapled stack of black-and-white documents instead of an attractive, full-color brochure might take the lack of embellishment as a sign of inadequate preparation or a lack of confidence in the proposal. For the French person, the elaborate American brochure might be seen as an attempt to mask a lack of substance with glitter and flash.

In presentations and meetings, particularly on complex or technical subjects, Americans often summarize their thinking in short bullet points, which they then comment and expand on without necessarily repeating what's on the slide. The bullet points serve to create structure and remind the speaker of what he or she wants to convey. For a French audience, depending on their level of English, this may be frustrating because not enough formal detail is provided.

French presenters, on the other hand, see slides as their primary method of conveying information, and tend to put everything they want to say and discuss into this written format. During the presentation, they may simply read the slides to the audience. American participants may see little value in such presentations, feeling that they could more easily read the document for themselves. We will share additional insights about French and American presentation styles in chapter 17, "Working across Cultures."

Cultural Superiority and Language Elitism. Despite the ambitious goal of Xavier Darcos—French Minister of Education from 2007 to 2009—to develop bilingual (French-English) students by the end of high school, France has a long way to go. While the French deride Americans' lack of foreign language competency, they often take a perverse pride in mangling "utterly unpronounceable" English words and are not themselves noted for being multilingual—or even close to the ministerial goal of bilingual. French students placed 69th out of 109 countries in the 2008 rankings of the TOEFL,[6] the Test of English as a Foreign Language, an English-placement test required by many U.S. universities as a condition of acceptance for foreign students. They scored 25th out of 43 European countries. It's important to note that these students are self-selected, since the TOEFL is not required by the French educational system; those who take the test usually hope to study (and possibly work) in an English-speaking country.

An article in *Le Monde*[7] speculated on the reasons for this poor showing, including the French educational system, which stresses the written language and acquisition of proper grammar rather than the more practical, spoken language. Interestingly, the article asked, somewhat tongue-in-cheek, if there might be a component of French DNA that somehow makes French people "fatally impermeable" to English!

Part of the resistance to (and difficulty in learning) English—and other foreign languages, for that matter—may be a mindset that sees the French language as the preeminent medium for human communication. Many French people feel that everyone should aspire to speak French. Any civilized, sophisticated, and educated person should possess this linguistic key to culture itself. Algerian-born writer Albert Camus elegantly expressed this notion in the famous quotation, *"Ma patrie, c'est la langue française"* ("My homeland is the French language").

France reinforces its sense of linguistic superiority by having an official body that actually makes decisions regarding what is and what is not proper French. The Académie Française,[8] founded by the Cardinal and Duke de Richelieu, was officially established by Louis XIII in 1635.

> He [Richelieu] believed that we could not do better than to commence with the most noble of all arts, namely, eloquence. The French language, which has suffered much hitherto from neglect on the part of those who might have rendered it the most perfect of modern tongues, is now more capable than ever of taking its high place, owing to the great number of persons who possess a special knowledge of the advantages which it enjoys and who can augment these advantages. The cardinal informed us [Louis XIII] that, with a view of establishing fixed rules for the language, he had arranged meetings of scholars whose decisions in these matters had met with his hearty approval, and that in order to put these decisions into execution and render the French language not

---

[6] *www.ets.org*

[7] *www.lemonde.fr/societe/article/2009/08/25/les-etudiants-francais-toujours-aussi-nuls-en-anglais_1231684_3224.html*

[8] *www.academie-francaise.fr*

only elegant but capable of treating all the arts and sciences, it would only be necessary to perpetuate these gatherings. (Isambert 1906, 182)

One of the relatively few institutions of the Ancien Régime to have survived virtually intact to the present day, the Académie's primary activity is to produce a comprehensive dictionary of the French language. "Every Thursday afternoon, for eight months of the year, the forty members of the Académie [optimistically called the Immortals] meet for one hour to discuss the dictionary. The last edition—the eighth—was published in 1935 and they have been at work on the ninth edition ever since" (Marnham 1994, 29). As of February 2010, they were up to *P*—through the word *plébéien*. The Académie's dictionary is available online at http://atilf.atilf.fr/academie9.htm.

For an institution whose operations move at the pace of a glacier, the Académie provides quite a lot of action in the political arena. The business of deciding who will or will not occupy a *fauteuil* (armchair) at the Palais Conti is fraught with politicking and issues that go far beyond literature or scholarship. Influential people in many areas of French life apply subtle and not-so-subtle pressure on the Immortals in the hope of gaining acceptance for their protégés.

Another example of the linguistic aspect of the *mission civilisatrice* is *la Francophonie*, which can be translated roughly as "the French-speaking world." The French government actively supports the teaching and preservation of French in former colonies and elsewhere, including Louisiana and parts of the Northeast in the United States. There is a parliamentary commission for la Francophonie, l'Agence de la Francophonie, which regularly holds a world conference. In 2002, Abdou Diouf, former president of Senegal, was elected secretary general of the organization, and he was reelected in 2006. World Francophonie Day is March 20.[9]

Merely speaking French is not good enough—one must speak it well, which means properly. French grammar tends to be prescriptive rather than descriptive, and poor use of language and spelling are detrimental to an individual's credibility. French schoolchildren are drilled with an exercise called *la dictée*, in which they transcribe a text read aloud by their teacher. More than just a spelling test, the dictée is a minefield of grammatical booby traps designed to trip up the unwary.

But the dictée phenomenon is not limited to the borders of France. Since 1994, there has been an annual international *dictée des Amériques* contest,

---

[9] *www.francophonie.org/*

organized by Télé-Québec, which draws significant participation throughout the world.

In the fall of 2008, over 1,300 students in *seconde*, the French equivalent of tenth grade, were given a dictée used in exams in 1976, taken from a popular novel and not thought to present any special difficulties. The results were catastrophic: two-thirds of the students scored zero (out of a possible 20 points) and only 14 percent managed to get a passing grade of 10. Worse than the raw scores was the kind of mistakes they represented, according to a professor who helped run the experiment. "80 percent of these mistakes are errors of conjugation and grammar, which are mistakes in the logic of the language itself."[10]

These concerns are very much in line with a general hand-wringing over the decline of standards in French. From test results to SMS French to suburban slang to English language TV shows and movies, it appears that the language is under assault from many sides. The erosion of their language resonates strongly with the French people, as they see the correct and elegant use of the French language as one of the glories of the civilization and an anchor of their identity.

Like many other aspects of French life, there is a correct way to use the language: *comme il faut* (as one must). The French educational system inculcates the concept that there is a superior, standard French against which all variations come up short (regardless of how popular those variations might be). As Canadians Jean-Benoît Nadeau and Julie Barlow point out, "almost all *francophones* [French-speakers] have a quasi-superstitious belief in the existence of a perfect normative French—mainly, but not only, in writing. Francophones' fierce attachment to the *norme* shows up in their sustained fascination with grammar and spelling contests" (Nadeau and Barlow 2006, 181). In context, the "spelling contests" are undoubtedly dictées—rather more than a simple spelling test.

Even French people who eagerly embrace *néologismes* (new words) and turns of phrase retain a belief in the *norme*. They're just less uptight about deviating from it, although some use slang in an ironic, apologetic fashion, just to make sure no one assumes they are misusing the language due to ignorance of the correct form.

At the same time, French is definitely evolving and changing, despite the efforts of the purists to maintain their notion of a language fixed for all time. It incorporates and quickly "Frenchifies" expressions from other French-speaking nations and from immigrants, artists, and visitors from around the world. Even the venerable Académie Française has stated, *"L'Académie ne refuse jamais la modernité. Elle ne refuse que ce qui peut menacer la pérennité de la langue."*

---

[10] *tf1.lci.fr/infos/france/societe/0,,4241551,00-dictee-nos-enfants-sont-nuls-.html*

(The Academy never rejects modernity. It only rejects that which threatens the permanence of the language.)

Perceptions of Arrogance. In her groundbreaking research on French and American perceptions of arrogance, Natalie Lutz reports one Frenchwoman's impression of an American colleague:

> I once met an arrogant American. He was so at ease. First of all, he took up a lot of space! He sat opposite me and leaned on the chair in a very relaxed way. As we talked, he was so at ease! He seemed to have no doubt that building relationships with others is easy. He was so confident and so comfortable! That's what made him come across as arrogant. (Lutz 2010, 72)

Certainly, the last thing the American gentleman wanted was to offend. He was just trying to put his best foot forward by being friendly and approachable. In the U.S., informality is often appreciated and creates a relaxed and friendly "vibe" that shows we are accessible and transparent. Meeting someone new calls for a display of this kind of "solidarity politeness" to put the other person at ease by making it clear we see him or her as equal to us. A casual air of confidence can put others at ease and show we are trustworthy. It also conveys that we expect we'll be able to get along with the new person just fine.

As opposed to confidence, expressions of modesty in the U.S. are usually focused around topics such as sophistication and intellectual acumen, which are often associated with elitism and snobbery. The French—for whom a core value is refinement and *savoir-vivre*—are on the contrary rewarded when they express such attributes.

And in fact, French culture prescribes a more formal and modest behavior style, especially when meeting someone for the first time. We might call this "deference politeness." Reserve, self-restraint, and formality show a degree of modesty since this type of behavior doesn't assume we'll get on famously.

Informal behavior is associated with the private sphere of family and friends. The private and public spheres in France are more clearly separated, which means that by expressing formality and respecting protocol, you show you know your place is in the public sphere, not in the private one. Informal behavior with those one does not know is also traditionally associated in France with unequal relationships, such as between the upper bourgeoisie and their servants or adults with children. An equal relationship is one where both parties do not assume that the other is "their friend" and maintain a respectful distance in the early stages.

Ironically, then, while both French and Americans behave in ways they assume will give the other a positive impression, their different attitudes toward formality can instead give a sense of arrogance. The American sees French reserve and formality as a confirmation of the French stereotype of snobbishness and quickly concludes, "What a bunch of arrogant, uptight, stuck-up snobs!" The French person, seeing American informality and casual confidence, can quickly see someone *arriver en terrain conquis* (arriving on conquered ground), saying in effect, "I own this place, and I own you." The French conclusion may be, "What an arrogant boor, throwing his weight around!"

Hygiene and Odors. The issue of cleanliness comes up again and again when French people and Americans come together. Americans complain that the French don't wash enough, while the French find that Americans are overly concerned with germs. While the French palate has developed to a point where it can taste a certain wine and determine what side of the mountain the grapes grew on, the American nose seems to be particularly sensitive to body odors. Proverbs such as "Cleanliness is next to godliness" suggest the almost sacramental nature of hygiene for Americans. Not surprisingly, American companies have developed a vast array of products to help people avoid offending others.

French people feel that a little natural odor is not necessarily objectionable. While France remains the world leader in fine perfumes, the idea of using deodorant to mask normal body odor has still not gained wide acceptance. In a European survey, researchers found that the French are among the most resistant to deodorant—only half of those surveyed use it—although they were close to average in their consumption of soap. Despite the gradual disappearance of the famous bidet in the home, the average French person takes one bath and 4.4 showers a week, making him or her one of the best-washed Europeans (*Economist* 1995, 56). Until they come to the United States, the French simply do not realize that natural body smell can be a serious problem. Therefore, Americans in France may simply have to adapt.

Thinking and Doing. The artworks of a culture express its values. It is no accident that one of the great masterpieces of American art is Grant Wood's *American Gothic*, showing a stern-faced farmer and his equally solemn daughter in front of their farmhouse. The man holds a pitchfork. These people clearly have work to do and are serious about it.

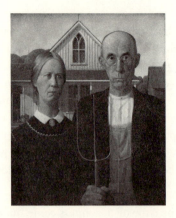

Grant Wood, American, 1891–1942, American Gothic, 1930, Oil on beaver Board, 30 11/16 x 25 11/16 in. (78 x 65.3 cm) unframed, Friends of the American Art Collection, 1930.934 Photograph by Bob Hashimoto, Reproduction, The Art Institute of Chicago.

It is no accident either that one of the great French masterpieces is Rodin's *The Thinker*, a statue of a man sitting—and thinking. French society values thought and ideas for their own sake. They may or may not have any practical application, and either way is fine. For the pragmatic, "can-do" Americans, this attitude is hard to understand and even more difficult to appreciate. What good is something that serves no practical purpose?

Auguste Rodin, S. 1131, bronze, 71.5 x 43.5 x 56.5 cm, Christian Baraja, Musée Rodin, Paris.

This thinking versus doing orientation is often the source of friction between French and Americans, but it is rarely recognized, particularly in business, where the pragmatic American approach clashes with the slower-paced, intellectual French one. We will examine this in some detail in chapter 15, "Dialogue between Two Worlds."

In the next section, we look at French and American ways of living and relating to the world.

PART II

Face-to-Face

FIVE

With the Self

B ecause of significant differences in the perception of "self" between French and Americans, we will give this subject special attention. This chapter is divided into three parts: a cultural approach to the self and individualism in the two cultures, a discussion of important American "self"-related notions and their French equivalents, and an analysis of the concept of privacy and its repercussions on interpersonal communication.

A CULTURAL APPROACH TO THE
SELF AND INDIVIDUALISM

What do I call my "self"? Language clearly illustrates the centrality of the self in the United States. More than one hundred words begin with the prefix *self-*, including *self-conscious, self-esteem, self-centered, self-realization, self-denial*, and *self-reliance*, to name just a few. The equivalent of these words cannot always be expressed succinctly in most other languages, and French is no exception. The only usage of *self* adopted by the French is the Franglais *self-service*; *le self* means a "self-service restaurant."

The French equivalent of the American *self* would be *le soi* (as in *confiance en soi*, self-confidence), but the word has never been elevated to the rank of a concept or value. Therefore, it is difficult to talk about a person's *soi* and, to most people, it might refer to a person's ego. The notion of "big ego" (*il a un gros ego*, he has a big ego) is generally understood in French—just as it is in English—as someone who has an excessive, inflated image of himself; a person who is *égocentrique* is a self-centered individual. In more technical terms, the "ego" refers in Freudian psychology to what the French call *le moi* or the Germans *das Ich*.

A more appropriate way to relate to the French person's self would be to describe his or her personality, which can naturally have hundreds of facets. *Personnalité* (personality) is in fact one of the most accurate cultural translations of *self* in French.

The difficulty of expressing the concept of *self* in French culture may also suggest that French people are not self-directed, in other words they are more outer-oriented to the extent that other people or environments may define and mold their identity at a young age—certainly much more than what usually happens in the U.S. We will come back to this idea when we analyze self-related notions such as self-esteem.

This does not mean that the French do not express their "selves." Their means of doing so, however, is very different from what an American would understand as "self-expression" (*expression de soi*). In general, French people tend to be more concerned with who they are, individually and socially, than with what they can do or what they have achieved. They think of themselves in terms of what school they went to, what position they occupy in a company, or what social level they have reached either by birth or by acceptance in a specific circle. A simple word or title often says it all, and people easily associate the person with the context and the meaning of that context.

Many American sociologists believe that because of the erosion of traditional values in American society, the self has taken on the importance of a "cultural quantum," occupying center stage in a person's life, with activities and preferences chosen and carried out in order to satisfy or fulfill that self. Marketers often tap into this phenomenon, trying to make the consumer feel that he or she is a unique individual with unique tastes and needs. American society encourages us with numerous success stories based on the achievements of a single individual, the self-made man or woman. Even the popular notion of leadership implies individual success where a person stands out from the crowd in order to lead the group.

For Americans, the importance of achievements is paramount. The American expression of the self takes the form of action or "doing," whereas a French person would rather express his or her "being" with insights, ideas, creative observations, or opposition to a group's decision—a way to assert one's uniqueness. What the person is really capable of doing or has achieved is secondary. The

French language does not have a simple equivalent for the action-oriented word *achievement*. The closest translation would be accomplishment or realization, in the sense of making something real (e.g., *réaliser un rêve*, to make a dream come true). A bumper sticker summary of the French mentality could read, "I am a human BEING, not a human DOING!"

Difference in France is valued because it brings creativity and originality to the fore. In this sense, the French value individuality: the right to be different, to express one's opinions and, most importantly, the subtle art of standing out from the rest of the group while remaining part of it. This contrasts with the American approach to individualism, understood as self-reliance and independence, where actions are taken in order to benefit the self and fulfill its desires. Individualism works differently in the two countries, and generalizations about Western cultures being individualistic need to take this into account.

A vivid example of French individualism in action took place on an overnight flight between Washington, D.C., and Paris. A seasoned traveler in a two-seat section offered his seat to a young woman who wished to chat with his neighbor. As the central five-seat section next to him was occupied by only one Frenchwoman, he thought he could simply sit there for a few minutes. "I'm sorry," the woman told him, "but these are my seats and I'm just about to lie down so I can get some rest." At that point, the Frenchwoman's husband came from behind and sat in the first seat of the middle section, preventing the startled traveler from sitting there. He thought, "Okay, I'd better give in or things will heat up *à la française*. It's not worth getting into a fight with these two morons!"

French individualism is expressed toward others in the sense that it tends to negate other people's contributions or even their presence. A person lighting up a cigarette in a nonsmoking area could be sending this implicit message to others: I don't care about your well-being and I don't care if smoke is going to bother you.

A French person who keeps bringing up his or her arguments in a group well after a consensus has been reached—and the person arguing may also be part of the consensus—sends the message: I don't care about the harmony of the group; my personal ideas are still more important and more valuable than the group making a decision.

A person "borrowing" a book in a public library in France—and, as we've noted, not returning it—is indirectly saying, I don't care if no one can use the book after me. I need it for myself and, after all, the city is there to provide for the public good. They will replace the book anyway.

This attitude may seem close to simple selfishness, but it is deeper than that. At its root, French individualism negates the "Other." As British writer Richard Hill noted, the French have "a visceral urge to assert their individuality on the other" (1994, 53). In the examples above, an individual affirms his or her individuality by negating the Other, which can be a person, a group of colleagues, or the general public. The Other is not instrumental to one's growth and development, and one neither needs nor expects positive feedback from the Other in order to thrive. In many situations, the basic assumption is that little can be gained from the Other, and one's ideas or personal satisfaction remain more important in any case.

We can say that for French people, the Other is part of their contextual environment, but without much value. Often, the Other is a stranger, an unknown person, or the general public. It might also be a colleague or an acquaintance that impedes one's satisfaction or happiness. However, family and intimate friends are never considered Others. They are rather an extension of the self. Family ties and obligations of friendship must be honored and leave no room for the standard expressions of French individualism described above. In other words, the type and strength of personal relationship involved determines who is Other and who is not, who belongs to the in-group and who does not.

This kind of detachment and extreme independence is foreign to Americans and distresses them when they encounter it in the French. American individualism does not negate the Other. Instead, it needs the Other in order to reinforce the self. Feedback provided by colleagues or supervisors boosts a person's self-esteem and compliments are continually sought. The Other—and his or her opinion—constitute essential nourishment for a person, and Americans place a great deal of value in what Others have to say about them. For example, many Americans have been concerned during contentious conflicts—such as the 2003 war in Iraq—that their image in the world was seriously damaged, and no one seemed to like them any longer. To most French people, this idea of being liked, especially on an international level, would not be relevant and would not get into the picture while making a decision.

The importance of the Other in American culture is illustrated by a strong need to be liked and a tendency for people to avoid, or at least soften, negative criticism when providing feedback. In general, one is expected to be a "nice guy" who promotes peoples' ideas and spreads a positive attitude. From a French perspective, American individualism appears closer to self-centeredness.

Paradoxically, France, as we've noted, is a country where solidarity matters, regardless of lack of concern about the Other. People are willing to pay huge social dues to support the unemployed and the poorest citizens. Even the tax system reflects this value with a not particularly popular tax on the wealthy called *Impôt de Solidarité sur la Fortune* (Solidarity Tax on Wealth).

The French might complain when the country is caught up in massive strikes but are generally not outraged. Other "revolutionary" efforts to make things happen are, in typical French fashion, also usually well received by the public. More than two-thirds of Parisians polled during the historical, massive strikes in December 1995—the most significant strike in the past twenty years—supported the claims of the employees who completely shut down the public transportation system for three weeks in Paris. While commuters were inconvenienced and lost time and money, they did not judge the situation only in terms of how it affected them individually, since the actions were being taken for the greater good of a specific group or for the benefit of the entire region.

Americans hardly ever experience the paralytic effects of a true strike, but when they are forced, for example, to struggle through traffic jams on the way to work because of a shutdown of public transit, they take it almost as a personal attack. "How dare those clowns prevent me from getting to work? Just who the hell do they think they are?"

The French lack of regard for individual Others—even the tendency to affirm one's self by negating them—does not, then, generally extend to domestic social and political affairs, where the French are usually more likely than Americans to stand together against an institutional Other such as the government or top management. The paradox between French solidarity and individualism can be summed up as follows: "On a personal level, I don't care if my cigarette smoke irritates you, but I will hold up the other end of your protest banner as we march together against the government!"

The contrast between French and American individualism can be further illustrated by the kinds of heroes each country idealizes.

French heroes reflect the importance of doing something great for the people or the nation. Jeanne d'Arc, Charles Martel (who stopped the Arab invasion at Poitiers in 732), and General de Gaulle are typical French heroes. By their talents and actions, they saved France from foreign invasion and bestowed upon the entire country a sense of pride and glory. The Abbé Pierre, an activist priest known for his fight against homelessness in France, and Soeur Emmanuelle, a French-Belgian nun who devoted most of her life to assisting impoverished people in Cairo, Egypt, represent the beloved French heroes of modern times. Although both of them have passed away (the Abbé Pierre in early 2007 and Soeur Emmanuelle in October 2008), their dedication to helping the homeless and fighting poverty has made them very popular figures in France. Another modern hero—certainly in the eyes of many young people—might be sports figure Zinedine Zidane, who led the French World Cup team to victory in 1998. Eight years later, Zidane's popularity was boosted beyond the sports sector thanks to an infamous head butt against an Italian player in the last game of his career during yet another World Cup final. All these people have brought fame, honor, or glory to France and, from a French point of view, have made it more worthy of respect in the eyes of the world. Of course, Americans also admire similar heroes such as Thomas Jefferson, Abraham Lincoln, Eleanor Roosevelt, Martin Luther King Jr., John F. Kennedy, Rosa Parks, and others who improved the lives of millions through their personal efforts and struggles.

In recent years, though, another type of American hero has emerged, possibly in connection with media hype and the adulation of celebrities: the individual who succeeds by surmounting some barrier to self-realization or by surviving personal challenges. People like Michael J. Fox or the late Christopher Reeve could hardly reach the high levels of popularity in France that they enjoy in the United States. While they have raised awareness and millions of dollars for research, their battles began with their own struggles against disease or injury—in other words, with their own self-interest. What makes them admirable in American eyes is that they set an example, inspiring others in their situation to fight and remain hopeful.

Chesley "Sully" Sullenberger, the US Airways pilot who landed his jet on the Hudson River in early 2009, turned into another type of hero for his fellow Americans. Many French people would think that, while his professionalism and self-control are certainly praiseworthy, he essentially did what he had to do in any weather condition: land his plane.

Similarly, "rags to riches" self-made individuals such as Andrew Carnegie would be admired in France more for their philanthropic efforts than for fighting their way from poverty to wealth. These people's individual actions and struggles wouldn't make them especially worthy of respect; they merely fought or are fighting for their own survival, something anyone would do in a similar situation. Although their endeavors are valuable, they did not save any lives or work for the good of others and thus, in French eyes, did not achieve anything extraordinary.

But in American eyes, these heroes represent role models who inspire people. Because of the examples of strength and courage they offer to Others in their daily lives, they have become popular. An American then uses these examples—these Others—to strengthen and develop his or her own self. Because they serve as great models of self-reliance and self-help, the behavior of such American heroes affects every individual.

IMPORTANT AMERICAN "SELF"-RELATED NOTIONS AND THEIR FRENCH EQUIVALENTS

Since the self and its attendant concepts have a central and unique role in American culture, it is useful to examine some self-related notions that have no direct equivalent in French culture.

Self-Help and Self-Reliance. These two notions exemplify the importance of a person standing on his or her own two feet in American culture. These ideas are taught early on to young children, who are expected to strike out on their own and be responsible for themselves as early in their lives as possible. Even though these concepts are positively received in French culture, they do not carry the same weight as in the United States. "God helps those who help themselves" translates into French as *"Aide-toi, le ciel t'aidera"* ("Help yourself and heaven will help you")—but in everyday life, help is primarily understood as being given from one person to another.

The wide range of books on "self-help" in any American bookstore would puzzle a French person accustomed to a different and more relational support system, and would certainly raise the question, "Why do Americans need so much help from themselves?" Small self-help sections, though, featuring translations of American works are beginning to appear in large Parisian bookstores. At the FNAC, France's largest and trendsetting bookstore, however, the self-help books were not up front with the best-sellers, but were in a subsection of "Esoteric Readings." Gibert Jeune, a popular Parisian bookstore uses a similar approach; it lists Self-Development books in its *Librairie Esotérisme* on the Quai St. Michel (Left Bank), along with Shamanism, OVNIS (UFOs), and *Cartomancie* (fortune-telling). A more appropriate way to address the "self-help" question in France is to talk about *développement personnel* (personal development)—not exactly the same thing, but closer to the concept.

Self-reliance does not translate directly into French either. The word *indépendance* expresses a person's ability to function on his or her own, and a reliable person is by definition someone you can count on. It is difficult to express in French that a person should count primarily on her- or himself.

A sense of independence is certainly favored by French parents when socializing their children, but not to the point that a ten-year-old child would be encouraged to set up a lemonade stand in her neighborhood or offer to wash your car. Youngsters rapidly learn to live and navigate within the parameters of French society. In other words, being self-reliant means not just going along with the complexities of French society but also being able, through a combination of cleverness and daring, to use it to one's advantage. A person with this capability is called *débrouillard(e)*—or *le roi/la reine de la débrouille*—which translates culturally into English as "resourceful." *Brouillard* literally means "fog," and *une personne débrouillarde* knows how to untangle things, where to go, or whom to reach to make things happen and avoid hassles. The typically French notion of *débrouillardise* refers especially to the ability to deal with complex situations and to find one's own way out of the maze of red tape in French society.

Esteem and Self-Esteem. Americans base their awareness of self on the assumption that their individual actions will bring results and lead to greater personal development and advancement. The importance of action is reflected in notions such as self-realization or self-actualization, which are synonymous with growth and development.

Self-esteem, then, is a direct and significant result of recognition by Others. Consistent with notions of individualism discussed earlier, esteem works the other way around in France. The term *self-esteem* can be created in French (*estime de soi*), but it does not exist in common parlance and is not used as in the United States. *Estime* in France is an expression of the respect and appreciation you show toward others, not yourself. You can have a lot of esteem for someone, and "to esteem" is a transitive verb in French (*J'estime cette personne*). Esteem is a feeling of admiration and respect one develops for another person once a relationship of some sort has been established.

However, French attitudes toward the recognition of the importance of self-esteem seem to be evolving, as illustrated by the popularity of the book *Estime de Soi: S'aimer pour mieux vivre avec les autres* (Self-Esteem: Love yourself to live better with others), published in 1999 in Paris. Written by two psychiatrists, Christophe André and François Lelord, it cites primarily U.S. source materials in the bibliography. The success of the book led Christophe André to publish several other books, including *Imparfaits, libres et heureux: Pratiques de l'estime de soi* (Imperfect, free and happy: Practicing self-esteem) in 2006 and *Les états d'âme: Un apprentissage de la sérénité* (Frames of mind: How to learn serenity) in 2009. Reviews for *Imparfaits, libres et heureux* have been full of praise. One of them reads, "To be oneself, finally. Not to worry about the effect we create. To act without fearing failure or judgment. Not to tremble thinking about rejection. Quietly finding one's place amongst others. This book helps us to advance on the self-esteem path, to build it, to fix it, to protect it. It helps us to accept and love ourselves, even our imperfections, not in order to resign ourselves, but for the sake of our evolution."

Similarly, while the concept of self-esteem might be considered "not applicable" in French schools and homes, attitudes are starting to shift a little and French psychologists, as well as other professionals, understand the importance of a child building a healthy, expressive self. A French school psychologist in New York stated that the "French practice" of self-esteem is expressed through the action of *valoriser un enfant*, to value a child. However, it is culturally interesting to note that a child cannot (or should not) value herself. An outside authority, parents or teachers, bestows upon her this *valorisation* (valuing).

Another explanation for the absence of a self-esteem concept is that French society tends to look down on pride (*fierté*) when expressed at the personal level; being praised by others is fine (though not very common), but praising oneself highly generally leads you into trouble. The French language distinguishes between negative and positive prides. One can demonstrate suitable modesty and self-restraint by keeping his achievements and other records for himself, or he can demonstrate what the French call *orgueil*, a form of negative pride. Boasting about one's accomplishments in order to prove that one is superior would be considered "sinful pride," or a *péché d'orgueil*.

As Sacha Guitry (French actor, film director, and writer) said, "Vanity is other people's pride" (*"La vanité, c'est l'orgueil des autres"*). Swiss philosopher and poet Henri Frédéric Amiel echoed Guitry's words when stating, "There are two degrees of pride: one where we approve of ourselves, and another where we cannot accept ourselves; the latter is most likely more refined." (*"Il y a deux degrés d'orgueil: l'un où l'on s'approuve soi-même; l'autre où l'on ne peut s'accepter. Celui-ci est probablement le plus raffiné."*)

Although the verb *to esteem* and the notion of esteem for someone else are given in an English dictionary, the current usage of *esteem* shows how American culture has shifted toward a more self-oriented pattern of appreciation. This sense of self-esteem may not resonate with French people, but they will fight fiercely to preserve a core characteristic of their self: *leur honneur* (their honor).

The French Sense of Honor. An American woman teaching English to adults in France had an unnerving conversation with a prospective student.

> He wanted to sign up for an intensive two-week program and was convinced that he could just about become bilingual in that time. When I asked him why he wanted to learn English so quickly, he explained that he had applied for a job with an international development project and that fluent English was required. He had apparently sworn on his honor that he spoke fluent English, so now he had to learn it, and fast. *"Vous comprenez, Madame, mon honneur, j'y tiens!"*

("You understand, Madam, that I have a great sense of honor!") I was so flabbergasted that all I could say was, "Then why on earth did you lie?"

Honneur in French is specifically the feeling that one has moral dignity, personal pride, and esteem in dealing with others. It is something that must be defended, but not always in the way that Americans might expect. In the example above, the student felt he had to defend his honor by learning English, bringing reality into line with his oath. For the American teacher, he had already lost his honor by making an oath that was false.

Many foreign observers agree that the French value personal honor and integrity above all. A French person's honor refers both to his or her personal pride and to notions of individual dignity. It represents a person's most important moral asset. *"Je déclare sur l'honneur; je jure sur l'honneur"* ("I declare/swear on my honor") gives the strongest proof of the person's good faith and honesty. It would be roughly equivalent to a more popular form of oath taking in the United States: "I swear to God."

The following quotations about *l'honneur* illustrate its importance in French society.

> *Les dons les plus précieux de l'esprit ne résistent pas à la perte d'une parcelle d'honneur. (The most precious gifts of the intellect cannot stand up to the loss of a speck of honor.)*
>
> —From *Manifeste du surréalisme* by André Breton

> *L'honneur, c'est comme les allumettes: ça ne sert qu'une fois. (Honor is like a match: it can only be used once.)*
>
> —Said by Marius in *César* by Marcel Pagnol

Perdre son honneur (to lose one's honor—for instance, in the example above, if the employer finds out that the applicant doesn't speak English) would certainly be the most terrible thing that can happen to a French person. Depending on the circumstances and the environment, it might also mean the person will lose face, a very embarrassing situation in a culture that strongly values relationships and community. In France if one becomes known as a liar, one's reputation is tarnished and, as a result, that person may never again be taken seriously. Saving face in the United States is less a question of establishing facts and more a matter of maintaining one's image. Spin management and skillful counterattacks are more important than a simple denial—or even proof—of wrongdoing.

To safeguard one's honor is as important in French culture as preserving one's psychological privacy. Yet, the French notion of privacy isn't quite the same as what Americans fight for in their efforts against invasions of privacy.

PRIVACY AND PROTECTION OF THE SELF

Privacy has been defined by L. Robert Kohls as the "ultimate result of [American] individualism" (1988, 8). Privacy in the United States involves more than just keeping one's nose out of other people's business. Americans demand the right to be left alone, to have time and space to be alone without interference. Such a concept simply doesn't make sense in more collective cultures and many French people find it odd that someone would want to be alone just for the sake of being alone. Phrases do exist in French to express such a need: *Laisse-moi tranquille!* or *Fiche-moi la paix!* However, they might be better translated as "Stop nagging me!" or "Get off my back!" Such a situation is quite specific and usually very brief, and you can *ficher la paix* to someone without leaving the room.

Conversely, there is a stronger expressed need for privacy in France than in the United States in terms of physical (protecting one's territory) and psychological privacy (protecting one's private realm). Foreigners notice how the French protect their physical property with fences and closed shutters at night. Also, the French invitation to "make yourself at home" entails many more restrictions than the American equivalent. Houseguests in France have limited access to various areas in their host's house. If they need an extra towel, for example, they ask their host or hostess to get it for them rather than rooting through cupboards to find one. Most American houseguests, on the other hand, try to be helpful and not treat their hosts like servants, while American hosts normally expect houseguests to help themselves—within reason—to what they need from kitchen and bathroom cabinets or the refrigerator.

Interestingly, there is no single word in French to translate the American concept of privacy. French people tend to think of the concept of privacy in the sense of keeping their private lives, well, private. Depending on the context, people might use words and phrases like *freedom, private life, personal intimacy,* and even *individual liberty* and *dignity,* as illustrated by the Disneyland Paris incident (see page 5). A famous wiretapping case involving the *Renseignements Généraux* (the French equivalent of the CIA) during Francois Mitterrand's reign was labeled as *atteinte à l'intimité de la vie privée* (violation of the intimacy of private life). Such elaborate phrases might sound pompous or euphemistic to

Americans, whose language allows them to sum up the incident more suc-cinctly.

French psychological privacy—the need to keep things to oneself or a ten-dency not to open up—is also a characteristic that often strikes Americans in France. There sometimes seems to be a wall around peoples' private lives, the height of which varies according to the person they meet. A total stranger will get very little attention, not even a smile, while an acquaintance may receive bet-ter treatment. An American psychologist who lived in France for several years described the French personality with a brilliant metaphor:

> The French personality is like a solid house surrounded by a beautiful formal garden and protected by a high wall in which are set pieces of [jagged] glass. It is difficult to get in the gate, but once you are inside, you are cordially received in a fascinating atmosphere. One is overwhelmed. Then the problem arises about how you're going to get out. (Wylie 1981, 60)

We often use the metaphor of a coconut and a peach to contrast French and American personalities. The coconut has a tough and not very appealing shell that contains pleasant meat and liquid within. The peach, on the other hand, is soft and inviting but has a hard core that is difficult or impossible to get into.

French culture strongly emphasizes a characteristic called *pudeur* in relation to interpersonal communication. The closest English translation would be "self-restraint." French people learn early on that personal information, or information that could possibly hurt others, should not be revealed or mentioned to just anyone, and that a certain degree of intimacy must be reached before a person can open up. The amount of private information French people deliver in public is therefore much less than in the United States. Talking about one's private life, or personal or family problems, to a person you do not know intimately would be considered inappropriate and weak, not to mention shallow.

As an example, compare the behavior of people sitting next to each other on domestic flights in France and in the United States. In France—and in fact, in most of Europe—people sitting next to each other rarely speak and quickly find a book to read or another "safe" occupation that maintains the psychological wall around them. Even if they decide to enter a conversation, it will always be very casual and neutral. Americans, on the other hand, are much more inclined to strike up a friendly conversation with seatmates, sometimes getting into relatively personal subjects.

A French person who reveals details about his or her private life to *un inconnu* (an unknown person) would be considered promiscuous in the sense that he or she is sharing intimate information with a total stranger in the same way he or she would with a spouse, parent, or close friend. This is not acceptable to the French, who open up only to their families and to friends with whom they have long and trusted relationships.

Americans would react similarly to a person who gives the same holiday gift to everyone—office colleagues, family, and friends—regardless of the significance of the relationship. Imagine someone giving identical boxes of chocolates to coworkers, spouse, children, the mail carrier, and parents. People with a close relationship expect that a little more care will go into the choice of a more personal gift.

Because of differing public and private spheres, it is sometimes a challenge for Americans to bridge the cultural gap with their French acquaintances and arrive at a mutually satisfying level of intimacy. French people, on the other hand, sense very easily at what point they would invade another's privacy and tend to treat Americans the French way—not asking questions at all, or asking in a very round-about way, which may seem like beating about the bush.

A few years ago, Alain, a French graduate student at a Midwestern university, became involved in a French-American exchange program. At one point, he was asked to help clarify some issues that were still unclear after lengthy telephone calls between a French mother and an American mother regarding their children's exchange visits.

While speaking with the French mother, Alain realized she was suffering from a serious disease. The American mother got the same impression, but neither of them dared to ask any further questions. Alain later escorted the American boy to the French family's town. Although she was obviously undergoing serious medical treatments, the French mother never mentioned anything to Alain or the young American boy and acted as if she were just fine. A year later, Alain learned that the mother had died from lung cancer. On hearing the news, the saddened American mother had a revelation: "This is French privacy."

While many people in the United States might like to share their grief and suffering in order to receive emotional support, such an attitude was deemed inappropriate by the French mother. She did not want to bother anyone outside her family with news of her frail health. Such an attitude may seem aloof and cold to Americans, but they should not take it personally. Preserving one's intimate circle and privacy is at the core of French culture.

In this area, President Nicolas Sarkozy has "rocked the boat" and deviated from traditional French cultural patterns. As a presidential candidate, he made a point of opening the doors to his private life, and photos of him and his family in casual attitudes and settings appeared in the press. His colorful love life was also openly discussed and, at one point during the campaign, his wife left him to live with a Frenchman in the U.S. She returned in time for the elections and to become briefly the First Lady of France before divorcing him early in his presidency. A whirlwind romance with model-turned-actress-turned-singer Carla Bruni reached the level of movie-star gossip ("hand in hand on the beach"—try to imagine President and Mrs. Chirac in such a situation!) and led to Nicolas Sarkozy's third marriage.

Since then, Sarkozy is keeping his private life more private, but a great deal of criticism has been leveled at him precisely because of his openly flaunting what French politicians traditionally keep—and continue to keep—to their inner circles, as the following anecdote shows.

An affirmation of French traditional patterns involved Dominique Strauss-Kahn, head of the International Monetary Fund (IMF) and one of the nation's most influential Socialist leaders. Following his admission in early 2009 of an affair with a subordinate, and before an internal investigation was concluded, various French ministers were quick to point out that this behavior had nothing to do with his extraordinary professional skills, which would continue to serve the IMF during a difficult period.

Finance Minister Christine Lagarde summed it up: "Personally, I think that private life should remain private and I hope that in this situation [Strauss-Kahn] will retain all of his talent, all of his aura and all of his reputation because it is quite simply essential that we have someone strong, solid and recognized as such heading the IMF." No harm, no foul.

Unlike Americans, the French don't seem to make a connection between a person's attitude and actions in his or her private life and what might happen in public; this is an area where the cultural gap is simply real.

SIX

With the Family

THE FAMILY CIRCLE

As in many European countries (particularly in the Latin ones), the family plays a central role in French socialization and in French life in general. The French are not as likely as Americans to relocate away from their families and, when it is economically possible, prefer to stay in the same geographic area. The concept of family tends to include extended family as well, often three or four generations.

> A cultural assumption shared by many Americans is that dependence, if not bad, is at least suspect. American parents raise their children to be independent, to stand on their own two feet. Somewhere deep in [the American] psyche there lurks the conviction that in the end we have only ourselves to fall back on. . . . In [French] culture, parents raise their children to be dependent on the family, not in the sense of being helpless but in the sense of relying on the family for advice and support (both financial and emotional) and regarding the family, rather than oneself, as the primary focus in life. (Wylie and Brière 1995, 81)

French families neither expect nor encourage young people to strike out on their own as early as possible. University students continue to live with their parents if they can, and if they cannot, they return home for weekends and holidays.

A French student in the United States was amazed to find that many of his classmates had chosen the university precisely because it was located at some distance from their parents' home. Some of them had actually come from large cities with better schools, which he took as evidence that their desire for independence outweighed their concerns for educational quality and reputation. Many American students pay some or even most of their own expenses, working part-time or receiving financial aid, and this may also play a role in establishing themselves as independent adults.

It may be important in this connection to note that American universities can be quite expensive, while public universities in France are practically free. This means that French students do not need to earn money for tuition. French parents generally expect to cover rent and living expenses while their children study so that they can focus on learning. The concept of psychological growth and maturity through fending for oneself does not usually enter the picture.

This tendency among the French to stay with one's parents as long as possible is reinforced during hard economic times. The difficulty of finding a first job and the perceived necessity of studying longer for a better degree make young adults more cautious about venturing out on their own. When problems arise, they experience an especially strong urge to get back to the family circle for support and advice. Even young adults who are working full-time may continue to live at home, and this raises no concerns about the adult child's capacity to achieve independence. When a couple marries or moves in together, however, they usually prefer to have their own place, ideally not too far away from either family. Families often gather for the sacred tradition of Sunday lunch, either in the parents' home or in a local restaurant. Look around the dining room if you have your Sunday lunch at a country restaurant; you will see grandparents, parents, aunts, uncles, and cousins spending hours in animated conversation. These traditions continue even with rising divorce rates and other social problems.

In the United States, the concept of family usually encompasses only the nuclear family, just the parents and children. This is the essentially autonomous unit, and these narrowly constituted families are expected to make their own decisions about where to work and live, what to do on vacation, and how to spend or save their money pretty much independently.

The importance of retirement communities in the United States reflects the expectation that "active seniors" still want to live and pursue their interests independently. Retirement facilities in France are not developed in the same way, although *villages retraites* with various levels of additional services have become more common. Regions like the Côte d'Azur, where the climate attracts retirees, do not usually provide separate communities to meet their special needs. Retired couples or individuals simply buy a house or apartment in the area and do not necessarily try to integrate with the locals or other retirees.

When an American couple marries, they establish their own home and set their own priorities. Parents may be consulted for important decisions, but if, for example, a good job is offered in another city or state, the offer is likely to be accepted. If a French couple or family have to move away for economic reasons, such as better job opportunities in Paris or other large cities, they will make an effort to return as often as possible on weekends and holidays. In fact, if a relative has a large home in the country, at the beach, or in the mountains, the entire extended family may gather there during the long summer vacation. This tradition is not reserved for the well-to-do, as it tends to be in the United States.

The *résidence secondaire* (country home or apartment) plays an important family and social role in France. Some people even prefer renting to buying their main residence in order to have their own cottage in the country or apartment at a seaside resort. This attitude also suggests the importance of quality time to be spent with relatives and friends outside the regular working and living environment.

Family time is so important in France that people rarely sacrifice it for additional income. Many Americans are eager to make extra money by working weekends, evenings, or even a second job. For the French, the additional income does not make up for the loss of time relaxing with family and friends. French employees may simply refuse to work overtime or on weekends, and this cultural position is reinforced by laws limiting the demands employers can make.

A major battleground in this area has been laws that prevent shops from opening on Sundays. Traditionally, most French businesses have been required to close on Sundays to ensure that employees can spend the day as they wish, relaxing with their families. Of course, exceptions were always allowed for essential services (for example, bakeries and *pharmacies de garde*), and for "cultural institutions" such as museums, theaters, and cinemas. This restriction frustrated certain businesspeople, such as the management of the Louis Vuitton shop on the Champs-Elysées, who had to watch thousands of Sunday tourists do nothing more than window-shop at their luxury boutique. In a brilliant use of Système D (see chapter 17, "Working across Cultures"), they set up displays of old luggage on the second floor, declared the Louis Vuitton Museum open to the public seven days a week, and reminded visitors to stop at the "gift shop" downstairs on their way out!

On a more serious note, the French National Assembly voted in July 2009 to allow shops to open on Sundays in tourist areas, spa towns, and large cities like Paris, Lille, and Marseille. The vote was fairly close (282 to 238), and the debate was fierce among the general population as well as politicians. The anti-Sunday-opening campaign united such strange bedfellows as staunchly Catholic institutions with the Socialist and Communist parties.

The amount of time French families spend together, as well as the physical proximity of relatives, supports a level of family involvement that many Americans might find irritating or even intolerable. Advice is offered, requested, and debated on many issues that in the United States would remain within the nuclear family or the couple involved. The extended family serves as an active support network. Relatives, including godparents, are resources for finding a job, an apartment, a car, and any number of products or services.

Isabelle, a young Frenchwoman living with her fiancé's parents in Atlanta and looking for a job, was surprised to realize that she would not receive the same level of help from her American prospective in-laws as she would expect in France. "They were willing to make introductory phone calls for me but apparently were unable or unwilling to ask friends and colleagues directly for a job. I had a name and phone number and it was up to me to take it from there." For Americans, self-reliance can be a way to grow; for Isabelle, it felt like abandonment.

Like the hexagon, the circle is an important symbol in French social geometry. It describes the grouping pattern of French families and friends, which has apparently remained unchanged for centuries. At the end of each story of Astérix, the whole village gathers for a huge banquet to celebrate the victory of its heroes. The table is an open circle, with wine barrels and wild boars roasting on a spit in the center. Only undesirable people—like the off-key bard Assurancetourix—are kept out of the physical circle, for obvious reasons. Anne Goscinny, daughter of one of Astérix's creators, explained the importance of the ritual banquet that closes each story: With the social circle reestablished, cohesion returns to the village and a calm descends to silence the aggressions of the outside world.

If you are invited to a French family meal, you become part of this social circle. All guests gather around the same table, sharing the same food and the same conversation in most cases, depending on the size of the table. A French meal can last for hours, and five- to six-hour meals for special family occasions such as an engagement, first communion, or baptism are common. For weddings, the dinner often continues throughout the night and, in some regions, ends with the traditional onion soup served at dawn.

This French tendency to form and preserve the circle is very strong. In one instance we conducted a seminar with a group of French expatriate women. Lunchtime arrived and a cold buffet was set out. All 15 of us stood up and formed a circle around the food, breaking that circle only to serve ourselves, and then getting back into our places. There was no forming of little clusters, as often happens in informal discussions in the United States.

In another instance, a French expatriate woman, recently arrived in the United States, was having lunch with a group of colleagues. She finished her dessert early and was eager to go out to smoke a cigarette, but she confessed to us, "I don't feel like I should get up and break the circle. We're having such a nice moment together that I would feel bad about it."

A barbecue in the U.S. was intended for French expats and American employees, along with their families, to get to know each other. However, each culture established its own social geometry and inadvertently offended the other. The Americans flitted from group to group, forming and re-forming little conversational knots, while the French set up a large circle with lawn chairs and started an informal sing-along of old favorites. "The French people just made this little fortress and shut us all out. Talk about unfriendly!" is how one American saw it; a French guest, on the other hand, wondered, "Why didn't the Americans take chairs and join us? Why were they so aloof?"

Finally, the French family is a source of identity and identification for its members. Being from a family with a good reputation is an advantage in many situations in France, while membership in a disreputable family may be an impediment. In the United States, people are supposed to be judged on their own individual merits and are therefore able to surmount more readily a disreputable family background. The French family's region of origin is also an important element in an individual's identity, even if no one in the family has actually lived there for generations. A French person's roots give him or her a vital sense of continuity and connectedness, a sense of place and a sentimental attachment to that place. This accounts for some of the French reluctance to move. Even moving "up" to Paris for improved job opportunities, though necessary for personal advancement, may be done with a heavy heart and plans will be made to go "home" as soon as economically possible.

In a large country such as the United States, where mobility is an integral part of life, coworkers in San Antonio, Texas will not be aware of the social status of a fellow worker's family in Pasadena, California and if they are informed of it, they are unlikely to be impressed or concerned. What you do as an individual is what counts and forms the basis of identity for most Americans. In other words, the family as a source of identity reflects the more communal aspect of French culture and its grounding in the past, while identity in the U.S. is an individual matter, grounded in the present and the future.

CHILD REARING

An American told us about a particularly striking contrast he had noticed between French and American cultures.

> In Paris, I was walking down the street just behind a young mother and her two kids. As we passed by a middle-aged woman and her small dog, the kids—about five and six years old—growled playfully at the dog. The owner turned around and scolded the kids brusquely and loudly. It was severe enough so that the children instantly fell silent. They ran up to tell their mother, who was walking ahead, what had happened. At first she thought they meant that the dog barked at them. When she realized it was the woman who had "barked," there was no real difference in the reaction—a grand indifference. A normal, acceptable happening.

> In a coffee shop in New York City at 7:30 A.M., a young mother in her early thirties, with a two-year-old toddler, entered and greeted a friend, then sat down. The focus of the entire breakfast was the child. Both women encouraged the kid to react. Each loud screech was greeted by laughs, approval, and encouragement for more vocalizing, "Oh, aren't you cute!" The child strolled freely around the entire café, approaching other tables, with benign smiles from the mother and friend. Nobody in the café really seemed to mind (except me). (Wallace 1999)

Another example was noted by French-American author Pascal Baudry, who observed French and American mothers watching their children at a playground in the U.S. The American mothers cheered their kids on, encouraging them to climb the playground equipment by saying, "Come on! You can do it!" The French mothers tended instead to issue warnings: "Watch out! Don't climb so high, you're going to fall!" The contrast was even more striking when a child actually did fall and ran crying to mama for comfort. The American moms dried their children's tears, gave them a hug, and encouraged them to give it another try. "Don't give up, you can make it this time!" The French moms reinforced the idea of caution and authority, saying, "See what happened? I told you not to climb so high! Now stay here with me and don't get into more trouble."

French parents do not simply "raise" or "bring up" their children. When speaking of child rearing, the most commonly used term in French is *éducation* and the verb is *éduquer*—to educate, with a much broader definition in French than in English. A child's *éducation* refers to his or her socialization within the family and the wider community as well as formal schooling. It implies that French parents are, to a far greater extent than American parents, responsible for both training and teaching a child what is necessary in life to become a successful

64

individual. *Eduquer* includes the notion of parenting, with the implication that the parents are the authority figures because they have knowledge and experience that the child does not.

The relationship between parents and children has significantly evolved since the 1970s in France, and younger parents tend to be more considerate of their children's developmental needs, while promoting dialogue and a more equal balance of power. Children nowadays have a degree of autonomy and liberty that was unknown to their elders. However, there remains a sharp contrast between the way American and French parents raise their children.

In very general terms, American child rearing emphasizes the child first, while French child rearing emphasizes the family and society, and to some extent the child. American parents usually try to give their children every opportunity to express themselves. They try to see things from the child's perspective and will inconvenience themselves to encourage their children's development. French parents are no less doting or loving than Americans, but they see their role as training and socializing the child to adapt to the adult world. As adults, they have the responsibility of guiding their child toward maturity and helping him or her see the world from an adult perspective. French children are normally toilet-trained by age two—without apparent catastrophic effect on their adult sex lives—thus accommodating themselves to their parents' convenience and reputation in the community.

An American mother at a Paris café found there was no children's menu for her eight-year-old daughter. "Monsieur," she politely asked the waiter, "what do children eat here?" "Madame," responded the waiter, "here, children eat what they are TOLD to eat." Once again, the message is that the child must adapt to adult and societal needs, rather than the other way around.

Children who misbehave in public in France reflect poorly on their parents and their child-rearing abilities. They have a responsibility to society to control and socialize their children, and total strangers may feel free to remind them of this by commenting on a child's behavior, or even by scolding the child themselves, since the parents are not fulfilling their duty.

A child who is behaving beautifully in public is "well behaved" in America, responsible for his or her own actions. Such a child in France is *bien élevé* (well reared) by the parents and thus reflects well on the parents who did such a good job. The emphasis and locus of control in the United States is the child. In France, it is the parents. Similarly, a French parent whose child brings home good grades will say, "We're so proud of you!" underlining the importance of parental input in the child's life and the centrality of the family rather than the individual. An American parent might say the same thing or might emphasize the child's independent actions and achievements by saying, "You should be proud of yourself!"

Conversely, a French parent who says to a child, *"Tu peux être fier de toi!"* ("You can be proud of yourself!") is using sarcasm to underline the fact that the child has done something wrong. This is typical of French negative feedback, where the blame is clearly and implicitly put on the person who has failed to do what was expected of him or her. Like many other aspects of French child rearing, negative feedback continues to play an important role in adult life, influencing many areas.

As we mentioned, while there has been talk of self-esteem in French child rearing and schooling, the concept of *valorisation de l'enfant* seems to resonate more strongly. The locus of control is still outside of the child: someone else has to *valoriser* (a notion close to nurturing); as a general rule, you don't do this for yourself.

French schools normally do not provide the range of extracurricular and enrichment activities found in the United States. It is expected that the family will organize such things for its children, providing them with music or art instruction and athletic activities through specialized clubs. Parents do not normally take active roles in their children's clubs, which are subsidized and run by local municipalities. French mothers and fathers are not expected to be Girl Scout troop leaders, Little League coaches, and so on.

Beginning in childhood, there is already less overlap than in the United States between the private sphere of the family and the social sphere outside. Like the tendency to give negative feedback first, this is another characteristic that reappears in the work situation in France, where public and private remain distinct. Given this attitude, it's hard to imagine a "family values" public debate in France. Family values are the prime realm of each extended family, and the school (read, the government) or the community never interferes in such private matters.

American parents encourage their children to make choices and to think for themselves at an early age. Quite young children may be allowed to decide which restaurant table a family will sit at, what they will wear or eat, and other matters that French parents would never think of throwing open for debate. This is in accordance with the value American culture places on autonomy and independence. Independence is gradually instilled in French children, but the parents retain the essential element of control and guidance. For example, even very young American children often receive an allowance to help them be responsible for their own money and manage their own affairs. French children under the age of eight or ten rarely get their own pocket money.

An amusing contrast between French and American parenting styles occurred in a bicultural family. The four-year-old son didn't want to eat his broccoli, and asked his American mother, "Why do I have to eat broccoli? I don't like it!" His mother patiently explained that vegetables are full of vitamins and minerals and would help him grow up to be big and strong. They went back and forth like this a couple of times until the French father looked sternly at his son and said, "You have to eat your vegetables because I said so."

The degree to which Americans value equality also plays a role in child rearing. Some American parents feel they should be their children's friend, even their "best friend." Children are often asked to participate in their own upbringing by making decisions regarding which school to go to and which courses to take. Parents may negotiate with their children about when to do their homework and when bedtime should be. Such collaboration would strike French parents as patently absurd, since it is based on an assumed egalitarian relationship between parents and children. Parents in France are in charge of their children and have the duty to guide their growth properly. One French father explained, "You can't be your kid's pal and some things are not negotiable. I think [my child] understands authority, even if at age 13 he doesn't always accept it" (Virard, *Enjeux*, March 2006, 51).

A French mother newly arrived in the United States was in for a shock when she registered her son in the local middle school. The principal asked him directly what he wanted to study from the à la carte elective curriculum. Even harder to swallow for the mother was that she was apparently expected to sit silently through this process and was not consulted regarding her son's decisions.

Conversely, Americans in France often get the impression that French parents behave in a fairly authoritarian manner with their children and do not pay enough attention to them and to their developmental needs. A French child who tries to interrupt an adult conversation by saying, "Mommy, look at me! Look what I can do!" is likely to be reprimanded and told that the grown-ups are talking. A French person talking to an American parent might be surprised and somewhat insulted if the interrupting child, rather than being corrected, becomes instead the center of praise and attention: "That's wonderful! You're getting to be such a big girl! Now let Mommy get back to her conversation." Many Americans consider that the child's needs are primary in such a situation, that the parent's efforts should be directed at encouraging the child's self-expression and independence and building her self-esteem. French adults generally consider that the child's interests and needs in most cases should not supersede adult concerns and, accordingly, teach the child to understand and accept limitations on his or her sphere of action and expression. By not allowing children to interrupt, French adults help them to learn proper manners and behavior. Such knowledge is essential to their success in school and in adult life.

Teaching the rules of proper behavior—appropriate table behavior, conversation with adults, social functions outside the home, restaurant visits, and so on—takes up a lot of the parents' time. Mealtime plays an important role in a child's socialization. In France, the function of a meal is not only to feed oneself and others but also to communicate with others. All family members usually gather around the same table for a substantial evening meal. It is very uncommon for members of traditional French families to pick what they want from the refrigerator or to eat sandwiches while watching TV. Such antisocial behavior would in fact eliminate most family interaction, as it often does in the busy American family. In the French home of one of the authors, children were not excused from the table until after dessert. Then, and only then, was it possible to watch TV in the living room.

PERSONALITY DEVELOPMENT

The combination of differing socialization processes and family values in the two countries produces very different personalities. As noted earlier in the section "Perceptions of Arrogance," Americans learn to present themselves with casual self-confidence. Little Americans begin their public-speaking careers with "show and tell" in preschool or kindergarten, where they are expected to stand before the group and present something interesting, and to do so in an interesting way.

French children are not used to this kind of public exercise, and generally they do not learn to present themselves and their interests in public. A common parental admonition is, *"Cela ne se fait pas!"* ("This is not done!"), which teaches and reinforces the rules when they are transgressed. As a result, French children (and eventually adults) tend not to *se mettre en avant* (draw attention to or assert oneself), and may appear more self-effacing than Americans.

Some of these personality differences have been highlighted by Laurence Wylie:

> By age ten, then, the French children have become *bien élevés* (well reared). They have learned about limits, boundaries, delineation, and appropriate behavior . . . . They have learned control over themselves, over their bod-

ies. They have acquired tremendous inner psychological independence, I think, that American children do not have. I think they have not learned what American children do learn, that is, the emphasis on striking out for themselves, venturing out, trying new things. (1981, 58)

... And, when verbal expression is not permitted, there is the expressive power of the eyes, the body, the importance of mime. And finally, there is fantasy. I think that French children have an inner personality, an inner independence, an inner life that American children lack. And they illustrate and embellish it in a way that gives French literature and cinema a particular and very beautiful cast. Each individual is surrounded by his own [psychological] wall, enclosed in his own circle, but through these escape mechanisms, he can exist even though there are social controls. (62)

Thus, French children learn early on that there are two main compartments in their lives: an outer world full of social rules, codes, and regulations to obey if one wishes to please parents and society at large, and a more intimate, inner world full of imagination, fantasy, personal feelings, and ideas. A French child is encouraged to develop this inner world, to nurture and protect it. But the secret garden is not open to everyone. To maintain this private territory, French children need to establish personal space—through physical separation into one's own room, for example—but often the sense of psychological separation is enough. When adult guests are present, quite small children play happily by themselves nearby, free from the influence of others, including their parents.

This distinction between internal and external worlds is not as obvious in American culture, where children—and adults—tend to express more easily and more consistently what goes through their minds, what's going on in their lives, and what they expect from others.

The effect of child-rearing practices on personality development cannot be underestimated, and many of the misunderstandings between French and American adults are the result of differing ways of being brought up. Since our early years are so critical to how we perceive ourselves in relation to our environment, it is no wonder that Americans and French people come to different positions or conclusions in so many situations.

SEVEN

With the School

This chapter discusses the goals and structure of education in France and the United States, including the influence of culture on education and vice versa. It also includes a section on higher education, highlighting the dichotomy between grandes écoles and university systems. Appendix A describes the French curriculum and school system from preschool to higher education.

THE FRENCH PASSION FOR SCHOOL

The other partner in French education is the school system. The philosophy, aims, and methods of French schooling both illustrate and support many French cultural values.

Public schools are free of charge and compulsory from the age of six to sixteen, although most children go to *l'école maternelle* (preschool and kindergarten) starting at age three. La Maternelle is divided into three sections, according to the children's ages. The first two years correspond to U.S. preschool or nursery school (ages three and four), while the third year (age five) is equivalent to American kindergarten. Government-subsidized and managed day-care centers look after younger children.

School is the most important of a French child's activities. How the child performs and masters knowledge in the early grades will determine to a large extent what he or she will achieve later in life. Most teachers agree that CP (*Cours*

Préparatoire; first grade) is where the child must acquire a solid foundation and learn basic reading, writing, and mathematics. Parents are aware of the stakes and tend to put a high degree of pressure on the child from the beginning. An elementary school student normally hears a daily barrage of questions from concerned parents: "Did you do well today?" "Did the teacher give you any grades?" "Did you get any bonus points?" "What do you have to do for tomorrow?" "Show me your school correspondence booklet."

Americans working on a children's film in France discovered that culture played an important part in the reaction of parents of prospective child actors:

> [T]he idea that a child can survive missing three months of school . . . is apparently mostly an American phenomenon. "The American parents said, 'What's three months in a child's life compared to the experience? . . . .' And the French parents said, 'Oh, my God, three months in a school year?'" (Hohenadel 1998, 22)

French parents have good reason for concern. The French school system does not give children much slack and demands a minimum level of performance for promotion to the next grade. Although things are changing, starting at age thirteen or fourteen insufficient average grades may result in a child's being held back to *redoubler* (repeat) a grade, not an unusual occurrence. For this reason, students in their final years of high school may range in age from sixteen to twenty, depending on how many grades they have skipped or repeated. Although there is presently a strong countertrend in the United States demanding that children must be intellectually ready to move on, "social promotion" is fairly widespread. This means that a child with inadequate grades is promoted to avoid damaging self-esteem and to prevent teasing by other children.

School in France is like a series of hurdles the child must negotiate with the assistance of devoted supporters: parents, teachers, school administrators, and advisers. It's hard for Americans to imagine the level of competitiveness in French schools, especially when the child enters high school and approaches *le baccalauréat*. In June 1998, an assistant to the minister of education referred to the *bac* as the rite of passage to adulthood (France 2, 14 July 1998). French parents are concerned with preparation for le bac well before their child enters his or her last year of secondary school.

A French person's academic career plays a more important and profound role in his or her life than it does for an American. The various academic tracks diverge quite early, and the system is unforgiving: it is virtually impossible to move from a lower-level track to a higher one. Academic talent is noted and nurtured, but average and less-able students are in effect consigned to lower-level manual and service jobs. As early as age eleven or twelve, students may be assigned to shortened study tracks leading to vocational qualifications. Once the evaluation has been made, it is pretty much final and changes are extremely rare. The bac alone is far from a guarantee of success, since only the Bac S (science specialization) really opens important or prestigious doors. The level of concern French parents show about their children's schooling is a reflection of its decisive role in their future success or failure.

French teachers and parents are less concerned than their American counterparts that their children enjoy school, since it is essentially a place to acquire knowledge. Teachers sometimes try to assign special projects, but French students tend to see this as additional work required of them—maybe even an assigned punishment—rather than a chance to explore and discover.

Educational reforms are a regular preoccupation of French governments, teachers, parents, and, of course, students. School reforms are passionately discussed, from the *Assemblée Nationale* (equivalent to the U.S. House of Representatives) to the corner café to the family dinner table. Reforms may mean changes in the pacing of the school day, week, or year to match children's "natural rhythms"; they may involve minor pedagogical changes or major philosophical ones. Reforms have completely revamped the organization, attitudes, and methods of nursery and elementary schools. One reform outlines plans for teaching foreign languages starting in elementary schools; still others propose radical rethinking of the entire educational system from nursery school through secondary school.

Despite increasing autonomy for individual schools and *académies* (large regional school districts), most educational decisions are still made and applied on a national scale. Since all French public schools are run by the central Ministry of Education, the curriculum is the same throughout France, although some class time can now be spent according to local priorities—the study of regional languages and cultures, for example.

The typical school day in France runs approximately from 8:30 A.M. to 12:00 and 1:30 P.M. to 4:30 P.M. It is also very intense. Children attend school Mondays, Tuesdays, Thursdays, and Fridays and, in some cases, Wednesday or Saturday mornings. Many schools offer extended supervision after normal hours (*l'étude*), and most children eat lunch at school, except in smaller country towns and villages, where everything shuts down for two hours and the whole family gathers at home. In recent years, some schools have remained open during the summer vacation, offering remedial and enrichment activities with volunteer teachers.

FRENCH CULTURE AND
FRENCH SCHOOLING

We can gain some interesting insights into the French educational system and philosophy by examining the list of required school supplies provided at the website of the Ministry of Education.[11]

First, it is significant that the school supply list is established at the national level by the Ministry of Education to ensure centralization and uniformity. These decisions are not left up to the académies, although schools can require additional supplies for specific classes. Second, the list is broken down into subcategories of "consumables" and "equipment," reflecting the French tendency to catalogue the world and everything in it into precise groups and classes. Third, exact specifications are provided for each item, so that a notebook must contain exactly 96 pages, 21 × 29.7cm of 80–90 grams per square meter weight, with a stapled spine—emphasizing structure and rigorous methodology.

These characteristics demonstrate the French approach to education. Knowledge flows from the top down—from ministry to académie to school to teacher to student—and while there is more room for self-expression than in previous generations, the assumption is still that teachers are there to teach and students to learn. Students who arrive in school with this formidable set of supplies and equipment will not be allowed to use them in any way that takes their fancy. They will be taught how to use the various items to reinforce educational structures and methodologies (how the brain is "formatted," how children learn to learn). For example, the list specifies ballpoint pens (medium point!) in four colors: blue, black, red, and green. One color is for general notes, one color is for underlining, another is for important dates and names, and so on.

Thinking and intellectual skills are of paramount importance in a culture that, according to seventeenth-century philosopher Blaise Pascal, defines man as *un roseau pensant* (a thinking reed). In the same vein, seventeenth-century philosopher Nicolas Boileau said, *"Ce que l'on conçoit bien s'énonce clairement, et les mots pour le dire arrivent aisément."* ("What is well conceived is expressed clearly, and the words to say it come easily.") First comes thought; once that is done properly, the rest is easy.

Philosophy is a required subject for all students in their final year of secondary school. It is the first exam that launches the bac session every year. The following are the questions for various bac specializations from 2008.

---

[11] See the listing at *http://media.education.gouv.fr/file/Toute_l_actualite/35/5/Liste_fournitures_61355.pdf*

Four hours. Spelling and grammar count. Go.

- Literature specialization: Commentary on Sartre's *Notebooks for an Ethics*, or an essay on either "Can perception be cultivated?" or "Is scientific knowledge of living possible?"
- Science specialization: Commentary on Schopenhauer's *The World as Will and Representation*, or an essay on either "Does art transform our consciousness of what is real?" or "Are there other ways besides demonstration to establish a truth?"
- Economic and Social Science specialization: Commentary on Alexis de Tocqueville's *Democracy in America*, or an essay on either "Is desire possible without suffering?" or "Is it easier to know others than to know oneself?"
- Technology specialization: Essays on "Is it possible to like a work of art without understanding it?" and "Is it up to the law to determine my happiness?"

Schooling at all levels tends to be focused on the transfer of information from teacher to student and is essentially a one-way process. Logic and clarity are stressed in all subjects, and French teachers present knowledge in a way that favors deductive reasoning. First, the abstract and theoretical framework is established, then particular cases and illustrations are discussed. A first-grade French teacher introduces parts of speech by first giving functional definitions of nouns and verbs, then providing examples of each in simple sentences, and finally asking the child to mark nouns and verbs in exercise sentences. In the United States, by contrast, a first-grade teacher would be more likely to encourage inductive reasoning by first giving examples of nouns and verbs as isolated words, then having the children find nouns and verbs in sentences, and finally providing definitions to solidify and reinforce learning points.

The amount of homework also differs in the two systems. French children take home a substantial amount of work. By the final year of high school they are expected to spend as much time on homework as they do in class (35 hours each, for a total of 70 hours per week). Parents are usually heavily involved in their children's schooling, particularly in higher grades, and closely supervise their progress. To a certain extent, a student's lack of preparation or poor results reflects badly on the parents. American schoolchildren are expected to be fairly autonomous in completing their homework. Although some parents do substantial amounts of research or typing, parents who more or less do their child's assignments for them are considered to be undermining their child's learning and independent development.

Schools in the United States generally make every effort to include parents as active participants in their child's education. Students and parents may be seen as clients who must be satisfied, and whose input should be taken into account to improve the services offered by the school. Parents may volunteer at schools to help teachers in the classroom, as chaperones for field trips, as tutors for children needing extra help, as fund-raisers, as sponsors for after-school clubs, and so on. French public schools, on the other hand, are considered the reserved domain of teachers and the state. Parent-teacher associations exist, but parents are not directly involved in their child's school life. These contrasting expectations caused friction at a French-American school in the U.S. French parents were surprised to find that their participation was expected in volunteer work at the school and in special fund-raising events. Newly arrived French teachers were also at a loss, since they had never had volunteer parents in their classrooms before and didn't know what to do with them.

One French MBA student in the U.S. was surprised to experience this client-centered approach to education when he was asked to help organize a two-week study tour to Europe for his fellow students. Two professors accompanied the group: one group leader and one assistant, who was expected to lead the trip the following year. After the trip, the assistant asked participants for formal feedback via a survey on what could be done to improve the trip for the next group. The French student's response was, "What does he need to ask them for? He was on the trip, he can make his own judgment!"

Several incidents at a U.S. French-American school highlighted another major difference in parental expectations across cultures. In general, French parents showed more deference toward the teachers and respected their authority as the final word in decisions concerning their child's schooling. American parents were more likely to question teachers and challenge their decisions. Some even went so far as to request changes in the curriculum. In one exceptional case, French parents and teachers were shocked when an American parent told a teacher point-blank that his child would not complete the homework she had assigned.

French exams almost never take the form of a multiple-choice test. This would contradict the basic school philosophy, which demands reasoning backed by knowledge and facts. Therefore, depending on the subject, a small problem, a short essay, a creative exercise, a *dictée* (dictation), or a *contraction de texte* (précis) tests the student's knowledge and skills. Except for courses in the French language itself, pure memorization leads only to failure. *Bachoter* (to cram facts without understanding) is one of the worst educational sins a French student can commit. French, especially French grammar, is essential and is stressed throughout the first ten years of school. Language is in fact the foundation that supports sound reasoning. Teachers remind their students that the three essential elements in French are "clarity, clarity, and clarity." Students learn to write so their work flows well and is articulate.

Grading and feedback in France do not reflect concern with building (or lowering) a child's self-esteem. Generally, grades are lower than what we normally see in American schools. On a scale of 1–20, 19 and 20 are "reserved for God" in France. This contrasts with the American system where a perfect A+ (and sometimes even A++) can be and is achieved. Paradoxically, for a culture that values privacy, grades in France are a matter of public record. Students' grades are posted for all the world to see, and university exam results may appear in local newspapers in rank order. In addition, the results of the baccalauréat exams are available on the Ministry of Education's website with no registration or password required.

Teachers comment publicly on an individual student's work, usually when returning homework assignments. These comments may be quite sarcastic; in any case, words will not be minced: "Dupont, stop playing video games and concentrate on Corneille, it will do you good." "Corinne, this is much better than last time, but work on your punctuation." An English teacher at a French high school was tutoring a student who needed extra help in preparing for the English oral exam section of the bac. "Work on your math," he said. What he meant was that the student's English skills were so poor that his only hope of passing the bac was to bring up his math score.

The way in which French children are taught to think and learn tends to stay with them as adults. To a large extent, they expect superiors to be experts and to have the information required. A manager who asks subordinates how to solve a problem is not likely to be held in high regard. Imagine a schoolteacher asking her pupils what they think they should learn.

While we cannot describe the French educational system in its entirety (see the table and detailed explanation in Appendix A), we would like to spend a few pages highlighting the higher education system.

HIGHER EDUCATION

The first twelve years of compulsory education focus on instilling general culture in the child and on "formatting" the brain. The following four to six years are reserved for specialization. In fact, French students make important decisions about their future much earlier than Americans do, and changing majors during the equivalent of American undergraduate study is uncommon in France, except in the case of failure. Parents are well aware of the risks involved and take their children's progress during their last years of high school very seriously. Competition starts early in French schools, and education is the major way, if not the only way, to reach the higher ranks in society.

The French language reflects the difference between regular or standard education and the more specialized higher education. Standard education is still called *éducation,* regardless of the level, but higher-level learning takes on the name of *formation* (training). When someone is asked in a job interview or during a professional presentation, *"Qu'est-ce que vous avez fait?"* (What have you done?), it refers to the person's higher education, not to his or her employment. In reply, just the name of the school says it all. *"J'ai fait Dauphine"* means the person studied at one of the best business schools in Paris, which is part of a public university. *"J'ai fait Sciences-Po et X"* is a more impressive response. It means that the person studied political science at a highly respected Parisian institution and, even better, comes from the school of the brightest, *Polytechnique,* which has trained and nurtured engineers and top managers for over two centuries.

While the standard curriculum from primary school until the *terminale* (12th grade—see appendix A for details) is a symbol of French uniformity and universality, the higher education curriculum is a real maze where the direction you end up taking depends on various elements: your intelligence (i.e., your grades during the three years of high school and your results on le bac), the amount you can afford for your studies, the advice and support you received from your parents and, above all, your personal vocation.

French higher education takes place in two major types of institutions: public universities and public or semiprivate schools called *grandes écoles.*

UNIVERSITIES AND PUBLIC EDUCATION

The greatest strength of French universities, many of which were founded in the Middle Ages, is that they provide education at a very low cost: annual tuition is less than $500 U.S. A PhD candidate pays about €350 tuition a year. French universities are therefore extremely crowded and poor study conditions have been the major complaint of students over the past decade. Students, professors, and researchers often take their complaints to the streets during various strikes and other protest actions. Although not as prestigious as the grandes écoles system, admission to a university is still very competitive. You'll see hundreds of students queuing up for hours in front of university buildings once they get the results of their bac. Seating is limited, so it is important for them to register early in hopes of being admitted to the university of their choice. One unintended consequence is that even such renowned schools as the Sorbonne tend to be overcrowded and under-maintained. Jean-Robert Pitte, president of the Sorbonne, once joked that each student has an average of 2.6 square meters of space (24 square feet). In contrast, a *poulet de Bresse* (a high-quality chicken, with the *Appelation d'Origine Contrôlée* label) requires 8.3 square meters (90 square feet) to earn the AOC label![12]

The university curriculum depends on the student's major. In most subjects, students can earn a three-year degree (*Licence*), which is less and less popular and seems to be phasing out slowly. Depending on their interest and stamina, students may also opt right after the bac for a four-year degree (*Master I*) or five-year degree (*Master II*). Finally, a doctorate (*Doctorat*) is available for those wishing to study until the age of twenty-six or twenty-seven and specialize in research. This new system (Licence, Master, Doctorat) has been implemented to harmonize with other European countries' curriculum.

Fewer students in France go for a doctorate than in the United States. This degree does not carry the status it does in the U.S., and people hoping to teach in a top lycée or at a university are more likely to prepare for the *aggrégation*. This is a very prestigious competitive exam that opens many doors, including those of tenured professorship. But the *agrég* is, above all, proof of a high level of knowledge that very few people can attain. However, a doctorate remains a degree for professors, researchers, and professionals of high caliber.

LES GRANDES ECOLES

A unique feature of the French educational system is the grandes écoles (great schools). While many countries have top-level educational institutions that tend to mold and graduate their nation's future leaders, the effects of the grandes écoles system reverberate through and layer French society in ways that are both deep (profoundly affecting both society and graduates) and often invisible to outsiders.

The yellow brick road to the top in France—in business, politics, and many other fields—leads not to public university but to one of the grandes écoles,

---

[12] *www.understandfrance.org/France/Education.html#ancre104317*

many of which were founded in pre-revolutionary France to fill the need for engineers and technical specialists to design roads, canals, and other public works. Engineering thus retains an exceptionally high status in French culture and is usually the core function in any industrial company. After the Revolution, Napoleon continued the tradition by founding the *Ecole Polytechnique* to train military officers for his expanding empire.

In the wake of France's defeat in the Franco-Prussian War, the *Institut d'Etudes Politiques de Paris (Sciences-Po)* was founded to strengthen the civil service and government administration. Similarly, after World War II, de Gaulle created the *Ecole Nationale d'Administration* (*ENA* or National School of Administration; top-level school for future politicians and civil servants), for which Sciences-Po became a sort of feeder school.

Business management schools began to join the ranks of the grandes écoles in 1820 with the creation of the *Ecole Supérieure de Commerce de Paris (ESCP)*, later joined by the *Ecole des Hautes Etudes Commerciales (HEC)*, the *Ecole Supérieure des Sciences Economiques et Commerciales (ESSEC)*, and others. Most are public or semiprivate, often operated in conjunction with local chambers of commerce.

Several characteristics distinguish grandes écoles. They tend to be small to medium-sized institutions, with a maximum of four hundred students per *promotion* (class/year). They have a highly selective admission process and the period of study is relatively long (five to six years compared to two to four years at university, depending on the degree achieved). The faculties as well as the students tend to be the brightest and best, and the grandes écoles attract faculty from many sources. Education methods and materials are often more flexible and innovative than in universities, and schools maintain close ties with related government ministries and industry. A great deal of research tends to be carried out in the grandes écoles rather than the universities.

From the ranks of grandes écoles graduates come the presidents, vice presidents, and boards of directors of virtually every major private and public company in France, and quite a few smaller ones as well. One twenty-four-year-old graduate of Ecole des Mines (top engineering school) was asked by an American colleague what his degree represented in his eyes. "Essentially," he replied, "it means I'm set up for life."

The grandes écoles are not a part of the public university system, yet they are fully integrated into the French educational system. There is no official definition or listing of grandes écoles. However, the *Conference of Grandes Ecoles (CGE)*, an organization created in 1973, regroups 222 grandes écoles (including 13 located abroad), 21 leading private or state-owned French firms and 48 professional societies or alumni networks (www.cge.asso.fr/cadre_ecole.html).

It has been estimated that only about 1 percent of students in French higher education study at one of the grandes écoles, and 5,000 students graduate from them annually. A grande école education is seen as offering a double guarantee. First, that the graduate has the "right stuff" intellectually, a thorough grounding in everything from literature to legislation that will allow him or her to function at the highest levels of government or business (and to move effortlessly back and forth between private and public sectors as the need arises). And also that the graduate is virtually set for life, assured of access to the best jobs in his or her field—sometimes without even going through recruitment by human resources.

Admission to the grandes écoles is generally via *concours*, a highly competitive school-specific exam that requires two years (or possibly more) of study at *classes préparatoires aux grandes écoles* (preparatory classes for the grandes écoles) or *prépas*. *Prépa* classes are located in lycées, although students actually do university-level work. These classes are extremely difficult and stressful; they are designed both to prepare students for the kind of work they will face at a grande école and to weed out those who are not up to it, either intellectually or by temperament.

Prépa is based on survival of the fittest. Students considering classes préparatoires are forewarned, even by the schools, that the workload is heavy and intense, that regular attendance is required, and that one must have *courage et bonne santé* (grit and good health) to survive the ordeal.

Prépa is also known as *la voie royale* (the royal road), leading to admission to a grande école and a successful career. Only the top-ranking students get in, based on the number of openings available and their scores on the concours. If a student is not admitted to a grande école, he or she can take an equivalency exam and get credit toward a degree from a French university or do a third year of prépa and try the same concours again. Those who are admitted can also relax just a little: although the curriculum at the grandes écoles is demanding and rigorous, it is generally agreed that prépa is worse. In fact, a French diplomat in a North American city confided half-jokingly during a cocktail party, "We have to work so hard to get into ENA and then to graduate—surely you don't expect us to do anything strenuous after that!"

A mediocre student will not be admitted to a first-class institution thanks to his or her family's history with the school or donation of a new gymnasium; however, though the system is a meritocracy based on brains alone in principle, other factors affect the selection process. While the procedure stresses intellectual prowess, it has traditionally been easier for the children of wealthier families to get in, as they have access to better schools, tutors, and other advantages, as well as a greater push from parents who understand the system. Their more fluent self-expression and exposure to the world at large through travel or other cultural experiences also give them an advantage in the dreaded oral exam (*le grand O*), in which students' *culture générale* is assessed as part of the admission procedure.

Today, grandes écoles exist in many fields, but in line with the history outlined above, the most famous are associated with engineering, public administration, political science, and business. ENA is one of the most prestigious ways to reach the top, in either the government or the public sector (state-owned organizations). Its graduates form a mandarin class and are known as *énarques*. ENA has been virtually a prerequisite for French presidents, prime ministers and other high-level public officials—although, here again, Nicolas Sarkozy breaks the mold, not having graduated from ENA or any other grande école (although he did study at Science-Po).

The crème de la crème of the system is *Polytechnique*, known familiarly as "*X*" from the crossed cannons on the school's coat of arms. Think of X as a combination of Harvard or Yale in terms of tradition, prestige, and influence; MIT or CalTech in terms of rigorous mathematics and engineering curriculum; and West Point in terms of its military element. Students at X are actually in the French army and are paid while they study. They are also required to appear in uniform for special events, such as the parade down the Champs-Elysées on Bastille Day.

The story of a young X graduate, hired into a large French manufacturing company and sent to spend three years at the company's American affiliate in California, provides an insight into the mentality of grandes écoles graduates. He adapted well to the more informal atmosphere and his staff appreciated his straightforward and down-to-earth approach.

In the fall of his first year, plans were made for a Halloween costume party in the department, but this was a few years before attempts had been made to introduce Halloween in France. So the Frenchman asked an American colleague who had lived in France and spoke French what it was all about. "Do I need to do anything special? Am I expected to wear a costume?" The American replied that he didn't have to, but that his staff would certainly appreciate his willingness to join in the fun. "What should I wear?" was the next question. The American thought for a moment and then asked, "Did you bring your uniform from X to California with you? You could wear that—just leave the sword at home!" To the delight of his American colleagues, the Frenchman appeared on October 31st in full Napoleonic regalia. But the most telling part of the story came later, when the American who suggested the idea said, "For me, it was kind of amazing to think that this unpretentious young man thought that he might conceivably have some use for his X uniform in Southern California—and brought it with him!"

In the United States, the prestige of the school one graduates from is important, but mainly in finding a first job and in terms of the contacts one has later on. For a grande école graduate, the benefits never end—and not just in matters of job security. For example, at *Electricité de France*, the French national electricity utility, new hires come in on one of four bands, depending on their level of education. Each band allows for advancement in rank and salary based on the number of years the employee stays with the company; grandes écoles graduates from the top schools start in the highest band (A in the diagram below) and stay that way until they retire. As in many other large French companies, it is simply not possible for someone coming in on a lower band to reach the top levels.

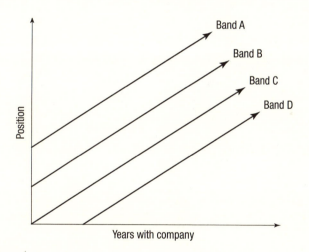

For the best of the brightest, there is one more selection process. The highest-ranking graduates of each school choose an *Ecole d'Application* (literally, "application school", where students focus more on an occupational specialization) from among the other schools. Graduates are then members of these *Grands Corps* (literally, great bodies) and high-level civil servants for the rest of their careers. The Corps manages their career and provides them, under secondment (temporary transfer), to whichever organization they are working for.

There has been criticism of the hermetic nature of the system and its ten-dency to perpetuate itself, as those who benefit from it go on to lead the country and its institutions with remarkable intellectual vigor without calling into ques-tion the system that allowed them to get there and the benefits they enjoy. At the same time, there have been serious efforts in recent years to get disadvantaged students on the voie royale through various programs that first make them aware that the grandes écoles are a possibility for their future and provide mentoring and other support to help them gain entrance.

EIGHT

With Friends

French people and Americans both value their friends, but ideas about who is a friend, how friends are made, and what friendship means are very different. Since these differences are the source of frequent misunderstandings on both sides, it is important to analyze and clarify them.

THE LANGUAGE OF
FRIENDSHIP AND LOVE

In English, we can distinguish among acquaintances, colleagues, and friends, at least linguistically. In the United States, though, people rarely do so, using the word *friend* to refer to someone they met yesterday or to someone they have known since childhood. About the only distinction normally made in the U.S. is between a "casual" friend and a "close" or "best" friend.

The French language allows for the most subtle of gradations in the nouns we use to speak of people we know, and French culture requires they be used.

un(e) ami(e): a friend
une connaissance: an acquaintance, someone you know superficially
une relation: mainly a colleague or other professional contact
un(e) camarade: a good pal from youth, school, university, or military service

un copain (f. *une copine*): a buddy; etymologically someone you share
  bread with
un(e) pote: like *copain*, but more familiar
un(e) petit(e) ami(e): boyfriend or girlfriend; may be in a romantic sense
  depending on the context
un(e) ami(e) d'enfance: a friend from childhood
un(e) ami(e) de toujours: an always and forever friend
un(e) meilleur(e) ami(e): best friend
mon ami(e): normally means "my lover" but depends on the context
un(e) cher(e) ami(e): a dear friend—more distant than a simple friend,
  oddly enough

Notice that the gender is evident in written French, but it may be obscured in
spoken French.

Paradoxically, the French verbs of friendship and love offer a much smaller
choice than English. One French verb, *aimer*, does yeoman's duty, expressing all
the gradations of feeling from mild affection to passionate love. This may seem
odd given the French romantic reputation. The French do not use the word *love*
outside a fairly intimate relationship. French friends do not say that they love
each other or sign their letters with "love" or "lots of love from," as American
friends do. They might say *"Je t'aime bien,"* but this means only "I like you." In fact,
most adverbs used with *aimer*—for example, *bien*, *beaucoup*, *infiniment* (literally,
"well," "a lot," "infinitely")—actually weaken the verb rather than intensify it, as
is usually the case in English.

An American woman who had lived in France for some years enjoyed a
very pleasant—and platonic—relationship with one of her neighbors, an older
Frenchman. Before she left to return to the States, she wanted to tell him how
much she had enjoyed their friendship and how much she liked him. She said,
"Monsieur, je vous aime." His reaction to her passionate declaration was probably
"She's getting ready to leave, and *now* she tells me!"

Another example revealing the differences between French and American
usage comes from Michel, a young Frenchman studying for a master's degree at
an American university. He had briefly met the twenty-year-old sister of a classmate during a visit to the classmate's home. Some of their discussions included
what struck Michel as deeply personal revelations on her part. They wrote to
each other after he returned to school and she signed each letter "Love, Laura."
She even sent a greeting card signed "Love always, Laura." The intimacy of her
tone suggested to Michel that her feelings for him were very romantic indeed,
and he found himself falling in love with her. He even wrote her two or three love

letters but received no response. He was horrified to learn through his classmate that she already had a steady boyfriend.

MAKING AND BEING FRIENDS

Americans "play it by ear" with their friends and take friendships as they come. Most American friendships begin with some kind of physical proximity, often involving a shared activity. While working out at the gym, chatting over coffee after church, arranging carpools to kids' soccer practice, hanging out at the mall, or borrowing garden tools, and through similar everyday connections, Americans discover common interests and affinities they can pursue with invitations to meals, to a movie after work, or to a football game on Saturday. American friendships may last a few weeks or a lifetime; they may be superficial or deep.

The French, with their passion for classification, have very clear boundaries for their relationships with specific people in specific situations. For example, French neighbors are not automatically counted as friends or even as acquaintances. Because most French people, particularly in large cities, lack the personal space that Americans take for granted, rules—written and unwritten—exist to protect people's privacy. And these regulations are strictly enforced, as any foreigner who takes a shower after ten at night is reminded by apartment neighbors. A Parisian joked that French children grow up traumatized because they are constantly told to avoid disturbing the neighbors: "In the U.S., you scare kids with the Bogeyman, but I think French kids imagine the Neighbor as a child-eating creature with bloody fangs and claws. Maybe that's why we avoid neighbors when we grow up."

A good French neighbor does not disturb others, follows rules concerning common areas of the building, and generally keeps a low profile. An Englishman living in France reported this story to us:

> A neighbor in the next flat, a psychiatrist (I knew this only because of the plate on his door), saw me frequently for about a year. One evening we entered the lift together. He asked, *"Quel étage?"* ("Which floor?") I replied, *"Cinquième, comme d'habitude"* ("Fifth, as always"). At the time I felt I had struck a small blow for Britain.

Whatever the cause, the virtue of neighborliness is not appreciated in France as it is in other cultures. An American woman living in a small town in southwestern France learned that her landlady's elderly mother was very ill. The landlady had gone to another region to look after her, leaving her husband and adult son to fend for themselves. "I put together a big lasagna, took it across the street in a pretty casserole dish, and told them that they could leave the empty dish on our stoop. They looked confused and a little embarrassed. They thanked me profusely, though, and so did my landlady when she got home, but I think they were really baffled by the whole thing."

While colleagues from work may become well acquainted in France, the relationship may be limited to drinks or dinner after work. It is not normally expected that people who work together will develop close friendships. It's fine if workmates do happen to become friends—and it indeed happens—but there is no expectation that they will nor is there any obligation to do so.

Close friendships are rarely made across social classes. An interesting exception to this is Le Club Med, which advertises itself as "the antidote to civilization." A story tells of two Frenchmen who met during a vacation at a Club Med village in Greece. They developed a warm friendship and spent a great deal of time together during their stay. In keeping with the French tendency to separate work and private life, they did not even mention what they did back in France. It was only when they exchanged addresses just before leaving that they discovered one of them was the director of a company while the other was a night watchman at the same company. The story does not reveal what happened once they got home, but chances are they both understood they could not possibly maintain the friendship (Ardagh 1970, 441).

So, where *do* French people make friends? French friends are often made early in life, at school or university, in the workplace to a lesser extent, and, until 1997, during the mandatory military service for men. The French tendency to stay close to home and the small size of the country, compared with the United States, make it easier to maintain such long-term friendships, particularly at the depth French friends expect. Once French people have struck up a friendship, they have made an emotional investment in each other. This is something that must be attended to and not taken lightly. The French do not confer the status of *ami* quickly or easily, and rightly so. Friends in France are bound by mutual obligations and mutual responsibilities. They expect friends to do certain things for them in certain circumstances, and they expect friendships to be deep and long-term.

Another linguistic indicator of the quality of the relationship between two people is whether they call each other "tu" or "vous." *Tu* is normally reserved for family, friends, classmates, and similar close relationships, while *vous* is pretty much everybody else. Although young people seem to use tu more easily than older generations, there is still a distinction. While two people on a vous basis can be friends, moving from vous to tu indicates a shift in the relationship. This distinction is difficult for Americans to understand, so it's generally best to let your French colleagues take the lead. If someone calls you tu, it's usually safe to call him or her tu in return. Company culture may also play a role: at Electricité de France, the French public utility company, the norm is to use tu with everyone. The difference extends beyond the pronoun, as the verb forms also have to reflect the appropriate level of communication. The phrase, "Can you do that please?" can be expressed in French in two ways:

> *Peux-tu faire cela, s'il te plait?*
> *Pouvez-vous faire cela, s'il vous plaît ?*

Notice that even the way you say "please" varies!

Different conceptions of the nature of friendship sometimes create problems in French-American intercultural interactions. The following diagram shows this difference graphically: the walls surrounding the core personality in each culture are in fact concentric circles, so you would see two target-shaped figures if you looked down on the diagram from above.

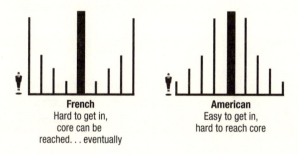

French
Hard to get in,
core can be
reached. . . eventually

American
Easy to get in,
hard to reach core

Americans are open, friendly, easy to approach. They are instantly on first-name terms, and they invite virtual strangers into their homes with a generous ease that amazes the French. But if the first walls are easy to step or jump over, the barriers rise as you get closer to the core. The core itself may never be reached, even by a spouse, children, or intimate friends. Because the bonds that link friends do not necessarily go very deep, American friendship is not necessarily considered a major commitment—although it may be, depending on its duration and the circumstances. Coworkers may share some fairly deep revelations with each other, but once one of them moves on to another company, they do not necessarily spend much time together or even keep in touch.

The French, on the other hand, are not so easy to get to know. There is a tall barrier between those who are outside and those who are inside. But once you have scaled the outer barrier, they become lower and lower, so that you may, after a considerable amount of time and shared history, reach the core. To return to the diagram, there may be a difference between which level you think you are in and which level someone from the other culture thinks you are in. For example, French visitors to the United States are astounded to be admitted quite readily into the family circle. They take this as evidence that the other person has made his or her psychic investment and that the potential for a deep friendship is there—which is normally not in fact the case.

Friends in France operate according to the unspoken rule, "Say what you mean and mean what you say." They expect promises to be followed up and do not understand that "I'll give you a call" or "We'll get together sometime for lunch" in the United States can easily mean "We may never see each other again." Many French people living in the United States, after finding that such statements are not firm commitments, hastily conclude that Americans are phony and unreliable. From the American perspective, on the other hand, such a comment reinforces a pleasant and positive encounter without an obligation to follow through. Autonomy is maintained and respected, and the choice of continuing the relationship by getting together again is left open.

THAT'S WHAT FRIENDS ARE FOR

As mentioned earlier, the American culture is strongly oriented to doing. Accordingly, American friends often get together to share a specific activity. If friends share a particular hobby or interest such as quilting or fishing, it is likely that this activity will be the focus of their time together.

Friends in France may also share specific activities or tasks, but they do not always feel the need to do so; simply being together is enough. This reflects the French cultural orientation toward being. A group of friends may get together with no particular purpose in mind. During their time together they may discuss possibilities such as a picnic at the beach or a film. These plans are hashed out and critiqued by the entire group, perhaps in a café over endless cups of coffee, and may or may not be followed up; the discussing is more important than the doing.

Rick, a young American, was puzzled by this when, as a foreign student newly arrived in Poitiers, he was invited to spend an evening with a group of French students:

I thought, "Great! The natives are friendly." So all of us—about a dozen kids altogether, male and female—met up at this café and started to talk about what to do. Somebody suggested a movie, but a couple of other people had seen it already, or heard from someone else that it wasn't very good, and then every-one talked about movies for awhile. Then somebody else suggested we go out someplace to dance, which led to a critique of every dance place in town, but no consensus. Same thing when I suggested we could go out and grab a bite somewhere. In the end, we spent the whole evening supposedly deciding what to do until about three in the morning, when everybody went home.

What this young American could not see was that the group was doing something very important: developing and reinforcing the ties of friendship that held them together.

The important thing [in a French conversation] is to establish ties, to create a network, tenuous as it may be, between the conversants. The exchange of words, in the "thread" of conversation, serves to weave these ties between the speakers. If we imagine a conversation as being a spider's web, we can see the exchanging of words as playing the role of the spider, generating the threads which bind the participants. The ideal (French) conversation would resemble a perfect spider's web: delicate, fragile, elegant, brilliant, of harmonious proportions, a work of art. . . . We [French] create the fabric of our relationship in the same way and at the same time that we "make" conversation. (Carroll 1987, 25–26)

While Americans value their connections to family and friends, they feel that ultimately they must act in their own best interest and stand on their own two feet. The individual is the basic building block of society. In a culture that values independence and autonomy, close and interdependent relationships may seem dysfunctional, if not actually pathological.

In contrast, as far as the French are concerned, Marx was right about at least one thing: the smallest unit into which humanity can be divided is two, not one. One is a fiction. A friendship in the French sense blurs the boundaries between friends. It develops as an organic whole: two people merge with noth-ing in between. A relationship has no existence beyond the people who live it, since they simply embody it. Friendship in French culture cannot be understood as a step-by-step approach where both parties are making progress toward an implied goal of becoming friends. As French people spend time together and get to know each other, their *cercles* simply begin to overlap.

In the United States, even very close friends are careful to respect each other's individual space. Balance and reciprocity based on mutual respect for the other's independence and individualism are vital foundations for friendships among Americans, who generally act on the principle that adults are—should be and want to be—independent, not beholden to anyone. "Owing" someone as a result of the other person's kindness is a debt Americans take seriously. The common American expression "I owe you one" has no French equivalent. Accordingly, they strive to maintain harmony in the nature and type of their exchanges.

French friends see obligations not in the context of reciprocity but rather as elements in the network of their relationships. "Perhaps Emmanuelle will not 'return' what I do for her today, but she will certainly do something for someone else when the chance comes up, and someone else may do something for me, or for another person altogether." In the end it's not important, because the goal is not to maintain some kind of cosmic bookkeeping. For those outside your network, your obligations are minimal; for those inside, you simply don't count up what you do or receive.

Raymonde Carroll suggests that, for the French, their networks are what defines them, whether the actual effect of the network is positive or not.

> The cultural premise which might take the form "I exist in a network" molds my French way of seeing. I am as much fed, carried, made significant by the network of relationships which defines me as I can be trapped, stifled and oppressed by it. Without this network, I am out of my element, and I suffer all the more as I am not conscious of this.
>
> Similarly, an American cultural premise . . . could take the following form: "I exist outside all networks." This does not mean that these networks do not exist or that they have no importance for me (an American), but that I make myself, I define myself. Whoever I am in American society, wherever I come from, whatever I have, I create the fabric of my identity, as is evoked, in a more limited context, by the expression "self-made man."
> (1987, 145)

The importance of networks or webs in a French person's life can hardly be overstated. Perhaps the closest equivalent in American culture would be a large and very close-knit family. Imagine, then, that a French person operates within several overlapping webs of this nature. We can see that working this way requires an enormous effort in relationship building and maintenance, in responding to the needs of others in the network, and in directing requests to the proper person in the proper way. But speed is not of the essence, since it is the relationship that counts, after all. The focus is how good you feel and not so much what you have achieved; the process, not the task.

A French person also needs to be quick to operate in this way, and very intuitive. Life looks like a vaudeville plate-spinning act: one has to keep an eye on all of the plates at once, giving them enough of a turn to keep them going without knocking them off the stick. But things don't always go smoothly, and sometimes one has to step carefully over shattered crockery. Friendships in the United States, based as they are on shared tastes, opinions, or interests more than on commitment, need to be relatively free of friction. Edward T. Hall and Mildred Reed Hall suggest,

> The American drive to be liked, accepted, and approved of by a wide circle of friends and associates means they must inevitably sacrifice some of their individuality. The French are less likely to hide their real selves, and hence the French are equally less likely to be good team players in business or elsewhere. (1990, 152)

American friends try to offer positive support to each other and to establish harmony. If they disagree, they may downplay their differences, agree to disagree, or try to smooth things over to maintain good relations. Bickering, argument, and open disagreement are signs that people are not getting along well and that the relationship may be in danger of falling apart.

French friends do not seek to maintain harmony but rather to cultivate distinction and avoid boredom. They expect to disagree, to criticize, even to argue. A friend may be very direct, even frankly critical, but this is part and parcel of interpersonal relationships and not necessarily meant or taken as insulting. The French find it tedious to always be in agreement and for this reason may be attracted to friends who are quite different from themselves. Since the relationship is not based on agreement, it is not threatened by disagreement, and French friends expect one another to comment honestly on their actions and choices. Support can be expressed in confrontation as well as by acquiescence. The bond between friends is not fragile and can stand up to this tension, even be strengthened and deepened by it.

Americans, raised to avoid sensitive subjects in conversation, are often taken aback by the vehemence and even rudeness (as they see it) of French conversations about precisely those sensitive topics, for example, politics. One American woman had gone to a great deal of trouble to prepare a special meal for her first dinner party in France. While her cooking was a success, the evening, she thought, was catastrophic:

> I almost died when everybody started arguing about politics. It got so bad I just about crawled under the table and waited for the battle to end. But later, as everyone was leaving, they all said what a terrific time they'd had, how delicious the meal was, and how much they looked forward to getting together again.

FRIENDLY SUGGESTIONS

As an American looking to make French friends, you would do well not to rush the process. Take your cue for pacing from your French acquaintance, and try not to "come on too strong" in the early stages. Remember the implicit personal commitment inherent in French friendships, and either take it seriously from the beginning or make it clear you are not interested.

Once you have decided to pursue the friendship, by all means put your heart into it. Your French friend certainly will. However, you do not need to stress this overtly as you might in the United States with statements such as "It's great to get together with you. I really enjoy the time we spend fishing (or shopping)." The explicit way in which Americans talk about their friendship sounds artificial to the French, almost like you are trying to convince them of something.

Keep in mind the obligations of friendship from a French perspective, and the fact that you and your friend are part of each other's inner circle. You may be fortunate enough to be included in get-togethers with your friend's old classmates or family. When this happens, try to "go with the flow" and don't get anxious if things seem vague or are not moving forward. Just being together is an important part of friendship.

Finally, try to be consciously aware of your unstated assumptions and expectations in personal relationships, and watch for signs that these match—or don't match—those of your friend. Many Americans learned some version of the Golden Rule as children: "Do unto others as you would have them do unto you." But the Golden Rule does not apply in intercultural relationships, since the other person may not want to have done to him or her as you would have done to you. Find out what it is your friend *does* want—celebrating a birthday at happy hour with a bunch of coworkers or a quiet dinner with family and close friends—before taking off in the wrong direction. This might be called the Platinum Rule: "Do unto others as they would like you to do unto them."

NINE

With Romance

While the French can't actually take credit for inventing love, they have certainly raised it to an art form. Frenchmen and -women have a spectacular reputation in this area, and most of them seem to have accepted upholding it as their personal responsibility. The French are also given to discussing and philosophizing on the affairs of the heart and body in ways that are unimaginable in the United States. Two well-known French writers and thinkers, Françoise Giroud and Bernard-Henri Lévy, developed an entire book from a series of conversations concerning love, desire, seduction, jealousy, infidelity, marriage, and falling out of love. They discuss these themes using literary and historical references as well as personal observations and experiences. This type of discourse can trace its lineage back to the Courts of Love of the Middle Ages.

One thing they emphatically agree on is that relationships between men and women in France are certainly better than in any other country. Giroud observes that stable, adult men do not feel that their virility is threatened by women taking power, while others may be knocked off balance by powerful women. "Fortunately," she adds, "there are fewer such men in France than elsewhere!" (Giroud and Lévy 1993, 212).

LOVER OR FRIEND—THE
ART OF SÉDUCTION

Americans tend to view romantic and intimate relationships as deeper levels of friendship. Wedding invitations in the United States may read, "Today I will marry my friend"; greeting cards may say, "Happiness is marrying your best friend." In President Obama's acceptance speech, he referred to his wife, Michelle, as "my best friend for the last sixteen years." These sentiments are baffling to the French who, as good Cartesians, distinguish between relationships of friends and relationships of romantic and intimate partners. These categories do not overlap, and each has a different set of rules and expectations.

Elisabeth Badinter, a Frenchwoman who has written widely on gender issues, summarized the French attitude thus: *"La pire des choses dans une relation homme-femme, c'est d'être camarades"* ("The worst thing in a male-female relationship is to be friends"). She notes that *séduction*—in the French, not the American, sense—is a vital component in most male-female interactions in France (1995).

Séduction in French means attracting by means of irresistible charm. Seductiveness is only one aspect of desire. It can be playful, serious, or a combination. It is a quality of men as well as of women, although women are particularly skilled at it. Séduction is a game that just about everybody plays when they feel like it. In order to walk down a busy street in Paris, a well-dressed businesswoman was forced to squeeze between a large crowd of men on the sidewalk and the window of the electronics shop where a wall of TV sets was tuned to the Tour de France. Many men made comments about her blocking their view of the race. With a knowing smile and a toss of the head, she laughed and said, "Well, *messieurs*, if you would rather look at bicycles. . . ."

The unstated assumption—not shared by Americans—is that men and women will want to please and charm each other, but that such mild flirtatiousness is harmless and essentially playful as long as the participants remain in the category of friends. Thus, a Frenchwoman may go out to a restaurant, for example, with a man other than her husband without necessarily raising eyebrows. For Americans, the lack of clear category boundaries means that in many cases such a situation is suspect, at best.

Hannah, an American woman who had lived in France for many years, returned to the United States with her French husband, Jean-Paul. One rainy weekend, he was away on business. Knowing that the wife of a French couple they knew was also away, she phoned the husband and suggested they get together for Sunday brunch and a movie. "Better than rattling around the house all alone."

Hannah realized that she had been operating in French mode when her next-door neighbors—an American couple—came into the restaurant.

> I saw them out of the corner of my eye, then they disappeared. They were hiding behind the hostess stand. I realized they had seen me with Olivier and, knowing Jean-Paul was out of town, had jumped to a really wrong conclusion. Fortunately, we know each other well enough that I could go over and coax them out of hiding, introduce them to my friend, and explain everything. I think.

Frenchmen and -women can be flirtatious with each other without breaking any taboos, while in the United States, communication between the sexes is straightforward and monitored internally to avoid any shadow of sexual innuendo—unless that is what is intended. Men and women in France can remain friends while they flirt, but in the U.S., flirting instantly changes the tone of the relationship and may even make it impossible for the friendship to continue. Since the American boundaries between friendship and romance are fuzzy and do not provide an external definition for the relationship, the interaction between men and women must provide an internal one. Thus, the tone and pattern of their communication have to make it clear that they are "just friends." The firmer French boundaries provide the external definition for the relationship, which gives freer play to the interaction between those involved.

An American character in a French novel notes that Frenchwomen seem to have such easygoing, uncomplicated relationships with the men in their lives, regardless of the nature of the relationship. "Karen had talked about it with Daphne—these Frenchwomen had a certain 'something' in their relationships with men. It was inexplicable, but it worked. And Karen found that 'something' suspect" (Hermary-Vieille and Sarde 1997, 299).

In recent years, gender issues in the United States have become so fraught with tension that, in many situations, Americans simply try to neutralize their interactions by eliminating any recognition of sexual difference. Asking the French to behave in a gender-neutral fashion is like asking them not to breathe. Rather than trying to erase or eliminate gender differences, both Frenchmen and -women prefer to emphasize them.

> [Corinne] always thought that the difference between men and women was precious, something to be preserved. She adored little games of seduction with men . . . and then, Corinne loved men . . . she had a hard time understanding the visceral antipathy toward the male that she noticed in [some American women]. (295)

Frenchwomen in the United States often complain of feeling ignored by American men, who neither look at them appreciatively nor display the *galanterie* of Frenchmen. American women are confused by this attitude. For them, calling attention to women's sexuality in a nonsexual relationship or setting is by definition an affront because it reduces women to the status of objects. And, when in France, they are appalled by precisely those behaviors that seem to charm Frenchwomen. "When I arrived in Lyon," recalled one young American character, "I just couldn't take the wandering hands, the staring, getting touched in the metro" (291).

THE DATING GAME AND THE COUPLE

It is essential for French and American men and women to understand the differences in how people see relationships beginning and developing, and how these different viewpoints affect their encounters with members of the other culture. For example, French students coming to the United States are baffled by American dating behavior. In French culture there is no equivalent to the concept of a date and no parallel in what we can call the courtship ritual. In the U.S., the first couple of dates are usually seen as a no-strings-attached trial period; the couple goes out together to find out if they get along and if they like each other enough to pursue the relationship.

In France, a woman who agrees to go out with a man is considered to be past that initial stage. She and the man have, in effect, agreed that they want to see more of each other. They may spend a pleasant evening and each one go home alone, or they may spend the night together, but both definitely feel there is at least potentially some substantive interest. This has come as a surprise to more than one American woman, thinking she was going out for a first date with a friend. The Frenchman may seem pushy, aggressive, and moving too fast, but for him the first steps have already been taken. He cannot understand why she seems to be moving backward. Similarly, a Frenchwoman invited for a date by an American man may be surprised by his tentativeness, since she assumes they are a step beyond where he thinks they are. He may think she is the "fast" one.

In the U.S., people have a tendency to consider, discuss, and "work on" their relationships almost as if the relationships had an existence independent from the people involved in them. A romantic relationship generally proceeds in a step-by-step, linear fashion, as shown in the diagram below. So a woman who asks a friend, "Hey, you and Bob have been seeing each other for a long time now; what's up with you two?" may get an answer such as, "Well, we've talked about getting married but there's nothing definite just yet."

**Relationship Building:
A Sequential Process**

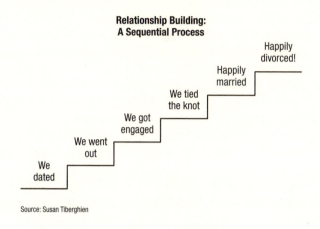

Source: Susan Tiberghien

Relationship Building: An Osmosis

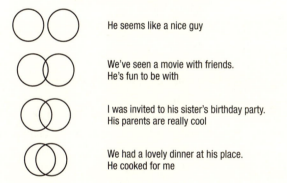

He seems like a nice guy

We've seen a movie with friends.
He's fun to be with

I was invited to his sister's birthday party.
His parents are really cool

We had a lovely dinner at his place.
He cooked for me

Recall the importance of the *cercle* in French social geometry. It shows up again in the way romantic relationships tend to develop in France: *cercles* gradually overlap, and friends usually need to read between the lines to understand how things stand. For example, a woman whose friend tells her, "I was invited to his sister's birthday party. His parents are really cool!" will understand that the new girlfriend has been invited into her boyfriend's family—something that may not happen in the U.S. until the American couple is actually engaged. Admission into the respective family *cercles* is often an important development in the formation of a new couple.

Younger high school and college students in the United States as well as in France tend to "hang out" in mixed groups, but the pairing up of couples generally happens at an earlier age among Americans. The formal and ritualistic aspects of a U.S. dating relationship are also puzzling to young French students and professionals. An American woman who eventually married a Frenchman became aware of the differences as a student in France.

> There was little pairing off and dating. When I explained how in the States a boy and a girl first dated, then went steady . . . then got engaged, they wouldn't believe me. They shook their heads and said it sounded like standing in line. So wherever we went, we'd pile onto the scooters, the eight of us, the girls with their arms around whoever was in front of them. (Grearson and Smith 1995, 202)

One Frenchwoman in the U.S. was baffled by the concept. "During this 'dating' process, people seem to be trying to give a good impression, putting their best foot forward. This doesn't give a realistic picture of who the people are, so that once they start living together or get married, disappointment is inevitable." The images were just too good to be true. By hanging out with groups of friends, French couples are much more likely to get an authentic picture of the other person before they become romantically involved.

Of course, people eventually do pair up in France. The contrast between French and American cultures emerges in the reaction of the new couple's group(s) of friends. In the United States, positive support is usually offered; the woman's female friends ask for all the "juicy details," while the man's male friends joke about his finally being "roped and branded." The French group, on the other hand, usually "retaliates" against the new couple's breaking the circle by humorously "roasting" them. They may be taken aside discreetly and asked, "Are you really serious about this? Have you seen her without makeup?" or "Maybe his other sixteen girlfriends knew something you don't!"

In fact, this teasing is partly a recognition of a change in status. Rather than being just two people in a group of friends, the man and woman have declared that they should now be considered a couple. And for the French, a couple is a particular social entity.

> "[T]he couple" is a social category (for the French). It is the affirmation of certain social values: to be part of a couple is to proclaim sexual bonds that are approved, made legal, legitimate, or licit by marriage, living together, or simply by the tacit, public approval of social as well as sexual ties. Forming a couple is a social act, unlike having a lover. Indeed, needless to say, forming a couple is different from coupling. This means that in order to exist, my couple relation-

ship must be "spoken": we put others in the habit of combining our names by doing so ourselves, by our discourse in front of others, and by our behavior in the presence of others. (Carroll 1987, 61)

In November 1999 the French National Assembly approved the *Pacte Civil de Solidarité* (PACS, or Civil Pact of Solidarity), legal status somewhere between living together and marriage. Once they are "pacsed," couples—heterosexual or homosexual—have most of the same rights and responsibilities as married spouses. They have a common fiscal regime and can file joint tax returns after three years together. If one partner is not already covered by the social security system, he or she is included in the other partner's coverage. There are some differences; for example, inheritance is not automatic for PACS partners (but it is possible if an agreement—*régime de l'indivision*—has been drawn up). Unlike their married counterparts, *pacsés* cannot adopt children or gain French citizenship through the arrangement. Foreign PACS partners can, however, acquire French nationality under certain conditions.

YOU SAY TOMATOES, I SAY LES TOMATES

Words that mean the same thing in different languages may carry very different nuances. Dugan Romano, a writer on intercultural marriage as well as a participant in one, notes that love may mean different things to different people and "is defined differently by different cultures—something that many intercultural spouses have learned to their surprise and, often, dismay only after they are married" (2008, 17).

All relationships require communication, but intercultural relationships require communication on many different levels. One of the difficulties in personal intercultural relationships is that so many different aspects of people's characters come into play. Does my wife behave in this way (which strikes me as odd and possibly offensive) because she is French, because she is female, because she is Parisian, or is it just a personal quirk? As one American wife of a Frenchman observed, "I finally found out that he wasn't a jackass after all, just a typical Frenchman!"

Conversely, we may excuse behavior in a partner from another culture that we would find unacceptable in a person from our own. Romano quotes the French wife of a Kuwaiti: "I forgave him all sorts of things I'd never let a French guy get away with because I thought that was just the way they did things in his country. Was I mad when I found out that in some ways he was a boor even in his own language" (97).

Where does the culture end and the person begin? Is it possible to distinguish between the two? Probably not, and it would not be an especially useful distinction even if we could. "In order for intercultural couples to overcome their communication handicaps, they have to work harder at listening, using the heart and mind as well as the eye and ear to avoid misunderstandings" (127).

Apart from the language issue, which can be enormously significant for couples, perhaps the biggest difference in communication between French and Americans lies in their styles: direct or indirect, implicit or explicit, linear or nonlinear. An American woman recalls her French boyfriend's unusual implicit marriage proposal:

> I came home from work one evening to find him filling out reams of bureaucratic paperwork concerned with marrying a foreigner in France. I asked, "Planning to marry a foreigner?" Deep in concentration, he nodded. "Anyone I know?" I pressed. Finally, he looked at me like I was the village idiot and said, "You, of course." I realized later that as far as he was concerned, the question had already been answered, so there was no need to ask it.

One French-American couple jokingly provides each other with "scripts" of what they want to hear the other partner say: "Now you should put your arm around my shoulders and say, '*Pauvre bébé*, you must be exhausted. Sit down and let me get you a little *apéritif*—what would you like?'"

Susan Tiberghien, an American married to a Frenchman, wrote a delightful piece called "At Home in Two Languages." After detailing a typical day as it would be lived in French or English, she concludes,

> Bilingualism or split personality? Once the two patterns fit, the choice is mine. I wake up and write down my dreams in the language I dreamed them. I read the newspapers in both. I live my day as it comes along. I say either *"tu"* or *"vous,"* whichever one I wish. And I make "I love you" sound just as beautiful as *"Je t'aime."* (Dicks 1995, 140)

When things are going smoothly, we find differences enriching and enjoyable: "Americans are just so open, so free from all the traditional French restrictions"; "The French have such great style."

When things are not going well, we quickly find fault with whatever cultural characteristic is annoying us: "These damn Americans just don't know how to behave. Look at the way she throws herself into the chair." "It's just a slice of leftover pizza—why does he have to set the table as if he were eating a five-course banquet?"

> Couples often react to each other as though the other's behavior were a personal attack rather than just a difference rooted in ethnicity. Typically, we tolerate differences when we are not under stress. In fact, we find them appealing. However, when stress is added to a system, our tolerance for difference diminishes. We become frustrated if we are not understood in ways that fit our wishes and expectations. (McGoldrick, Pearce, and Giordano 1982, 21–22)

The husband and wife in an ideal American marriage walk hand in hand through life, smiling sweetly at one another. The French ideal is harder to picture, but the couple may very well be gesticulating wildly, yelling at each other at the top of their lungs—but at least they're not bored. In French culture, as we have seen, harmony may not be a desirable state. Where the American partner may feel the relationship itself is at stake and try to defuse a tense situation by compromising or placating, the French partner may not feel that even a serious argument means major problems. As far as he or she is concerned, nothing truly fundamental has been threatened by the argument.

In an intercultural relationship, it may be easier and less threatening to interpret differences as a culture clash. The statement "It's a cultural problem" can paper over cracks in a relationship. Many people, particularly those with little personal intercultural experience, mistakenly believe that culture is simply a given, somehow carved in stone. When the strain reaches a crisis point in an intercultural marriage, the couple generally focuses on the cultural differences, often exaggerating them, and blaming them for every problem. A cultural conflict may be less threatening than a personal one. It may be easier to think that one has married the wrong culture rather than the wrong person.

TEN

With Work

In this chapter, we analyze some fundamental differences between the French and American conceptions of work and its place in an individual's life and identity. Specific discussion of intercultural issues in the workplace will be provided in chapter 17, "Working across Cultures."

As an introduction to this chapter, and as a way to set the stage, we would like to present research data about the number of hours worked annually in France and the U.S. between 1950 and 2008.

According to data from the Groningen Growth Development Center (GGDC) and the Organization for Economic Cooperation and Development (OECD), the number of hours worked per year has declined since 1950 throughout Europe, as well as in the U.S. and in Japan. A comparison of the charts for the U.S. and France shows that the decline has been steeper and gone deeper in France (see chart below). In the aftermath of World War II, the French worked over 2,200 hours annually, much of it dedicated to rebuilding the country's devastated infrastructure. The French total reached an all-time low of 1,533 hours per year in 2003 compared to 1,788 for the U.S., and has risen slightly since then. The numbers for both countries appear to have leveled off since the beginning of the twenty-first century. Americans work approximately two hundred more hours per year than the French, or about twenty-five eight-hour days.

Hours Worked Per Year

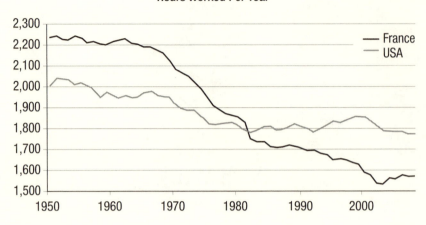

I WORK, THEREFORE I AM

The cliché is accurate for most Americans, who live to work. Americans tend to define themselves by their job or profession and find it quite normal to introduce themselves in this way: "Hi, I'm Maria Lopez, and I'm HR Manager at X Company." If asked to describe themselves further, they usually list their activities: "I'm a Cub Scout Den Mother, I play tennis, I'm the vice president of the church women's group, and I volunteer at Children's Hospital." Americans' activities, and particularly their jobs, are how they establish and affirm their identity. Not surprisingly, American employees are expected to give the highest priority to their work, sacrificing personal and family time if necessary.

> Research on the meaning of work in the U.S. shows the centrality of work in people's lives. In one study, about two-thirds of the people interviewed said that they would continue to work even if they had enough money to live decently until the end of their lives. The researchers concluded that "people want to work because they are intuitively aware that work, be it 'bad' or 'good,' helps to shape them." Work gives people a sense of direction and allows them the opportunity for personal creativity and fulfillment. (Asselin 1994, 19)

Manual work also plays a central role in American-style egalitarianism. Seeing the wealthy or the powerful engaged in manual labor reconfirms the American belief that all people are created equal. The White House once sent out a press release with a photo of former President Clinton and Vice President Gore helping to rebuild an African American church destroyed by arson. They were dressed in worn jeans and polo shirts and shown wearing work gloves and handling power tools. Clinton was shown on a stepladder wiping the sweat from his eyes while Gore drilled a hole in the wall. The photo resonated positively with the American public because of the typical American values it illustrated: self-reliance, taking action, pitching in to help a neighbor in need, informality, and the notion that no one is too high-and-mighty to do such a job.

In contrast to Americans, the French work to live. They are more likely to introduce themselves in terms of where they live or have lived, their family's roots, what school they went to (especially if it is a prestigious one), and personal interests such as the type of music or books they prefer. In short, French people tend to make a much looser connection between who they are and what they do.

The French public would be surprised to see a photo of their leaders engaged in manual labor as Clinton and Gore were. It would be considered inappropriate and undignified. When an enterprising American couple purchased the traditional Quimper Faïence factory in Brittany, they put on jeans and pitched in with their employees to clean the place up. This was so unusual that the local newspaper sent a reporter to record the event.

The most rigorous manual labor a French public official or business director might sully his (more likely than her) hands with would be the ceremonial groundbreaking with a first shovel of dirt or laying the cornerstone of a new building. Both, of course, are more symbolic than anything else.

In addition to respect for and deference to hierarchy, the French admiration for things intellectual corresponds to a devaluing of manual labor. Those who make a living with brawn may be appreciated as good people and good workers, particularly when the bathroom is flooded, but they will never have the status of those who make their living with their brains.

Work is important to the French, but it is not the primary focus or source of satisfaction in life. Robert Moran and his colleagues note that, "[the French] are seldom willing to sacrifice the enjoyment of life out of excessive dedication to work. *Qualité de la vie* [quality of life] is what matters" (2007, 452). Depending on the position and level of responsibility, work may simply not be as high on the French employee's list of priorities as it is on the average American's list. Promotions mean more money, but also more work and responsibility, and may not be as eagerly sought in France as in the United States. Spending time with one's family and friends or pursuing personal interests may be just as important as professional advancement. Although there are some "workaholics" in French companies, someone who seems to have no outside life, attachments, or interests will be considered a bit odd. With quality of life as one of their top priorities, the

French may not be as psychologically devastated by the loss of a job as Americans often are. You have lost your position, which may indeed be very serious, but you have not lost part of your identity.

The importance of living a balanced life in France is reflected in the more laid-back attitude toward work and the work schedule. All employees receive by law at least five weeks of paid vacation per year. Depending on a company's policies and scheduling needs, the maximum allowable time off in one stretch is twenty-four working days. Generally, French vacations may last two to four weeks, in contrast to the American practice of taking vacation as long weekends or a week at a time, at most. Americans may be concerned that they will just have too much trouble catching up when they get back—or that someone will have maneuvered into their job while they're away. As the French say (but Americans live by), *"Qui va à la chasse, perd sa place."* (If you go out hunting, you lose your position.)

The desertion of Paris for the entire month of August is legendary, and much of the nation's business is virtually shut down as well. In addition, the eleven paid holidays per year (twelve in Alsace-Lorraine) are often extended through the custom of *les ponts* (bridges). If a holiday falls on a Tuesday or Thursday, the French often take Monday or Friday off as well, whether paid or not, to gain a four-day weekend. The number of holidays in May (three to four), combined with les ponts, can make for a very light work month.

In the United States, the phrase "quality of life" is often understood to exclude the quality of life in the workplace. In France, the broader concept of quality of life includes work. The French have a reputation for being bons vivants who live the good life, taking pleasure in it and stopping to smell the roses—even to eat them in elaborate confectionery. French people are not risking core concepts of self on their job performance, and their approach is therefore less intense. French managers may work late or on weekends to complete an urgent project, while subordinates generally leave at the usual time and get back to the project the following morning. Americans at all levels facing a deadline or a demanding task have an essential part of their identity at stake and will often work extra hours to meet the challenge.

Where American workers pride themselves on working hard ("We really worked hard today; we got a lot accomplished"), French workers are more likely to congratulate each other for working well: *"On a bien travaillé aujourd'hui"* ("We worked well today"). In this connection, it is interesting to note that there is no good equivalent in French culture for the term "work ethic." The closest would be *conscience professionelle*, or professional conscience. This term refers to an individual's professionalism and seriousness on the job but does not include the American concept of commitment to work, one's job, or the company. As in English, *éthique* (ethics) is used for a group of people who abide by the same professional rules under *un code déontologique* (a code of ethics).

MY RESUMÉ, YOUR CURRICULUM VITAE

We can gain some interesting insights if we examine the cultural values that underlie the preparation and evaluation of resumés in both cultures. Resumé writers in the United States are advised to use "action words" like *achieved, accomplished,* and *managed.* The resumé itself is a fairly hard-sell summary of what the individual has accomplished. People try to present themselves positively as active, dynamic, hard-working individuals. While actual fabrication of information is frowned upon, the writer is encouraged to edit or "manage" the information to impress the potential employer. An impressive, eye-catching presentation is important so that the resumé and its writer will stand out from the crowd. The message is, "Here is what I can do for your company."

French resumés are more straightforward, a relatively unembellished listing of raw data such as position held and dates of employment. Personal details such as age, marital status, number of children, and possibly a photo are often included. Although some details may be judiciously left out, there will be no effort at "impression management." In fact, a fancy presentation will be suspect: it looks too slick and suggests that the writer may be trying to hide something or is glossing over a lack of substance. The message here is, "Do you think the position your company is offering might suit me?"

This human approach stresses who the candidate is as a person, rather than just the skill set and experience he or she can offer. At the same time, the inclusion of personal details may result in discrimination, and many minorities in France have raised precisely this objection. There is some discussion of the *"CV anonyme,"* in which even the candidate's name would not appear (recognizably ethnic names sometimes land a resumé right in the trash). French insurance company AXA has used anonymous resumés to recruit its sales representatives since 2005 and is very satisfied with the practice. In 2009, 20 percent of its sales representatives were recruited using an anonymous resume and AXA is planning to extend the technique to administrative jobs in the near future. However, the practice is far from generalized and the idea remains highly controversial. In 2009, the government issued a call for one hundred French companies in seven *départements* to begin using anonymous resumés. By November 2009, fifty companies had already committed to the pilot program. According to Diversity and Equal Opportunity Commissioner Yazid Sabeg, the anonymous resumé is not an end in itself, "but is a useful measure to break the barrier of access to the first interview while neutralizing prejudices. And symbolically, it's a strong sign for a company" (Van Eeckhout, 2009).

One American HR recruiter in the U.S. developed an effective technique when reviewing French-style CVs. "In the U.S., I can't even *know* a person's race, age, marital status, and so on. When I get French CVs, I know that information will usually be on the upper right-hand corner. To ensure that I comply with U.S. law, I slide the document out of the envelope and fold back the right-hand corner without even looking at it. Then I look at the resumé."

By playing up a person's achievements and playing down personal details, American resumés aim for objectivity, for a straightforward indication of an individual's potential. If the candidate has the education, background, and skills to do the job, the rest is considered irrelevant. In France, the feeling is that education, credentials, professional background, and skills may not be enough; personality and temperament matter as much as qualifications. French recruiters look for a fit between the individual and the context of the job beyond the candidate's ability to accomplish the tasks. They look at the person's qualifications, of course, but they also look at who the person is.

EMPLOYMENT, DIPLOMAS, AND SOCIAL WORTH

In October 2009, Eric Maurin, a research director at EHESS (Ecole des Hautes Etudes en Sciences Sociales) and professor of economy at the Paris School of Economics, analyzed the evolution of work and employment in France from the period between the two recessions of 1974 and 1993 through the global crisis of 2008–2009. He concluded that a *frileuse* (fearful, timid) France is suffering from a social fear, *une peur du déclassement* (fear of downgrading), and that this fear has a huge effect on people's attitudes and behaviors, both psychologically and socially, and eventually on France's national and international policies via trade regulations and protectionism. In many ways, he concurs with the conclusions of Yann Algan and Pierre Cahuc, two researchers whose work we will look at more closely in chapter 14. Algan and Cahuc suggest that group or personal benefits and perks—what they call corporatism—make France a very inegalitarian, hierarchical society where people tend to defend their own narrow interests for fear of losing the social status attached to their position or rank. Until 2008, France had a two-tiered retirement system with different provisions for workers in the public and private sectors. This is a significant example of certain categories of workers enjoying special, hard-won benefits, often at the expense of other groups.

Eric Maurin defines *déclassement* as a phenomenon of social fracture or disenfranchisement when an employee loses his or her job and the financial security that comes with it. Suddenly faced with the precariousness of a job search and possible long term unemployment, an individual might lose his sense of social belonging and social worth.

In Eric Maurin's words, "the French notion of *'déclassement'* doesn't have a real equivalent today in Anglo-Saxon and Scandinavian countries. It is a symptom of our old inegalitarian and hierarchical society, still aristocratic in many ways, where ranks and honors are granted for life, and are meant to stay within the same family. Hereditary transmission of nobility and its privileges disappeared with the Revolution, but social honor remains nonetheless attached to the acquisition and preservation of status. The fear of social demotion is the passion of status societies caught in the winds of democratization, when ranks and honors cease to be protected by heredity, and ought to be gained by every generation" (2009, 8).

In a dynamic environment, free from overwhelming state intervention and protection, one can hope to find another job fairly easily. But the global crisis has hit France hard, and the French economy has lost over 400,000 jobs in 2009 while its GDP shrank by 2.2 percent and business investment went down by 7.7 percent.[13/14]

Many young graduates are also unable to find a job. In many cases, they need to rely on what the French call *petits boulots* (small jobs), which undervalue and underutilize their education, and cause their potential to stagnate or diminish.

Despite the gloomy figures, Eric Maurin asserts, it is not so much the actual levels of *déclassement* which trouble those who have a steady, well-protected job, but the fear of *déclassement* that haunts the French, especially the middle classes and executives. In a 2006 poll, 48 percent of interviewees believed that they might one day become *SDF—sans domicile fixe*, or homeless. Two years later, this proportion jumped to an alarming 60 percent.

Even more at risk are young people without a higher degree. "In 2008, among young people who left school during the five previous years, 47 percent of those without a degree were unemployed, as opposed to slightly less than 7

---

[13] *http://videos.tf1.fr/jt-we/la-pire-recession-depuis-l-apres-guerre-5690957.html*
[14] At the end of 2009, based on OECD data, France had 2,916,000 unemployed workers, or 10% of the active population—the same rate as the U.S. *(www.oecd.org/document/29/0,3343,fr_2649_34251_44564061_1_1_1_1,00.html* and *http://stats.oecd.org/Index.aspx?QueryName=251&QueryType=View&Lang=fr)*

percent of those having a higher degree. This is a 40-point gap, the highest in history. More than ever, failure in school is a disqualifying factor in life."

This discrepancy between educational "haves" and "have-nots" is corroborated by research about social inequalities resulting from social origins. Sociologist François Dubet, quoted in *Le Monde,* reports, "Out of ten children of executives entering middle school in 1995, eight were still studying [at university level] ten years later, and only one dropped out without passing the *bac*. Out of ten children of workers, however, three were studying at university level while half dropped out without taking the bac."[15]

France doesn't do well compared to other European countries. According to Eric Charbonnier, leader of the OECD Pisa study quoted in the same article, "Here [in France] a 15-year-old high school student from a disadvantaged environment has a risk of failure 4.3 times higher than one from the upper social classes. The average for OECD countries is 3 times higher."

Despite efforts to establish quotas and allow disadvantaged children access to better schools, this data confirms the stratification of employment according to social origin as well as the importance of a higher education degree—another indication that the elitist, inequitable grandes écoles system perpetuates discrepancy across social classes.

JOB SECURITY, DIGNITY, AND CONFORMITY IN THE WORKPLACE

In 2008, according to INSEE (National Institute of Statistics and Economic Studies), nearly 87 percent[16] of French employees (22.1 million) are protected under the terms of a *Contrat à Durée Indeterminée* (CDI), which makes it relatively difficult to fire them, sometimes even if they do not perform. The remaining 13 percent work as temps, apprentices, or under a *Contrat à Durée Determinée* (CDD), which specifies the period of employment and generally protects the worker from being dismissed before the time is over. Under the CDI, workers can be fired or laid off for two reasons only: either a *faute grave* (serious fault) or for economic reasons (restructuring, merger, etc.). Even in these cases, it may be extremely difficult to get rid of someone.

---

[15] *www.lemonde.fr/societe/article/2010/02/11/ecole-l-echec-du-modele-francais-d-egalite-des-chances_1304257_3224.html*
[16] *www.insee.fr/fr/themes/document.asp?ref_id=ip1272*

To bypass these legal roadblocks, a common practice is to put someone you want to get rid of—but can't—in the *voie de garage* (the image is of unwanted railway cars shunted off to a sideline) or *dans le placard* (in the closet—nothing to do with sexual orientation).

In practical terms, this would involve putting someone in a position where he or she has no real power or responsibilities—perhaps promoting him or her to the head of a department with no subordinates. The company follows the law, the employee is protected, and everyone else can get on with their jobs.

This level of job security is associated in France with the concept of human dignity, which cannot be sacrificed for mere commercial or financial consider-ations. There is a general assumption in France that employers will try to exploit workers if they are allowed to, and that the law and labor unions must prevent them from doing so and protect the workers.

The act of working and being productive in American culture is in itself an affirmation of an individual's worth. Americans take pride in what they do, and if they have to put up with adverse conditions to achieve their goals, they take additional pride in overcoming them: "We had to work around the clock and order in pizza at three in the morning, but the proposal looked great and we got the contract."

Such a comment from a French employee might sound to coworkers like a flimsy rationalization for aiding and abetting one's own exploitation. Intrinsic rewards such as pride in one's work and accomplishment are not enough in themselves to counterbalance personal sacrifice in a country where a wide range of employee benefits is mandated by French law. In addition to the vacations and holidays mentioned earlier, French employees have comprehensive health-care benefits, including prenatal care, child immunizations, regular checkups, and dental, vision, and prescription benefits, which they keep during periods of unem-ployment. There is also paid parental leave, job protection for pregnant workers or those on parental leave, subsidized day care, and family and child allowances. All of these are felt to support human dignity and are seen as a right, not a privilege.

Dignity in France, and especially social dignity, is closely related to the concept of solidarity. French citizens need to support one another against nega-tive forces that dehumanize individuals and deprive them of their dignity—for example, unemployment. Americans tend to see unemployment as an economic rather than a social issue, but for the French, it goes deeper. Because they are no longer active participants in society, the long-term unemployed are in danger of being marginalized, becoming second-class citizens cut off from the social world. Such a person is called an *exclu* (excluded person) in France, torn out of the social fabric. Attached to the notion of joblessness is a powerful element of shame. In the United States the fact of being without work may not in itself be cause for shame, particularly amidst the layoffs and downsizings of recent years, but failing to make every effort to find work, on the other hand, is considered shameful.

In March 2006, the French government tried to reduce high unemployment rates (particularly among young people) by passing laws to allow for a *Contrat Premier Emploi* (CPE, First Job Contract) for those under twenty-six. These laws made it possible for an employer to dismiss at will a CPE employee with neither warning nor severance within a two-year period. The idea was to loosen up the relatively rigid French job market and encourage employers to hire young people, since they would not be stuck with them if they did not work out.

Massive strikes and protests ensued, many led by the young people who would supposedly benefit from the CPE. They saw the possibility of being fired for any reason or no reason as an attack on their human dignity, and marched under slogans such as "WE ARE NOT KLEENEX"—in other words, something to be used and discarded. They demanded the same job protections as any other worker in France covered by a CDI. Eventually, the government was forced to back down and overturned the law.

These notions of dignity and respect are present in the French workplace as well, especially in the treatment of employees, which accounts in large part for the reaction of Disney employees in France to regulations regarding their dress and grooming. They felt that the company had no right to dictate such personal things, that they were being reduced from human beings to "employee units" devoid of personality. A common American reaction might be "If they don't like it, they can go work somewhere else." But Americans also agree that there are some things that no company can require of its employees. Imagine the outcry at American corporations if employees and their families were required to attend a specific church every Sunday morning as a condition of employment. The difference between France and the United States lies mainly in where the line is drawn.

Belonging is an important goal for American employees. Americans' pride in being part of the team makes them more willing—even eager—to play down individual differences and quirks. They may wear company logo clothing even outside the workplace or decorate their cars with company bumper stickers.

From a French perspective, it is sometimes hard to understand why employees with little loyalty to a specific company are willing to allow their employer to codify their professional attitudes and behaviors in the form of corporate values, vision, and mission statements. The French feel that work is important and provides people with a sense of social dignity, but top management had better not tell them how to behave or what to think.

As an example of this attitude, consider what happened during a contentious companywide meeting at the headquarters of a large French manufacturer. The CEO and founder of the company, a highly respected gentleman in his eighties, was making the case for austerity measures to improve profitability. He was publicly challenged by an assembly-line worker who argued that the need for such measures was proof of managerial incompetence and demanded the resignation of the entire board of directors. Such a confrontation is rare in France, but it is virtually unimaginable in the United States.

This anecdote illustrates a paradox that is not easily explained. While the French tend to be more respectful of hierarchy and more accepting of authority, they do not hesitate to voice their opinion to those occupying the highest levels, as the line worker did. The fact that workers generally cannot be fired for such outspokenness (only sent to the *voie de garage* or closet at worst) may encourage workers to speak up. In the United States, where the culture is generally less hierarchical and employees are more autonomous and empowered—but can also be fired at will—such a confrontation rarely occurs.

ELEVEN

With Politics

SETTING THE SCENE

Writing about politics and its cultural characteristics is a challenge because politics evolve very fast and are influenced by the few at the helm of the country.

At press time, Nicolas Sarkozy is in the third year of his presidency. Due to a change to the French Constitution in July 2008, no one can serve as president for more than two five-year terms, which means that, assuming Nicolas Sarkozy runs for another term in 2012 and is reelected, he will be president of the French Republic until 2017.

Nicolas Sarkozy brought change, ambition, and action to the country, as well as a very different, almost omnipresent "management style." The purpose of this chapter is not to look at his achievements (or lack thereof), but rather to consider the forces at play in the French political landscape.

As in many countries, these forces in France are split between right and left wings, with Sarkozy's party, *Union pour un Mouvement Populaire* (UMP—Union for a Popular Movement), enjoying a strong lead in the National Assembly. The opposition, as the French call it, has been seriously weakened, and the main opposition party (the Socialist Party) is undergoing a severe crisis after some long-lasting infighting and a crushing defeat during the European elections of June 2009. Other parties on the left are also part of the opposition (such as the Greens, the Communists, as well as several smaller "workers' parties"), but fending for oneself seems to be more important than offering a united front to counter the actions of the government. In the end, democracy and the people suffer. However, as the presidential election of 2012 approaches, the opposition has realized that cooperation is necessary to achieve victory in regional as well as national elections. There have been efforts, especially between the Socialists and the Greens, to offer a unified front—something which doesn't happen without bruised egos, local fights, and shifting alliances.

POLITICS AND EVERYDAY LIFE

The state plays such a central role in French life that politics is one of the most serious national preoccupations. Decisions made at the highest political levels can have an instant and significant effect on the daily routine of someone as distant as, for example, a farmer living near the Spanish border. For this reason, politics is more of an everyday affair in France than in the United States and is an eternal source of conversation and debate. Everyone has an opinion and expresses it with great energy, and this occurs just about everywhere. Arguments, even when quite heated, are enjoyed by participants and bystanders alike, particularly when laced with wit, irony, and a clever turn of phrase.

Television news broadcasts always cover political affairs in detail. From unions and employee demonstrations to the role of the state in education, every aspect of French economic and social life has some underlying political element. What matters to the French, though, is not just the actions of such and such a party, but also the ideology and purpose behind the action. Although the political gap between left and right has closed somewhat since the 1980s, each side retains a distinct ideology. In recent years, people have tended to define and choose their political affiliation not so much in terms of left or right sensibilities but rather in terms of a few important economic and social issues: the discrepancy between the "haves" and the "have-nots," unemployment and the loss of jobs to other countries, France's role in the European Union, immigration, and the debate over immigrants' rights. More wary than they used to be, the French tend to consider issues on a case-by-case basis before aligning themselves with any political party, and even then they do not necessarily support all aspects of the party's program. A phenomenon that confirmed this attitude among the "unhappy" is the emergence of a party in the center, the MoDem (*Mouvement Democrate*), whose leader, François Bayrou, won more than 18 percent of the votes in the first round of the 2007 presidential election. For many, the center is a good place to be because it allows you to look left and right and make any necessary move, depending on the election at stake, the leaders' position, issues of the moment, and political platforms.

American grassroots activism and lobbying of politicians are not features of French politics. This is not to say that backroom deals do not exist in France, but the notion of private, nonprofit, or corporate lobbying groups meeting with politicians to influence legislation before it is debated and voted into law is simply not the French way. Perhaps because of the Revolution and other popular uprisings, the relationship between the governed and those governing tends to be adversarial (hence the name *opposition*: *quelqu'un s'oppose à l'action du gouvernement*—someone who opposes the government's action) and comes into play primarily after a law has been proposed by the government. Then opponents take their case into the streets via protests, strikes, and other actions that can range from cheerful, colorful parades to violent confrontations with police and the *Compagnie Républicaine de Sécurité* (riot squad). In typical French fashion mirroring pre-Revolution times, lawmakers and other people at the top act and the people react. This process is reflected in the way policy decisions are made and handed down in business as well.

Political issues and the nature of political debate in France are a far cry from what happens in the United States where, despite the Obama administration's expansion of government programs and influence, demands for tax cuts and reduction of government intervention still have widespread support. Although working citizens in France pay close to half of their annual salaries in combined national and local taxes (including social security payments), there is no serious call for individual tax cuts. Instead, French politicians may wonder, "How much more can we ask French citizens to contribute to maintain the social security system and to keep France a strong leader among European countries?"

Budget cutting in the U.S. is normally undertaken to bring down the deficit or reduce taxes. In France, austerity measures were introduced in 1995 to ensure that the country could meet the economic criteria required for participation in the European Monetary Union. In addition, the necessity of ensuring minimal survival with dignity—for example, by increasing or prolonging social benefits—has stretched resources further in a country suffering from a stubbornly high unemployment rate of about 10 percent. High unemployment is a long lasting phenomenon that might be due more to a structural issue (how French society is structured and functions) than a temporary crisis—even a global one.

In a diverse country where immigration issues become more sensitive each day, the rise of the Front National (FN), an extreme right-wing party supporting the "French race," has raised the anxiety level of many citizens and political leaders.

In the mid 1990s, the party secured mayoral posts in a number of midsized cities, and many residents and observers noticed a corresponding drop in racial tolerance and an increase in instances of hate crimes. One of the many controversies generated by the FN was the criticism by its leader, Jean-Marie Le Pen, of the multiracial nature of the French national soccer team in 1996. His remarks provoked angry reaction from every political persuasion.

Even more worrisome, Le Pen came in second during the first round of the 2002 presidential election with 17 percent of the votes, ahead of then-Prime Minister Lionel Jospin. French citizens feared what was termed a "Republican catastrophe." During the two-week period between the two rounds of the presidential election, protests took place throughout the country to "save" the Republic. In the second round, Le Pen won 18 percent of the vote and lost against incumbent Jacques Chirac. The Republic was saved and many French people breathed a sigh of relief.

Although its influence fluctuates and varies from region to region, in the summer of 2009, the FN (now boosted by the involvement of Le Pen's daughter, Marine) came close to winning a widely publicized municipal election in the northern city of Hénin-Beaumont against a left-wing candidate who gathered support from all parties. Even the UMP came to the candidate's rescue after their loss in the first round of the election. Depending on the urgency of the matter, politics can indeed make strange bedfellows.

THE POLITICAL SPECTRUM

The French are baffled by the apparent paradox of American political life: in a culture that supposedly values a wide range of ideas and diversity of all sorts, why are there, for all intents and purposes, only two viable and credible political parties? The French could never make such simple political categorizations. They tend to see more nuances in addressing politics and other issues than do Americans—a spectrum of grey areas between extreme opposites. K.I.S.S. (Keep it simple, stupid) would not be an effective rallying cry in France.

Use of the terms *right* and *left* to denote political views came from the seating plan of the French *Assemblée Nationale* (National Assembly), formed just after the Revolution. Today there are 577 seats in the National Assembly, spanning a range of political parties from the far left (the quite popular New Anti-capitalist Party—NPA) to the far right (National Front), with everything in between.

The major conservative parties are the *Union pour un Mouvement Populaire* mentioned above, the party founded by Jacques Chirac (who passed the torch to

Nicolas Sarkozy) and that seeks to bear de Gaulle's legacy into the future, and the New Center (*Nouveau Centre*), which is a spinoff of the *Union de la Démocratie Française* (Union of French Democracy, or UDF), created by former president Valery Giscard d'Estaing and no longer in existence. While not sharing the American Republican ideology of self-reliance and spending as little as possible on social programs, the French conservative parties tend to support the interests of business owners and management.

The major left-of-center parties are the *Parti Socialiste* (Socialist Party, or PS) and Les Verts (the Greens). The *Parti Communiste* (Communist Party, or PC) is still very much part of the French political landscape, although its influence has decreased drastically since the early 1990s. Depending on the election and the degree of animosity among its partners, left-wing coalitions may range from independent Socialists to the New Anti-capitalist Party—a fairly wide spectrum still being tested and vying for credibility in French eyes. The left-wing parties generally support measures favoring the common citizens, protection of workers and families, and equitable distribution of wealth and resources. Left-wing parties have traditionally been more hesitant toward involvement in the European Union, fearing a loss of French cultural identity and erosion of workers' rights and protections by an increased dependence on market forces.

During the 1980s and 1990s, French voters opted three times for a dual political system called *cohabitation*, meaning that executive power would be shared by the president and the majority coalition parties that control the National Assembly. An approximate situation in U.S. political terms would involve, for example, a Republican president with a Democratic vice president, cabinet, and Congressional majority. At the time, the French felt such an arrangement would ensure a balance of power and distribution of responsibilities, but it has not reoccurred in the eight years since the 2002 National Assembly election.

Most parties, regardless of their orientation, agree that the state has an obligation to play an active role in citizens' lives. The American idea of "the less government, the better" strikes the French as illogical and impractical. This approach, they feel, gives too much weight to the private sector and to capitalism. Private enterprise will not and cannot replace the state as the equitable provider of social services, protection, and justice. Despite budget problems and heavy tax burdens, the central premise—that the state has certain obligations toward its citizens—is nearly sacred in French life. Because of the level of state involvement, governmental decisions often reverberate in everyday life in very concrete ways.

A 1993 quotation from Edouard Balladur, right-leaning former Prime Minister, nicely sums up French attitudes:

What is the market? It is the law of the jungle, the law of nature.
And what is civilization? It is the struggle against nature. (Wolf 2005, 3)

The majority of high-level politicians in France come from the ranks of the nation's most prestigious institutions of higher learning (usually the ENA, *Ecole Nationale d'Administration*—National School of Administration, a grande école). Education is the royal road to the highest ranks of civil service, including ministerial positions and the presidency. An ENA professor got a surprising reaction when he asked his twenty-five-year-old first-year students, "How many of you would like to become president of the Republic one day?" A dozen students (out of approximately 140) raised their hands. Nurtured by the system and to a lesser extent by families, political ambition starts early indeed.

The idea of a political career built on success as an athlete or a film star is incomprehensible to the French, who expect their politicians to be experienced, consummate political animals. Most French politicians begin their careers early in life and work their way up to positions of power in their parties. Even if they disagree with the opinions expressed, French citizens expect politicians to be educated, cultured, and articulate.

Personality, eloquence, and public speaking skills are important requirements for a political career. A proof of good education and intelligence and the ability to deliver a brilliant and articulate speech that goes right to the people's heart and soul is always a strong asset in politics. The French politico must have a fund of classical and historical references that indicate the speaker's level of culture and refinement. The late President François Mitterrand, a former lawyer, was often praised for his ability to produce an excellent speech on the spot with minimal preparation. Although sometimes part of the décor during political campaigns, American-style "cheerleading" is not enough and is not always appropriate. This kind of balloon-dropping, confetti-throwing political feel-good extravaganza—typical at U.S. party conventions—has no place in the more serious, intellectual French political scene.

In a culture built on networks, connections play a political role as important as the message delivered or the competence demonstrated. It is well known that leaders of major French public companies, which are still legion despite privatization efforts, owe their top positions to political affiliations. A highly controversial example in March 2009 involved the appointment of François Peyrol, Nicolas Sarkozy's former deputy chief of staff, as head of the newly merged group Caisse d'Epargne-Banque Populaire. This appointment sparked controversy, especially because the French government was set to put up to a €5 billion ($6.5 billion) subsidy into the merged group.

Changes in government or cabinet shake-ups often precede major promotions and demotions within the top-management strata of public (read, state-owned) institutions and companies. These decisions are generally made in very private meetings—the opposite of open, transparent decision making.

A notable exception to "business and politics as usual" was the case of Bernard Tapie, a go-getter entrepreneur who became a business raider after a mercifully brief singing career. Tapie's case is so far out of the accepted French mold that it is useful to examine it in detail.

Casting himself in the American model of the self-made man, Tapie was involved in everything from sports to TV shows to public political debates. He rose rapidly. The crowning achievement of his career was his election as both a French and a European deputy and appointment as minister of urban affairs under a socialist government in the early 1990s.

As might be expected, such a maverick was never really accepted by the French establishment. He was attacked for unethical and illegal practices, forced to declare personal bankruptcy, stripped of his positions in French and European politics, and sent to prison for bribing soccer players to throw a game. Before his imprisonment, he became a movie star for a few months, demonstrating a remarkable ability to bounce back. Atypical in France, he resembles, in a way, the American hero who at first makes it against all odds only to fail, then rise again. He has been very popular among members of the middle and lower classes in France and at times has been compared with Lee Iacocca.

Tapie still retains his exceptional status and a certain level of popularity. His path remains unique in French public life.

ATTITUDES TOWARD POLITICIANS

A life of public service in France is respected, though politicians themselves may be the target of vitriolic below-the-belt satire. One of the most popular programs on television is a puppet show entitled *Les Guignols de l'Info* on cable channel Canal Plus, in which political and other public figures of all persuasions are regularly skewered.[17] In their wickedly accurate foam rubber incarnations, French politicos are portrayed as bumbling cretins, rapacious power-hungry swine, and vicious back-stabbers. Sarkozy's small stature, for example, is not off-limits for the show's writers, and neither is his habit of stage-managing public events to hide it. The anchorman of the parody news program is a puppet version of retired

---

[17] *www.canalplus.fr/*

Patrick Poivre d'Arvor (familiarly known as PPDA), who was a news anchor on channel TF1 for over 30 years.

In a recent episode of *Les Guignols*, PPDA announces that factory closings are continuing across France due to the economic crisis, but the government is doing all it can to calm the situation.

The scene cuts to a group of workers holding their boss in his office (an increasingly popular method of forcing management's hand). One of them is on the phone, apparently negotiating. He announces to cheers, "They're sending a minister to negotiate with us!"

The minister walks in to great excitement—and it turns out to be Frédéric Mitterrand, the minister of culture (and TV personality, writer, filmmaker, gay activist, and nephew of the late socialist president François Mitterrand). The workers' negotiator reacts with surprise: "We were expecting the minister of industry or employment!"

Mitterrand slips a DVD into a handy player and, to a background of syrupy music, launches into an illustrated purple-prose panegyric on the incredible destiny of the boss, Gontran Mastinguet de Rocheville (a delightfully archaic, aristocratic name).

"How to understand Gontran Mastinguet de Rocheville without mentioning the inexpressible drama that destabilized his childhood: the brutal confiscation by a nit-picking and inhuman fiscal administration of the 65-meter family yacht he had always cherished?"

One by one, the employees break down in tears as Mitterrand evokes the emptiness that multiple luxurious homes could not fill. He goes on to explain that, thanks to sending jobs offshore to Bangladesh (thereby making himself a small fortune), Gontran Mastinguet de Rocheville's dream is once again within his grasp. "It's all up to you, the employees he's loved so well. Will this childhood dream be broken on the jagged rocks of proletarian egotism?"

"We don't want to hurt a child," the employees agree. "Let's let him leave." Exit Gontran Mastinguet de Rocheville, presumably to make a down payment on that yacht.

While *Les Guignols* could never be accused of subtlety, its jokes tend to become fairly elaborate and assume considerable familiarity with politics and current affairs in France and beyond. In the United States, politicians are also fair game for humor, but until recently it has been of a somewhat gentler nature. Traditionally the jokes have been quick sketches or one-liners that are easy to understand. One needs to be familiar only with headlines—and the more scandalous, the better. In recent years, programs such as *The Daily Show* and

The Colbert Report have changed political satire and in some cases are cited as viewers' primary source of "hard" news.

Regardless of the status and prestige they attach to prominent political leaders, French citizens tend to judge the effectiveness and integrity (as understood in French culture, sexual affairs aside) of a public person rather than the discourse and the ideas he or she professes. Fed up with increasing fiscal pressure and facing an uncertain future, the French have progressively lost faith and trust in the institutions that make up the Fifth Republic. Deputies and ministers are less credible, and unions have seen their ranks rapidly decline. In 2008, no more than 8 percent of the French workforce was unionized (5 percent in the private sector); this figure has held steady since 2003 (7.5 percent of women, 9 percent of men)—half the level of twenty-five years ago. However, unionization rates have stabilized and a slight progression of union activism has been noted via involvement in workers' councils, where French employees represent their peers vis-à-vis management of the company.[18]

This attitude of political discontent has frayed the social fabric, reinforcing feelings of malaise within French society. The French are still awaiting the strong, uncompromising leader, perhaps in the image of de Gaulle, who can give them a sense of confidence while enhancing the prestige and status of France in the world. Nicolas Sarkozy, in a difficult economic period of his first term, may have benefited from the French desire for a strong leader—a characteristic that most French people would recognize, regardless of their political convictions.

Although pointed criticism and cynicism are part of the public scene, the privacy of French politicians is guarded behind high walls that no reputable journalist would scale. Investigative journalism in the Woodward and Bernstein tradition is nonexistent in France, and British-style "tabloid tell-all" revelations tend to focus on movie stars and foreign royalty rather than politicians at home.

In France, politicians' privacy involves more than their sexual and financial activities. A major controversy erupted after the death from prostate cancer of former President François Mitterrand. His physician published a book revealing that the president knew long before his death that he was suffering from an inoperable disease. The book was banned after one day (and available immediately on the Internet from a *cybercrêperie* in Besançon) due to the family's protest. What shocked the French about the book was not so much the disclosure of Mitterrand's illness, or even that he was aware of his fate when running for a second term in 1988. These aspects of the issue never raised any serious ethical

---

[18] *www.cerclerh.com/editorial/syndicat1104.asp*

concern in the media. At the core of the controversy was the revelation of such a secret: the betrayal of Mitterrand's memory and of the trust he had put in his doctor. It simply violated basic rules that call for the respect of people's dignity and privacy.

Another privacy scandal made news when a prominent journalist revealed that President Mitterrand had not only a mistress but also an illegitimate daughter by her. Again, the French were shocked not so much by the material facts of the case but by the revelation and public dissemination of knowledge appropriately shared only by intimate members of the president's circle. The journalist's scoop did his career no good at all. As one Frenchman noted at the time, "In France, it's a scandal if a political figure *doesn't* have a mistress."

Mitterrand's mistress and their daughter Mazarine lived in the apartment adjacent to his, while his wife occupied the official residence. When the Socialist Party presented a new Twingo (a Renault subcompact) to the president, no one was surprised to see Mazarine driving the car shortly afterward. She and her mother even attended Mitterrand's funeral along with his wife and their two sons. This certainly raised eyebrows in France, but it is simply unimaginable for a similar scene to take place at the official funeral of a U.S. president.

While the sexual indiscretions of American presidents—Roosevelt, Kennedy, and Eisenhower, for instance—were once ignored by the press, such is no longer the case. The media now dig for dirt and make it extremely public. Americans finally tired of the excesses of the media in the Clinton scandal and impeachment trial, but not because they disapproved of the invasion of his privacy.

Yet, a new phenomenon, which occasionally touches politicians, has reached the shores of French society. It is something the French call *peoplelisation*—the elevation of someone into the ranks of celebrity, generally despite the lack of brilliant insight or significant contribution to society. This phenomenon reflects society becoming more artificial as evidenced by numerous "reality" shows and other kinds of media-generated hype.

A memorable example of peoplelisation comes from the liberation of Ingrid Betancourt, a French-Colombian citizen detained for over six years by the FARC rebels in the Colombian jungle. Upon her return to France in July 2008, she was immediately granted "hero status" by the media, awarded the French Legion of Honor during the Bastille Day garden party at the Elysée Palace, and during a trip to Lourdes, was looked upon as the new Bernadette Soubirous (the young Frenchwoman who reported eighteen apparitions of the Virgin Mary in 1858 and who was later canonized). Ingrid Betancourt was also nominated for the 2009 Nobel Peace Prize. In contrast, we know very little about the other fourteen hostages (three Americans and eleven Colombians) who were freed that same day in late June 2008, and even less about other French hostages who remain captive in the Colombian jungle and elsewhere.

In fact, Nicolas Sarkozy may have been the precursor of this "peoplelisation" movement when, as a presidential candidate, he courted the media and opened his family's doors for publicity purposes. One striking picture shows Sarkozy and his former wife posing in an office while their son plays underneath the desk. Certain American presidents deserve to be copied, and JFK may have indeed been an inspiration for Sarkozy during his campaign.

WOMEN IN POLITICS

Despite social barriers and a linguistic awkwardness (until 1998 a female cabinet minister was addressed using a masculine article as *"Madame le Ministre"*), Frenchwomen have made considerable strides in politics. Women were given the right to vote in France in 1944, and a woman votes under her maiden name all her life. A number of women have served at the cabinet level in various French governments, and one, Edith Cresson, was briefly prime minister in the early 1990s. As noted earlier, many social benefits and protections for working women and working mothers are already in place in France.

With 107 women elected deputies in the 2007 parliamentary election, the percentage of women in the National Assembly has reached 18.5 percent. This is a record high and yet France (like the U.S.) lags behind many countries in terms of women's representation in politics. France moved from the 86th to the 58th ranking in the world, far behind Scandinavian countries—in Finland and Sweden more than 40 percent of representatives in their parliaments are women.[19]

In comparison, 93 of the 260 women who have served in the U.S. Congress are members of the 2009–2011 Congress—76 in the House and 17 in the Senate, 17.5 percent and 17 percent, respectively.[20]

In November 2008, an intense internal election in the Socialist Party (France's second largest party) pitted two women against each other for the supreme position of secretary general. Martine Aubry, former minister of labor and daughter of Europe-builder Jacques Delors, narrowly defeated Ségolène Royal, Nicolas Sarkozy's opponent in the second round of the 2007 presidential election. This shows that women do get involved in politics at the highest level.

---

[19] *www.linternaute.com/femmes/carriere/0706-femmes-assemblee/58e-rang-mondial.shtml*

[20] *womenincongress.house.gov/index.html*

Many female politicians and commentators agreed in general terms that more women should be included in politics at the national level but rejected the call for quotas, maintaining that they are simply not necessary, since equality is already guaranteed by the Constitution. However, in 1998, the Constitution of 1958 was modified to ensure that women have equal access to politics by requiring political parties to choose equal numbers of female and male candidates.

Quotas indeed violate the French universalist principle. Some Frenchwomen echo the fears expressed in the American affirmative action debate: that a woman who gains a position because of a quota will be perceived as less than competent. People may assume she would not have achieved success on her own merits. Despite such concerns, women in the United States have been less reluctant to use quotas to their advantage.

> Nobody likes quotas, but that's the only way to make things change, to get women into positions of power so they can show what they know, what they can do. It's not quotas per se that are bad but the way they are used. The idea was to give women the chance to make their mark, not to shove incompetent women into important jobs they would be taking away from men. (Hermary-Vieille and Sarde 1997, 300)

Nevertheless, some Frenchwomen say that politics in France will always be a man's game and that the political arena is simply too misogynist for women to make much progress. Some Frenchmen—and Frenchwomen—maintain that politics is too dirty a business for women to get entangled in.

TWELVE

With Religion

CHURCH AND STATE

Separation of church and state is another precious republican value of the French. Since 1905, when church and state were officially split, many French citizens have been eager to keep the church away from any influence in the country's affairs. Nonreligious matters are termed *laïques*. While *laïque* can be translated as "civil" or "secular," there is a sense of mission about the word that the English equivalents do not transmit. Particularly in the area of public education, *laïcité* (nominal form of *laique*) suggests a dedication to the values of reason, openness, and tolerance.

In February 2005, a major French polling organization did a survey on the one hundredth anniversary of the *loi 1905*. Of a representative sample, 75 percent of French people aged 15 and older said that the laïcité is an important element of France's identity. When questioned about the specific principles of laïcité, respondents weighted them as follows:[21]

Putting all religions on an equal footing: 32 percent
Separating religion from politics: 28 percent
Protecting freedom of thought: 28 percent
Decreasing the influence of religions on our society: 9 percent

---

[21] *www.csa-fr.com*, "Les Français et la loi de 1905."

Church and state are separated in France to the extent that the state does not even recognize religious ceremonies as legal marriages. A priest or other clergy can marry only in the name of the Lord, not of the state. A couple must first be married legally by the local mayor or the mayor's representative. If the couple or their parents want a religious ceremony, it takes place later.

In 1996 France marked the 1500th anniversary of the baptism of Clovis, France's first Christian king, with commemorative ceremonies and other special events. Many French people questioned whether the state should be involved at all in a religious event, despite its historical importance. Should the whole thing have been toned down or played to emphasize history rather than religion? Should the government have merely allowed private and religious groups to organize the event rather than being a direct participant? Demonstrations and debate on such topics suggest that separation of church and state is still a very sensitive point. It attracted further attention during the pope's visit to France for the International Catholic Youth Days in the summer of 1997.

It is difficult for the French to understand the importance of religious activity in Americans' public lives and the place of religion in political debate. It would be inconceivable for election campaigns in France to show candidates and their families attending church. An editorial writer in a French newsmagazine not noted for left-wing radicalism expressed complete bafflement that the Republican Party in the United States wanted to support "family values" by allowing prayer in public school. He could not understand what possible connection there might be between family values and prayer in school. Furthermore, he was taken aback at the very idea of prayer in a public school.

Despite official separation of church and state and continuous litigation over the issue, religion plays a major role in U.S. public life. Individual French athletes may cross themselves before a race or a match, but in the United States you can witness a ring of burly professional football players holding hands and kneeling to pray together. Businesses may be listed in the "Christian Yellow Pages" with the implication that people patronizing them are assured of a high degree of ethical responsibility. The White House Christmas tree and Easter egg hunt are long-standing traditions, and the lighting of a Chanukah menorah by the president has been added to the list of celebrations.

CATHOLICISM À LA FRANÇAISE

In France, religion is virtually synonymous with Catholicism. French people tend to assume that nearly everyone is at least nominally a Catholic and may be quite taken aback when they find this is not so. For most of the French, Catholicism is simply a given. In fact, French Catholicism is more a matter of tradition than of faith, but anything else is considered marginal. Reference is often made to a "three times Catholic," who appears in church for baptisms, weddings, and funerals.

Religious events and milestones are often more important as family traditions than as spiritual ones. Baptisms, first communions, and weddings bring out distant relatives from all over the region or even the country; they become a kind of family reunion. Again, the extended family gathers around a special meal to celebrate and catch up on all the news and, above all, to maintain the network of relationships that binds them together.

Many French Catholics are finding renewed meaning in churches and spiritual groups that strive to preserve traditions, such as the Latin Mass, or that lead the way in activism for social justice. Both strains have run afoul of the Vatican, which is seen by many as the guardian of medieval traditions. The pope's condemnation of artificial birth control, his strong opposition to abortion in a country where it has been legal for more than thirty-five years, and his staunch support for the celibacy of priests are in opposition to generally accepted French norms. Not surprisingly, France has been called the "wayward daughter of the church" since the Middle Ages. The French tendency to disagree, argue, and rebel appears in religious matters as much as anywhere else.

Jacques Gaillot, an activist bishop, was removed by the Vatican from his diocese in Normandy and reassigned to the diocese of Partenia (a true *voie de garage!*). Neither the unpromising location of his new diocese—under a sand dune in North Africa—nor the low population of Catholics, or for that matter anything else, discouraged the bishop. With the help of some technically inclined friends, he is now spiritual shepherd to a cyberflock in the Virtual Diocese of Partenia, where he continues to send regular open letters to the pope. Hardly surprising, really, in a country that had its own pope for a while and bred some fairly spectacular heresies.

OTHER FAITHS

Religious freedom in France is important, but the concept is not understood in the same way as it is in the United States. The range of religious options found under "Churches" in the Yellow Pages of American cities would be incomprehensible to the French, who also have difficulty understanding the way Americans seem to shop around for a church or a minister they like.

Religious affiliation in the United States is often an important element in a person's identity. To say that an American is an Episcopalian, Southern Baptist, or Orthodox Jew reveals something about that particular individual. Saying that a French person is Catholic provides no such insight. Being Catholic in France is virtually generic. Religion in the U.S. is also more public than in France, and a greater range of religious expression is permitted without inviting odd looks from neighbors or coworkers. In France religious conviction, beliefs, and practices are in the private sphere and left to the individual and the family. However, if a French person wants to be considered part of the French mainstream, it is better for him or her to be either Catholic or atheist than to belong to some other "exotic" religion. As in many other areas, foreigners are accorded more leniency. They are not expected to convert to Catholicism as part of their assimilation into French society, but they are expected to keep their religious convictions to themselves.

The stronghold of Protestantism in France is mainly the eastern areas that border Protestant countries—Germany and Switzerland—and in the southwest. This region was the home of Henri III de Navarre (Henri IV of France), a colorful womanizer who converted to Catholicism in order to become king of France. His comment on his conversion was, "Paris is worth a Mass." French Protestantism, perhaps because of its smaller number of adherents, does not present the wide range of variations found in the United States. French Protestants have historically stood up against powerful, entrenched enemies, including governments and religious institutions. This was seen during World War II, when the devoutly Protestant village Le Chambon-sur-Lignon became famous for its unspoken "conspiracy of goodness." Under the very noses of the Nazis, virtually the entire population became involved in saving the lives of hundreds of Jewish children.

Islam is the fastest-growing religion in France, primarily because of the arrival of immigrants from former French colonies in North Africa. Mosques have been built in most major French cities and in quite a few smaller ones. As anti-immigrant and anti-foreigner prejudice has become more common in recent years, relations between Muslims—even those who were born in France or who have acquired French citizenship—and their neighbors have been strained. French-born citizens of North African Arab descent are known as *Beurs*, a word that means "Arab" in *verlan*, a sort of French pig latin, and which has entered mainstream discourse. The cultural discrepancy between France's secular traditions and the more theocratic practices of many Arab countries makes communication and understanding difficult. The sight of Muslim crowds praying in the streets on Friday afternoons does not sit well with many French people, for whom public religious expression represents a social disturbance and a refusal to fit into the French public mold.

Jews have been present in France for centuries. They have alternately thrived and been subject to bloody persecution as well as less physical expressions of institutional anti-Semitism. In 1998 France celebrated the one hundredth anniversary of Emile Zola's famous letter, *"J'accuse,"* in which he exposed pervasive official anti-Semitism. Unlike most of the rest of Europe, many French Jews are Sephardic, having their roots in the Iberian peninsula, North Africa, and Turkey. Interestingly, Napoléon instituted the office of the Grand Rabbi of France and reconvened the Sanhedrin, a traditional Jewish religious council.

THIRTEEN

French Regions

There are twenty-two administrative regions in France, which are usually a grouping of two to five *départements*. There is a historical context for this structure. The Kingdom of France was divided into forty provinces until 1790. In a move to assert its power and authority over local loyalties driven by feudal land owners, the central government in Paris created départements to replace and supersede the provincial organization. The new organization into the current-day regions was crafted in 1956, and regions were later structured by a law passed in July 1972.

Political reforms in recent decades have given French regions more autonomy. This change has diluted the authority and influence of a highly centralized power and has enhanced the revival of a variety of local attributes, customs, and practices. In fact, the concept of diversity that would first come to a French person's mind is regional diversity, as each region embodies specific customs, features (such as traditional costumes), tales, foods, and history—all of which contribute to unique regional identities. It should be noted, however, that this accent on diversity varies from region to region, as some have stronger personalities and more character than others. An interesting phenomenon to observe in the evolution of the French cultural landscape is the relationship of these different regions to a larger entity in progress—the European Union—while contrasting it with other regions in Europe (especially Spain and Germany) that benefit from more power and autonomy.

This chapter describes some of this colorful "French diversity" by showcasing four regions: Brittany, Alsace, Basque, and Midi-Pyrénées. While these are not all administrative areas, they represent distinctive cultural entities. Those French people we call Bretons, Alsatians, Basques, and Gascons may not be typical of the average French man or woman, which only emphasizes how difficult it is to pin down who an "average" French man or woman is.

LA BRETAGNE—BRITTANY
(*BREIZH* IN BRETON)

Brittany is composed of four départements—Finistère, Côtes-d'Armor, Morbihan, and Ile-et-Vilaine—and occupies the westernmost part of France, close to its British cousins. It is most significantly one of the six Celtic nations, a term that describes territories in northwestern Europe who share similar Celtic cultural traits and languages. The Celts have had immense influence over Europe dating from prehistoric times and, through its distinctive traits and customs, Brittany captures what is still alive of Celtic culture in France.

The traditional language of Brittany, Breton, was the dominant language of the westernmost part of the region until the mid-twentieth century, and it is still actively spoken by 5 percent of Bretons. Like many languages and dialects in France, Breton is spoken mostly by older people. Sixty-one percent of Breton speakers are sixty years old or older. But bilingual road signs can be seen in traditional Breton-speaking areas—a healthy sign of the revival of Breton culture. An interesting characteristic peculiar to Brittany is the presence of a dual-language educational system in some cities and villages. While this is still not very common, with less than 4 percent of schools using both languages, it has been on the rise in the past few years.[22]

Breton is taught in privately funded schools called *Diwan* or Seed, which play an important role in the preservation of Breton cultural identity. These schools do not receive government funding—which would go against the principle of the Republic, one and undivided—and this has been a controversial issue for a number of years.

There haven't been calls for the political autonomy of Brittany in recent years, but they resurface from time to time. More important, though, is that because of its rough climate and fierce opposition to centralized national power, the preservation of traditions, customs, and ways of living make Brittany what

---

[22] *www.ofis-bzh.org/fr/langue_bretonne/chiffres_cles/index.php*

it is today—a culturally strong region. The Breton anthem was officially played for the first time before a premier league soccer game in Rennes in 2009. During this event, the president of the Rennes football club, Frédéric de Saint-Sernin, stated that "the Rennes football club would like to move forward while asserting its Breton identity; any player signing into the club shall understand that it promotes a very strong regional identity." Paradoxically, the current coach of the Rennes football club, Frédéric Antonetti, is originally from Corsica, another region with a strong cultural identity.

Brittany has a long history. It has many megalithic constructions (structures made of large stones) from the Neolithic era and has been called the "core area" of megalithic culture. Later it was occupied by several Celtic tribes who fought— just like plucky little Astérix—against Roman invasion. The most famous of these Celtic tribes was the Veneti, a seafaring people who gave its name to the city of Vannes (*Gwened* in Breton). At the time when Rome conquered what was then called Gaul, Brittany was known as Armorica, a name still used today. Between the fifth and seventh centuries, many settlers from Great Britain fled to Brittany in the wake of the Anglo-Saxon conquest of England, giving Brittany a stronger and more permanent Celtic flavor.

Brittany's folk music, heavily influenced by its Celtic heritage, has experienced a tremendous revival since the early 1970s and is being modernized and adapted into folk rock and other fusion genres. Along with flourishing traditional forms, such as the *bombard-biniou* (a bombard is a type of flute and a biniou is an instrument similar to bagpipes) and *fest-noz* (night festival) ensembles, it has also branched out into numerous subgenres, such as evolving, electronic, interethnic, trance, meditation, and so on, that give visitors an authentic taste of the region.[23]

The annual Lorient Interceltic Festival, which takes place in Lorient in the center of Brittany, is a delightful cultural event with its traditional *vieilles charrues* (old carts) and one of the largest rock festivals in France. Another music festival, the Crozon Peninsula festival, is known as the Festival du Bout du Monde, the End of the World Festival, geographically speaking, as it takes place on the western coast of Finistère.

Like any Celtic land, Brittany is full of myths, legends, and tales attached to mystical places and events. Sunset's Heaven, the Submersion of Is, Marie-

---

[23] Look at *www.musiquesbretonnes.com* to learn about the history of Breton music and the range of various types of music.

Morgane, Cat's gold (a legend from St. Malo), and the petrified rocks of the island of Bréhat are among those myths and stories.[24]

Many consider Bretons to be stubborn, resilient, and very much attached to their cultural assets, which include the sea and their Celtic family—to the point that they would defend it *becs et ongles* (with beaks and nails). In 1980, Bretons successfully fought against building a nuclear plant in Plogoff. More recently, invasion of green algae is threatening agricultural operations along the Breton coast and this concern is preoccupying the entire region. Due to their history and the location—being at the crossroads of cultures and civilizations—Bretons tend to be very open to the rest of Europe while remaining suspicious of and united against any Paris (read, government) initiatives.

L'ALSACE

The Alsace region, situated between the Vosges mountains and the west bank of the Rhine River, is composed of two *départements*: Bas-Rhin and Haut-Rhin, lower and upper Rhine respectively.

Alsace is part of a larger region in eastern France called *Alsace-Lorraine*. Alsace-Lorraine (*Elsass-Lothringen* in German) was a territorial entity created by the German Empire in 1871 after the annexation of most of Alsace and the Moselle region of Lorraine in the Franco-Prussian War (1870–1871). The Prussian victory brought about the unification of Germany under King Wilhem I of Prussia. It also marked the downfall of Napoleon III, nephew of Napoleon I, and the end of the Second Empire, which was replaced by the Third Republic. As part of the settlement between France and Germany, Alsace-Lorraine (comprised of three départements, Bas-Rhin, Haut-Rhin, and Moselle) became an imperial province of Germany and remained under its tutelage until the end of World War I. As part of the Treaty of Versailles in 1919, Alsace-Lorraine finally returned to France.

Earlier, Alsace was part of the Holy Roman Empire until 1674, and therefore its inhabitants spoke German. This blend of French and German cultures has left its mark on modern-day politics in terms of a particular interest in national identity issues. The Germanic influence can be seen in the more rural, traditional parts of the region and in areas such as food and architecture, whereas today's institutions, regulations, and ways of living are heavily influenced by French culture.

---

[24] To learn more about this folklore, go to *www.bretagne-celtic.com/an/accueil_an.htm*

Partly due to its need for stability, Alsace is also one of the most conservative and most pro-Europe regions of France. It was one of the few French regions that voted "Yes" on the European Constitution. French, as well as Dutch, voters narrowly rejected the Constitution in the spring of 2005, leading to a political deadlock.

In addition to being at a cultural crossroads, Alsace also underwent various religious influences over the years, with Catholic influence from France and Protestant from Germany. A large majority of Alsatians are Roman Catholic but, due to a long-lasting German heritage, a significant Protestant community has flourished and is still alive today. The Protestant Reformation in the sixteenth century opened up avenues for different faiths, and various groups appeared in Alsatian villages, including Lutherans, Calvinists, Jews, Anabaptists, Amish, and Mennonites; although most Amish and Mennonites moved to North America during Napoleon's time.

Unlike the rest of France, Alsace enjoys a peculiar historical discrepancy. As mentioned earlier, France passed a law in 1905 that clearly separated the powers of church and state—a law that didn't apply to Alsace as it was part of Germany at the time. Laws that were passed in France in the period 1871–1919 were not de facto valid in Alsace when it was returned to France, and consequently the region still adheres to the Concordat of 1801 which provides government subsidies to Roman Catholic, Lutheran, and Calvinist churches, as well as Jewish synagogues. This means that public school education in those faiths is provided (although parents can refuse religious education for their children), the clergy is paid by the state, and the public University of Strasbourg offers advanced degrees in theology (masters in Protestant theology and religious sciences). Because of the clear separation of church and state, the only French universities outside of Alsace that offer theology classes are private Catholic institutions called *libres* (free). Another legacy from the German period is two extra holidays enjoyed by the residents of Alsace and Moselle: Good Friday and Boxing Day (December 26).

As one can imagine, controversy abounds about this regional exception and many other unique legal aspects of Alsace, and the fact that other religions—especially Islam, France's second largest religion—are not included in this provision.

Alsatian, spoken by about four in ten adults, is the second most-spoken regional language of France after Occitan in southern France. It is a form of Alemmanic, which includes several variations of German spoken along the Rhine valley as well as in western Austria. Alsatian is, however, not as popular among younger generations.

Although German was spoken in Alsace for a long period, French is clearly the dominant language and German is taught as a foreign language. Often assumed to be a bilingual region, Alsace has in fact moved toward a situation of total French domination. This has spurred a movement to preserve the Alsatian language, which is perceived as endangered, as an element of the region's identity. Alsatian is now taught in French high schools, but the overwhelming influence of French media and the Internet make the survival of Alsatian uncertain among younger generations. Increasingly, French is the only language used at home and at work, whereas a growing number of people have a good knowledge of standard German.

Storks have been a part of the Alsatian scenery for many centuries. Once very abundant, they return every year from Africa to announce the coming of spring. The bird practically disappeared in the late 1970s, but repopulation efforts, such as raising storks in special sanctuaries and parks, have proved successful. Storks are mostly found nesting on roofs of houses, churches, and other buildings. Some of them even stay all year long in Alsace, to the delight of the Alsatian population, as storks are the symbol of happiness and faithfulness. The stork, as commonly portrayed in popular images, brings babies wrapped in bundles, firmly held in its beak. An Alsatian custom used to have a child who wanted a little brother or sister place a piece of sugar on the window ledge to attract the stork, in the hope it would leave the precious bundle in exchange for the treat.

Traditional Alsatian foods include the *flammenküche*, a thin-crusted tart filled with cream, onions, cheese, mushrooms, and bacon; an alternative version is the *zweibelküche* or *tarte à l'oignon* (onion tart with bacon). Another time-honored dish is a type of stew called *baeckeoffe* (baker's oven), initially prepared at home with pork, mutton, beef, and vegetables marinated in wine for two days, then put between layers of potato and taken to the baker's to be cooked. *Choucroute* is sauerkraut (aromatic pickled cabbage) and served hot with sausage, pork, or ham, and a glass of local beer or dry white wine. Alsace is also famous for its *Route des Vins* (wine road), which takes you through many vineyards to enjoy mostly white wines that tend to be sweeter than most other French wines.

With all its diversity and nestled at the confluence of two countries and civilizations, Alsace enjoys a distinct cultural identity heavily grounded in the heart of the European community. No doubt the presence of the European parliament in Strasbourg will only reinforce Alsace's openness to Europe and the rest of the world. Strasbourg is also called the *Capital of Europe*, not only because it hosts the monthly plenary meetings of the European Parliament, but also because it is the seat of the Council of Europe that unites forty-seven countries. The Council was created after World War II and located in Strasbourg as a symbol of French-German reconciliation.

IPARRALDE (PAYS BASQUE FRANÇAIS; FRENCH BASQUE COUNTRY)

The French Basque Country or Northern Basque Country (*Pays basque français* in French, *Iparralde* in Basque) occupies the southwestern corner of France, adjacent to the border with Spain. Though it is administratively part of the département of the Pyrénées-Atlantiques, as far as some Basques are concerned, *Euskal Herria* (Basque Country) is a single cultural unit that just happens to straddle an international border. There are a total of seven Basque provinces; four on the Spanish side (*Gipuzkoa, Araba, Bizkaia,* and *Nafarroa*) and three on the French side: *Lapurdi* (Labourd), *Nafarroa Beherea* (Basse-Navarre or Lower Navarre), and *Zuberoa* (Soule). Together, the French Basque provinces are known as *Iparralde*, northern side, while the Spanish ones are called *Hegoalde*, southern side.

This complex and convoluted definition of Euskal Herria is an appropriate introduction to a region that has retained a strong cultural and linguistic identity despite all the efforts on both sides of the border to assimilate it into the wider French and Spanish cultures.

The touchstone of Basque identity is the Basque language, which is unrelated to any other language on earth: a true language isolate (a natural language with no demonstrable genetic relationship with other languages). It is the last remaining pre-Indo-European language in Western Europe. In Basque, the official name of the language is *Euskara*.

Every few years, researchers announce that a relationship has been established between Basque and some other language, from Iberian to Chechen to Georgian. None of these has panned out, and the origins of the language remain a mystery—except to Basques, who will tell you, "Before boulders were boulders, and before G-d was G-d, the Basques were already Basque."

The status of Basque is very different in Iparralde and Hegoalde due to differing minority language policies in Spain and France. The French *modèle républicain* favors linguistic unity. Since the nineteenth century, when primary schooling became compulsory in France, efforts were made to suppress regional languages. Dismissed as *patois* (uneducated, provincial dialects), languages such as Gascon, Basque, Alsatian, Provençal, and Breton were relegated to second-class status and their speakers looked down upon as peasants. Children were punished for speaking their native language in schools until the mid-twentieth century, by which time many of these tongues were effectively moribund. Like other minority languages in France, Basque experienced something of a revival beginning in the 1970s and 1980s as an expression of regional pride. Most residents of Iparralde are not Basque speakers; one study pegs the percentage of non-Basque speakers in the region at 63.4 percent (although this tends to be lower in the mountainous countryside and higher in the coastal cities).

The story in Hegoalde is a bit different. While Basque was banned during the Franco dictatorship (1939–1975), it has since been given official language status. Hegoalde itself comprises two regions, the Basque Autonomous Community and Navarre. Nurtured by government programs and subsidies, the Basque language has emerged from the shadows to stand as both a native and everyday language there. An *ikastola* is a public or private primary or secondary school where Basque is the primary language of instruction, while an *euskaltegi* is a language school (also public or private) usually catering to adult learners.

Regardless of their level of proficiency in Basque, Basques tend to be fiercely proud of their language and culture. Someone with impeccable Basque lineage is said to be "Basque in all his (or her) surnames," and one of the authors experienced Basque pride on being introduced to such a person in Donostia (San Sebastián). On hearing that the visitor was from California, the Basque inquired, "And what do you think of Spain?" Realizing this was a trick question, the American replied, "I've heard it's a lovely country and I hope to visit someday." As far as the United Nations is concerned, they were standing in Spain, but the Basques greeted the response with huge smiles.

There has been some violence associated with Basque nationalism in France, but it has never reached the levels seen in Spain. Basque nationalism can cover a wide spectrum of goals (or demands), ranging from greater local control for local issues to complete independence for all seven Basque provinces. Support is generally less enthusiastic on the French side, and has diminished even further in recent years. Basque political parties usually draw relatively few voters and even fewer members.

If you were blindfolded and taken to the Basque country, you would instantly know where you were as soon as you opened your eyes. From the distinctive Basque typefaces on signs to the green, red, and white Basque flag to white, low-slung Basque houses trimmed in red or green to the *lauburu* (Basque cross), the culture announces itself visually at every turn. Basque linens are prized far beyond the regional borders, as are woolens from Pyrénées sheep.

Perhaps the best-known Basque tradition is the *Sanfermin* at Iruñea (Pamplona), the running of the bulls made famous by Ernest Hemingway. Local festivals featuring traditional music, dances, and costumes are popular all over the region, particularly in the summertime.

Every Basque village features a wall (*frontón* in Spanish, *pilotaleku* or *pilota plaza* in Basque) for the game of *Euskal pilotaren* (*pelote basque*), similar to the game known in parts of North America as jai alai. Local variants include the number of walls surrounding the court (one, two, or three) and how the ball is hit (with a variety of paddles, basket gloves, or the naked hand).

Like many traditional cuisines, Basque food is rooted in the products of the land. The description *basquaise* in French cuisine means a dish prepared with tomatoes and hot or sweet red peppers. Meat from the inland farms and fish and seafood from the coastal areas are abundant, as are cured meats, liqueurs, and cheeses. Basques are legendary sheepherders and many immigrated to the American west to tend flocks there. A happy and delicious evening can be spent going from bar to bar sampling *pintxos* (tapas) or in cider houses (*sagardotegiak*), rustic restaurants where cider flows from huge barrels and guests must catch it in their glasses. Both reach their pinnacle of perfection in Donostia in Hegoalde. The famous *jambon de Bayonne*, an air-dried salted ham similar to prosciutto, carries the *Indication Géographique Protégée* (Protected Geographical Indication) that indicates its authenticity. Nouvelle cuisine has also influenced Basque cooking, resulting in lighter dishes using traditional ingredients and flavors.

Chocolate came into Europe via the Basque country, when the Jewish merchants fleeing the Spanish Inquisition found a haven in Bayonne. This city is still home to many traditional chocolate houses, where it is drunk hot and dark in many variations.

Metallurgy accounts for a large sector of the regional economy, as well as the manufacturing of everything from medical equipment to office furniture to safety shoes. Aeronautics, agribusiness, and electronics are also important. As might be expected, tourism accounts for a large part of the local economy, as the mountains and beaches draw visitors from France and overseas. Board sports such as surfing and windsurfing are popular, and many companies associated with sporting equipment and clothing, such as Quicksilver and Volcom, are based on the Basque Coast.

MIDI-PYRÉNÉES

The Midi-Pyrénées is an administrative region of France created in the twentieth century with Toulouse as its local cultural, economic, and political center. It is the largest of the French regions—larger than some European countries, including Denmark and the Netherlands.

Although the Midi-Pyrénées is an artificial creation, it encompasses or includes parts of several ancient French provinces, including Gascogne (Gascony), Languedoc, Rouergue, Quercy, and many small provinces in the Pyrénées Mountains such as the Comté de Foix. All of these are divided into smaller areas that take pride in and to some extent retain their own local identities. These distinctions were born of and are maintained by a varied geography that includes mountains and isolated valleys, one of the lowest population densities in Western Europe (with the exception of Toulouse), and a fractious history of local disputes between small areas and towns.

Toulouse is a dynamic city that offers everything the urban dweller could wish for, including a university that draws a lively student population. Known as *La Ville Rose* (the pink city) due to the bricks of its buildings—an unusual material for the south of France—Toulouse is also noted for its Southern laid-back attitude. Toulouse time is similar to Spanish time, with dinner taking place as late as 9:00 or 10:00 P.M., especially on long summer evenings.

With a million *Toulousains* out of a regional population of about 2.75 million, the city is a top-heavy regional capital, attracting resources, workers, and government subsidies that smaller cities and villages envy. Residents of the city tend to be younger and better educated than those in the countryside, leaving the rest of the region with an aging and less-affluent population. The population loss that has plagued rural France has occurred in the Midi-Pyrénées as well, but unlike those in most other regions, people tend to resist going to Paris and prefer to head for Toulouse, which means they at least remain in the region, closer to family and friends. This also serves to reinforce regional identity.

Unlike the rest of France, or for that matter, Europe, the game here is not soccer but rugby. The Southwest is called *Pays de l'Ovalie* (the land of the oval ball) and the game is watched and played by all ages at all levels.

Outside of Toulouse, the region is noted for its small, quiet villages and towns where the most important thing is *douceur de vivre* (sweetness of life)—taking the time to enjoy the region's delicious foods and alcohols, enjoying a conversation with family and friends, and letting life flow gently and happily. A 1995 film about the region called *Le Bonheur est dans le pré* (Happiness Is in the Field) focused on the relaxed charm of the area and its cheerful, if slightly quirky, inhabitants.

Many stressed-out city dwellers from Paris and other European countries have purchased second homes in the area to try and tap into the local serenity. Enough of them have written books about their experiences that a London bookshop featured in its travel section a table of offerings under the sign, "NONE of these books recounts the tribulations of renovating an ancient farmhouse in a charming European village!"

Like other French provinces, those that make up the Midi-Pyrénées once spoke their own regional language: Occitan, a Latin language divided into Languedocian and Gascon, and many subdialects. Occitan became a European cultural language of the twelfth and thirteenth centuries thanks to the troubadours. It was suppressed, along with other regional languages, but survived until the mid-twentieth century. Despite revival efforts beginning in the 1970s that included Occitan schools (*calendretas*), the language is now spoken only by a few elderly people and linguistic specialists. However, the French of the region has a strong local flavor, both in its "singing" accent and the many Occitan words and expressions still in everyday use. The accent sounds like singing to speakers of standard French, because in the Southwest the "e"s that are silent in standard French are pronounced, as they often are for singing in French. A word like *samedi* (Saturday) has two syllables in standard French due to the silent *e*, while in the Southwest it has three full syllables: sam-e-di.

Agriculture is the key to the region's economy. The vast size of the region includes a large percentage of arable land, and there are 60,000 active farms. The food industry is also the main component of the region's industrial sector, although many high-tech and aerospace companies are also located here, (notably aircraft manufacturer Airbus). Tourists from France and far beyond are drawn to the region's climate, beautiful landscapes, rich history, fine cuisine, and *douceur de vivre*.

Perhaps the most emblematic of the ancient provinces is Gascony (*Gascogne*), whose heartland is the département of the Gers, right in the heart of the Midi-Pyrénées. The exact location of the borders of Gascony depends on whom you ask, but essentially it is the area to the east and south of Bordeaux. Although Gascony as a political entity had pretty much disappeared by the Middle Ages (and was even part of England at one point!), the Gascons have retained a fierce pride in their culture.

To mention just one of the sources of that pride, Gascon cuisine is one of the pillars of French gastronomy. Drawing from the region's products, it is distinguished by its use of goose and duck fat. Seafood such as oysters and baby eels are prized, along with sheep cheeses from the Pyrénées and birds such as ortolans and wood pigeons. The *pastis gascon* (or *croustade*) is made by drawing out sheets of dough so fine that they are practically transparent. This is called the *voile de mariée* or bridal veil. These are then piled up and filled with Armagnac-soaked apples for a favorite dessert.

Armagnac is one of the oldest brandies in Europe and received the *Appellation d'Origine Contrôlée* in 1936. Despite recent efforts, its production has never reached the commercial levels of Cognac. It is still essentially a handcrafted brandy produced in small quantities by small distilleries, using the unique pure copper alembic (still) and a continuous distillation process.

Some Gascons have gained fame far beyond the borders of their homeland, or even of France. D'Artagnan, immortalized in Alexandre Dumas' *D'Artagnan Romances* (including *The Three Musketeers*) was based on a real person: Charles de Batz-Castelmore (c. 1610–1673), Comte d'Artagnan—and he really was a Musketeer! Born in Lupiac (Gers), his father and brothers were all connected to the Musketeers, so it was natural for him to follow in their footsteps. His faithful service to the crown earned him many special assignments, including espionage, which required the utmost discretion. A statue of d'Artagnan graces the monumental staircase in Auch, the *préfecture* of the Gers.

Another famous Gascon is Cyrano de Bergerac, who describes the rough-and-ready macho Gascon character in a famous passage from Edmond Rostand's play:

Ce sont les cadets de Gascogne
De Carbon de Castel-Jaloux!
Bretteurs et menteurs sans vergogne,
Ce sont les cadets de Gascogne!
Parlant blason, lambel, bastogne,
Tous plus nobles que des filous,
Ce sont les cadets de Gascogne
De Carbon de Castel-Jaloux.

The bold Cadets of Gascony,
Of Carbon of Castel-Jaloux!
Brawling and swaggering boastfully,
The bold Cadets of Gascony!
Spouting of Armory, Heraldry,
Their veins a-brimming with blood so blue,
The bold Cadets of Gascony,
Of Carbon of Castel-Jaloux.

FOURTEEN

With Society

FRENCH AND AMERICAN REALITIES

The structure of French society is fundamentally different from that of the United States. Many important elements distinguish them: their origins and history, the role of the state, their judicial systems, the importance given to other cultures, and on and on. Such differentiation is to a significant degree the result of diverging if not opposing worldviews. The following sections discuss the societal characteristics that most set appart these two worldviews.

Multicultural or Monocultural. Refugees and émigrés have traditionally found a haven in France, particularly if they bring outstanding artistic or intellectual gifts with them. At the core of the French welcome has been the assumption that foreigners arriving in France can and should assimilate to French culture. This is an example of the French universalist attitude, which requires that everyone in a given situation, regardless of origins and particular circumstances, be treated exactly the same, a principle enshrined in the *modèle républicain.*

Late in 2008 Nicolas Sarkozy painted a mixed picture of the modèle républicain as a model of integration. He said it has become instead a "model of social reproduction"—in other words, its main beneficiaries are the elites who keep it in place in their turn rather than challenging it. "The miracle of the Republic is that it has forged the unity of France without condemning us to uniformity." However, he added that the Republic "is not a model that is frozen for eternity."

The United States, too, has a history of assimilationist thinking. After all, Americans are the originators of the idea of the melting pot. But from the beginning of European settlement of the North American continent there has also been a strain of thought that valued pluralism and today promotes diversity. To many Americans, therefore, French assimilationism seems rigid and close-minded.

The July 1998 victory of the French team in the soccer World Cup seems to be a milestone in the recognition of the pluralization of French society. Front National leader Le Pen's 1996 outrage over the inclusion of nonwhite players on the national team was drowned out as the entire country united to celebrate the team's victory. Almost half of the players were born outside France, and the son of Algerian immigrants, Zinedine Zidane, became a national hero after scoring two goals in the final game. In a word play on the colors of the French flag (*bleu, blanc, rouge* or blue, white, red), the victory was hailed as *"black-blanc-beur"* (black-white-Arab). Local officials were pleased to report the theft of French flags from public buildings, and young people of all ethnic backgrounds were seen waving and wearing them across the country (Lacorne 1998).

According to one news source, the victory represents the "triumph of diversity in a country infected by right-wing extremists." Soccer suddenly became more important than politics, and some journalists claimed that "it became a constitutive element—and possibly the only one—of a tattered social fabric. The World Cup turned into the Holy Grail" (France 2, 13 July 1998). Yet, as the editor of the newspaper *Libération* remarked, "A World Cup victory does not change social reality, but it can change the image the French have of themselves" (*Economist* 1998, 43).

In fact, beyond sports and music, people of foreign origins are underrepresented in most political and social areas of French life. Apart from representatives of overseas French dominions, only two people of color are or were involved in local politics. Kofi Yamgname, born in Togo and citizen of both countries, served as mayor of Saint-Coulitz, a small town in Brittany, from 1989 to 2001, and as French deputy from 1997 to 2002. Kader Atteyé, born in France of parents from Djibouti, scored a difficult mayoral victory in March 2008 in the small town of Morey, with 180 inhabitants, in the provincial Saône-et-Loire *département*. Upon his victory, five of the eleven elected municipal councilors resigned, a decision which may have been related to Kader's skin color. One of the councilors who resigned said, "What we tried to explain to Kader before the election is that inhabitants didn't want to have a black mayor, because it would shake up their habits." There is no doubt that this did shake up the town's habits, as it would in many such small towns all over the world.

Although it is illegal in France to collect statistics on race or religion, Solis, a company that specializes in marketing studies of ethnic communities, has estimated the number of minorities in mainland France, with a total population of 62,400,000.

- 3.264m North African (5.23%)
- 1.080m Sub-Saharan African (1.73%)
- 441,000 Turkish (0.71%)
- 757,000 French overseas départements and territories (1.21%)[25]

Estimates for religious affiliation are as follows:

- 83%–88% Roman Catholic
- 5%–10% Muslim (~3,554,000)
- 2% Protestant
- 1% Jewish (~491,500)
- 4% Unaffiliated[26]

As noted earlier, the high number of Catholics bears no relation to actual religious practice or belief.

In its 2008 report on racism, anti-Semitism and xenophobia, the Commission nationale consultative des droits de l'homme (CNCDH or Human Rights Commission) noted an alarming increase in violence and threats against minorities and foreigners.[27] The total number of acts and threats for the year was 864. The breakdown included 97 racist or xenophobic actions and 370 threats; 100 anti-Semitic actions and 297 threats.

Many French Jews are concerned about rising rates of anti-Semitism. Forty-six percent of the hate-motivated actions and threats recorded by the CNCDH targeted the relatively small population of Jews, which means that many French Jews feel particularly vulnerable, especially as more of these incidents involve violence than in previous years.

Beyond the numbers, the types of incidents are also worrying. The 2006 kidnapping, torture, and murder of Ilan Halimi by an ethnic gang sent shock waves through France, and many in the French Jewish community are concerned that police are downplaying the anti-Semitic nature of some attacks.

France, with its traditional duty to spread its knowledge and civilization the world over while protecting its own borders from invasion, has never been

---

[25] *www.solisfrance.com*
[26] *CIA World Factbook*
[27] *www.cncdh.fr/IMG/pdf/rapport_racisme_antisemitisme_et_xenophobie_2008.pdf*

culturally open to other populations. In a well-known 1976 book, *Le mal français* (*The Trouble with France*), author Alain Peyrefitte points out that the inability of France to learn from other cultures is one of its most persistent ailments.

Traditionally a "nation of immigrants," the United States has incorporated elements from all the world's peoples into its unique cultural mosaic. This rich and dynamic mixture has been a source of both conflict and strength throughout American history. Whereas the dominant culture in France and many other nations is a given, many of the dominant culture's assumptions and practices in the United States have been called into question in recent years. Quite simply, the U.S. is a great and continuing experiment. The election of Barack Obama as the first African American president marks another step in this experiment—although some might argue that having a Kenyan father makes him an American of African heritage rather than an African American.

The American ideal of valuing diversity and identifying difference as strength is in direct conflict with the French goal of assimilation into the cultural mold. Although there are large numbers of assimilationists in the United States too, the society is not monolithic in outlook. France is far from this kind of multicultural reality. Cultural minorities in France are acknowledged and respected only to the extent that they fit into the French social and cultural mold and do not disturb the social order. The magic word for success as an immigrant is *assimilation*. That's all French society requires from immigrants, and if they abide by French rules, they will receive all of the legal benefits and advantages any legal alien or naturalized citizen can enjoy on French soil.

The pictures below illustrate the French and U.S. societal models.

French Societal Model

Assimilation

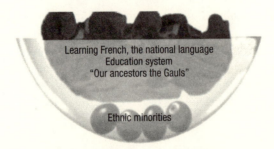

Learning French, the national language
Education system
"Our ancestors the Gauls"

Ethnic minorities

The French Republic—one and indivisible

U.S. Societal Model

Diversity "Made in the USA"

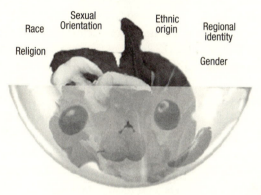

Race   Sexual Orientation   Ethnic origin   Regional identity

Religion   Gender

The U.S. patchwork:
Be whatever you are, and be proud of it!

The two main vehicles of assimilation into French culture are the French language and the educational system. Although these are very powerful elements of integration, their limitations have become obvious with North African populations who migrated to France after World War II. This is especially true for the French-born children of these immigrants, known as *Beurs*, as mentioned earlier. With little or no connection to their parents' homeland, they are torn between a Muslim family culture and French social pressure to assimilate.

The Islamic headscarf conflict in the late 1980s and early 1990s revealed France's malaise in dealing with nonassimilated cultural practices. It occurred at the core of the French psyche, in the public schools. Muslim girls came to school wearing their traditional headscarves, thus bringing a manifestation of their religious—therefore private—lives into a place that was public and most emphatically secular. In some cases, they were asked to study in the library. In others, they were simply dismissed from school until further notice. There was no set national policy to resolve the problem, and, at first, the decision was left up to each principal. In September 1994, though, students in public schools were officially forbidden to wear the Islamic headscarf. Muslim girls either had to conform to public school rules or attend a religious school. Finally, a law was passed in 2004 forbidding anyone to wear conspicuous signs of religious affiliation in public schools—including *hijab* for Muslim girls, *kippot* for Jewish boys, large crosses or turbans for Sikh boys, and large crosses for Christians. This conflict revealed the difficulty with which

French society accepts people who do not fit the image of the good *citoyen(ne)* (citizen). It required national legislation to resolve the issue.

While the law has clarified the situation in public schools, the issues of assimilation and adaptation continue to challenge French society. Debate continues on more radical forms of Islamic dress such as the *niqab* and *burka*, which cover a woman's face as well as body. As of late January 2010, based upon the declaration of the Prime Minister to the UMP party members, it is very likely that a law will be passed by the French parliament in the spring of 2010 forbidding women to wear the niqab or the burka in public places.

However, a couple of positive developments have occurred in this area. In December 2004, the HALDE (Haute Autorité de Lutte contre les Discriminations et pour l'Egalité, or Equal Opportunities and Anti-Discrimination Commission) was established as an independent statutory authority of the French government. It provides various legal means and assistance in identifying and combating discrimination, defined as unequal treatment based on eighteen discrimination criteria: age, gender, origin, sex, family/marital status, pregnancy, physical appearance, surname, health, disability, genetic characteristics, way of life, sexual orientation, union activity, and actual or assumed membership of an ethnic group, nation, race, or religion.

In 2008, Yazid Sabeg, a proponent of *discrimination positive* (affirmative action), was appointed commissioner for diversity and equal opportunities. A successful French businessman of Berber origin, he was born in Algeria and grew up in Lille, building a remarkable career despite official and societal obstacles. In his new role, he plans to create a more inclusive French society through increased educational and career opportunities for minorities, including various types of outreach programs and encouraging the use of anonymous resumés.

Universalism, Egalitarianism, and the Principle of Differentiation. Universalism is a republican value that informs the Declaration of the Rights of Man and Citizen, what the French call the social protection system, labor laws, and many other vital areas of social life. Based on this fundamental principle, the government enacts laws that give each individual access to the same rights and privileges. It does not in principle differentiate either positively or negatively based on the origin or specific situation of the person.

Affirmative action laws such as those that have been on the books in the United States—though they are beginning to disappear—will not be easy to implement in France. They exemplify the principle of differentiation, granting different rights and privileges for cultural or historical reasons on the basis of past oppression or discrimination. From a French point of view, this kind of differentiation would inevitably lead to the creation of separate societies, a precept that goes against the very principles that constitute the French Republic and its social fabric.

> The French Constitution forbids making any distinction among citizens based on race, origin, or religion. In this context, even moderate U.S.-style multicul- turalism can be seen as a potential threat to the integrity of the nation. Any attempt at enumerating minorities in France recalls the headcounts of the Vichy and colonial regimes. The net effect is to create almost a taboo around issues of ethnicity. (Lacorne)

Similarly, the gender gap as a distinct issue does not receive much attention in France compared with the United States, since French people tend to identify themselves as members of the same society and nation before asserting their gender differences. Despite outstanding intellectual leadership from such people as Simone de Beauvoir (*Le deuxième sexe*, published in 1949), feminist movements have received limited attention in France. Women are usually more concerned with who they are and with their femininity—what makes them womanly—than with demanding particular consideration because they are women.

In a discussion of the differences in gender relations between France and the United States, Elisabeth Badinter noted that universalism in France is based on a refusal to define a citizen by his or her particularity (1995). Issues that in the U.S. have been addressed primarily by women with a feminist agenda have been folded into more general efforts at social progress in France. This being said, French law and the social system do in fact tend to support women in their roles as women, wives, mothers, and workers with a variety of economic and social programs.

One Frenchwoman observes that during the 1970s, the women's liberation movements in France and the United States were about the same size and impor- tance. There was, however, a small but crucial philosophical difference:

> Frenchwomen emphasized the need to recognize differences between men and women. Equal, yes, but different. Most Frenchwomen expected to be validated precisely for their difference—and they still do. American women, on the other hand, wanted above all to become equal to men, with the same rights and responsibilities. . . . [I]n France, there was a struggle in the nineteenth century to free women from working down in the mines or at night. In the U.S., there is a struggle now to allow women to do all kinds of work, day or night. (Hermary- Vieille and Sarde 1997, 294)

But issues of gender difference and equality go deeper than matters of work, property rights, and maternity leave.

> Behind the different behaviors, there are two different models. Frenchwomen are universalists. Beyond the feminine differences they lay claim to, they consider themselves above all members of the human race. American women, on the other

hand, see universalism as an illusion in the absence of equal rights. That's why they have no problem placing themselves in the category of minority along with Blacks, Indians, or homosexuals. The term "minority" implies that they don't have the same rights as the majority. And the majority is white men. (293)

However, the French do differentiate in terms of social origin, which seems paradoxical in light of their cherished egalitarian principles. Despite the official abolition of class distinctions by the Revolution, social background, as we mentioned earlier, still plays an important role in determining an individual's options for education, career choice, and advancement. Authority and structure are essential in France. Because of the resilience of hierarchy in French society and traditional organizations (and, to a lesser extent, families), power and responsibilities are distributed according to clear lines of authority. In social settings as well as in the workplace, relationships between superior and subordinates are clearly established and respected.

As noted earlier, friends tend to be made at similar social levels, and descendants of aristocrats rarely mix socially with descendants of the wagon drivers who escorted them to the guillotine. Where such mixing occurs—the company's Christmas celebration for all employees and their families, for example—interactions between high-level managers and other employees are usually formal.

Americans in France are usually cheerfully oblivious of class distinctions, and this may create some uncomfortable situations for their French colleagues. An American department director who had recently arrived in France organized a Christmas buffet dinner at his home for his whole staff, including spouses and children. For him, this was a good opportunity to get to know his employees better. Some sixty guests attended, ranging from the janitor to the director of global research.

The party went on until two in the morning, and from the host's perspective it was a complete success. He was pleased that the guests represented "a good mixture of people." The French guests also noted the mixture but were less positive about it. Employees at the same hierarchical level pretty much stayed in their own groups, and, though most had a pleasant evening, they later recalled the uneasiness they felt at not knowing exactly where they stood and what was expected of them. While the American host was unaware of his guests' confusion, they were struck by the unusual attempt to blend public/work and private/social spheres across hierarchical levels.

Americans wishing to invite French colleagues from various levels to social functions, such as a backyard barbecue, should be aware of the reticence they are likely to encounter. This kind of gathering is not, strictly speaking, a taboo, and being a foreigner, you may be able to carry it off. It is important to keep in mind, however, that the rules are being bent, so bend them gently. Offering to share a "typical American cultural experience" will alert guests that the evening may be different from what they are expecting.

Justice. The legal systems of the United States and France have different historical and philosophical roots. American law is based on English common law, while French law is based on Roman law. English common law was codified by Magna Carta in 1215. Like so many other American institutions, it was brought by early settlers to the new colonies. Common law has been referred to as the common sense of the community, crystallized and formulated by our ancestors. It depends upon tradition and precedent for legal decisions, which are normally made by a jury of lay people. Judgment is inferred, determined by analogy with similar cases from the past.

French law as it stands today was essentially established by the Napoleonic Code, adopted in 1804. The code combined large portions of Roman law with the ideals of the French Revolution, including individual liberty, equality before the law, and separation of church and state. Legal judgment is rendered by trained judges rather than a jury composed of laypeople, and cases are determined according to written and codified law.

Three French researchers suggest that the differences between the American and French legal systems are nothing less than a different social method of approaching reality. They point out four important areas of variation between the U.S. and French systems:

1. participation by community members versus an official judge representing the State, though juries do exist in French criminal law;
2. an oral tradition versus a scholarly, formal, and written law;
3. reasoning based on similarity of cases versus reasoning based on the relevance of a text to the structure of a situation analyzed in abstract terms; and
4. inductive, holistic reasoning versus deduction and analysis. (Amado, Faucheux, and Laurent 1989, 34)

Many Americans mistakenly believe that under French law, a person is guilty until proven innocent. This is simply not so. French defendants are also presumed innocent, but it may be easier to prove guilt in a French court than in an American court. French criminal justice does not require proof beyond a reasonable doubt for conviction, as is the case in the United States. All that is required is what U.S. law refers to as a "preponderance of the evidence." In other words, the defendant is more likely to be guilty than innocent. In addition, the decision of a judicial panel in France need not be unanimous for conviction— dissent is admitted even here.

The French judicial system uses an examining or investigating judge, called a *juge d'instruction*, who is independent of both the executive branch and the Public Prosecution Office, which is supervised by the Minister of Justice. An investigating judge does not prosecute the defendant, but rather gathers facts and assembles any and all evidence, be it incriminating or exculpatory. He or she can question witnesses as well as suspects, and can order other investigations.

Separation of executive and judiciary powers has been crucial to ensure the independence of the French judiciary system, which is often confronted with cases involving political figures. However, some scandals and failures of the system have called into question the necessity and competence of such an investigating judge, to the point that there is a debate nowadays about the suppression of this function. One key case influencing this reflection or debate is the "Affaire Outreau" that we would like to highlight due to its unusual and dramatic nature.

THE OUTREAU AFFAIR

The Outreau affair is a judicial case that deeply marked the beginning of this century in France, sparking debate about the inadequacy of the judicial system. This affair was so catastrophic that then-President Jacques Chirac himself called it a "judicial disaster."

Outreau is a poor suburb of Boulogne-sur-Mer in the north of France. An alleged network of pedophiles was discovered in late 2001, involving parents of school-age children. Teachers and social workers noticed "strange sexual behavior" from four children in a local school. Parents were accused of pedophilia on the basis of some of the children's testimony, which was then backed up by confessions of some of the accused.

Eighteen people were involved and held in custody for up to three years. The first trial took place locally in 2004. Four of the parents pleaded guilty and were convicted to years in prison. Seven others denied their involvement and were acquitted. Seven other people were convicted, despite claims of innocence, and one of them committed suicide in prison while waiting for the appeal. The appeal took place before the cour d'assises de Paris (criminal court), and all six remaining accused were acquitted while the prosecution's claims were reduced to ashes.

One of the main witnesses in the case, who was also one of the convicted felons, revealed shortly before the appeal trial that she had lied about the involvement of other suspects. Several of them had nevertheless spent time in jail, and one had died. At the end of the trial, the prosecutor (*avocat général*) requested acquittal of all six accused. The defense renounced its right to plead and instead requested a minute of silence in memory of the deceased suspect. Even more disturbing, and in a clear loss of face for the judicial profession, the general prosecutor of Paris showed up on the last day of the trial and offered his apologies to the defendants on behalf of the legal system—before the verdict was delivered. His admission of wrongdoing was followed by official apologies from the president of France, the prime minister, and the attorney general.

The affair caused public indignation in France and raised questions about the reliability and credibility of the judicial system. Why give such an important case to an inexperienced judge fresh out of the Ecole Nationale de la Magistrature, the official training institute for judges and prosecutors? Why was so much weight given to children's testimony and psychiatric expertise that turned out to be erroneous? The responsibility of the media was also questioned as they were quick to hype the affair.

A parliamentary inquiry was launched in early 2006, the first time such an event was broadcast live on television. The inquiry was charged with examining the role of experts and child protection advocates, as well as the responsibility of judges and the media. Quite understandably, the hearing of the acquitted persons provoked a surge of emotion in the entire country for an affair that was designated as a *naufrage judiciaire* (a judiciary shipwreck).

A Cockeyed Optimist. Americans tend to think that people are basically good and that eventually bad people can turn their lives around and start again. The French traditionally believe that humanity is either evil or a mixture of good and evil and are convinced that people rarely change their basic orientation. These attitudes are pervasive in France and reinforce the belief of Americans—who in principle are inclined to trust people until they are proven untrustworthy—that the French are basically mistrustful or cynical.

It is often noted that Americans tend to be irredeemably optimistic, while the French are so deeply pessimistic that some talk about taking vacations in the United States for a "breath of American optimism." The French tendency to look at the half-empty glass is reflected in French language and philosophy. *"C'est la vie!"* (That's life!) expresses resignation about what cannot be changed.

The French language provides some interesting insights into this stern philosophy. A verb like *cope* has no direct equivalent in French, a "still life" picture is a "dead nature" (*nature morte*), and a "stillborn" child is "dead-born" (*mort-né*). The French terms may strike Americans as a bit harsh in their frankness, while the American words seem to the French like sugarcoating to avoid naming unpleasant realities.

Not surprisingly, fate plays a more important role in France than in the United States. People are born into certain conditions that are difficult if not impossible to change. A French person climbing to the top in the American self-made way is very much the exception rather than the rule. Since education is one of the most important factors in determining a person's social and economic level, almost everything has been decided by the time a person completes his or her education and enters the categories established by society. Although the word *entrepreneur* is French (a person who undertakes), entrepreneurship is not encouraged or nurtured by the French bureaucratic system or by the upbringing of French children. French parents do not suggest that their children make some pocket money mowing the neighbors' lawns or shoveling their sidewalks as American parents might do. There is little possibility in France—compared with the United States—for becoming a wealthy, nationally recognized person through one's own efforts.

La Délation—Turning In or Reporting Someone. There is an area of French-U.S. relations that offers varying perspectives, and which is closely related to notions of ethics, as well as public interest and the importance of the group versus the individual. The French noun is *délation*, and it is interesting to note that it doesn't have any equivalent in English (no nouns), except for the notion of reporting someone, or turning someone in.

Perhaps the basis of the confusion around this issue for French and Americans is a misinterpretation or misunderstanding at the level of basic definitions of the action, and the goals/intentions of the person involved. The French concept of délation generally means turning someone in or reporting someone for one of two reasons: either to cause trouble for or to punish the person who is breaking the rules, or to gain some personal benefit from turning him in—or both.

As a historical footnote, post-World War II French behavior has been heavily influenced by the actions of the Vichy government, which cooperated with Nazi Germany. Many minority groups suffered as a consequence, and thousands of Jews and other populations were turned in and sent to concentration camps. This was one of the most shameful periods in French history, a period for which France is still paying a price, and it left a deep stigma in the French psyche. Attitudes toward denouncing people changed drastically—to the point that délation of almost any kind is considered bad and looked down upon. The French tend to assume—or at least to suspect—that turning someone in is an act of ill will. Decent people don't do such things.

From the American perspective, turning in or reporting someone who is breaking the rules is usually seen as an action that helps the community as a whole. Antisocial behavior may pose a threat to the community, so everyone should help protect each other. Many neighborhoods in the U.S. have a "Neighborhood Watch" program, which involves people keeping an eye on other homes and vehicles and calling the police if they see anything suspicious. People pull together to help each other out and to keep the neighborhood safe. It's a very ethical thing to do.

French people coming to the U.S. tend to see such things through their own cultural perspectives, observe only the action of turning in or reporting someone without understanding the motivation and the absence of historical baggage behind it, and assume that Americans have an unhealthy taste for délation. Americans must be reporting people either to get them into trouble or for some kind of personal gain. How can decent people possibly behave like this?

A French graduate student at UC Berkeley was taking a series of exams. One of the instructions for the exam related to the importance of being honest, and not cheating. Students were instructed to report any classmates they saw cheating. To the French student, this was simply outrageous. "How can I possibly report someone who is in the same boat as I am?"

A French father in Virginia was upset at his seven-year-old son's primary school. During lunchtime, his son used a *gros mot* (a dirty word) in the cafeteria and was immediately reported to the school principal by a cafeteria aide for appropriate action; that is, behavior modification. The French father's reaction: "Why send him to the principal right away for such a small thing?"

On highway 45 North in downtown Houston, a sign in the HOV (High-Occupancy Vehicle or carpool) lane says, "Report anyone violating the rule. Please call 1-713-921-HERO." (HERO Hotline)

In the case of the exams at Berkeley, it didn't make sense for the French student to report his peers because of the collective nature of the experience: all students are in the same boat; this is "us" versus "them"—the administration, the top management of a company, or even the government. My primary affiliation will dictate my loyalty and therefore my behavior. In contrast, for an American student who is not cheating, the cheaters are certainly not "in the same boat." Their behavior is unfair to the entire class.

In France, it is also considered bad taste to "brown nose" (*lécher les bottes, failloter*) the teacher or the boss in order to attract his or her favor. This is seen as an attempt to distance oneself from a group, be it a group of students or a group of same-level employees or citizens. It is usually a sure way to sever ties with one's kin, to choose one's camp for good, and to *faire bande à part* (isolate oneself). Délation can therefore be seen as "sucking up" to authority, which is often seen as the adversary in "them" versus "us."

Respecting rules and regulations for the sake of the rules themselves and because the book "says so" is often considered too rigid a behavior in France because it prevents people from thinking. A French person would first consider what the rules and regulations are (the context), and what the consequences of breaching them would be. Would anyone get physically hurt if a driver uses an HOV lane against the rule? Most likely not. So better to yell or honk at him and forget about a phone call. In addition, being considered a HERO for reporting such a small thing would sound like hypocrisy to a French person, and this kind of honey would hardly attract a French fly. In a similar vein, a toll free number was set up in the French subsidiary of an American company to report cases of unethical behavior. To this day, the Human Resources department is still awaiting calls.

The French can act spontaneously in the public interest, but it tends to be expressed very differently. An occurrence of exemplary "public conduct" was offered by three French spectators during Bastille Day 2002 when *un désiquilibré* (an unbalanced man) tried to shoot President Jacques Chirac during the parade down the Champs-Elysées. Extreme situations do require exemplary behavior, and none of these three people hesitated for a second to stop the shooter.

TO BE OR NOT TO BE … PERFECT?

To Reach the Unreachable Star. Perhaps one of the fundamental differences in French and American worldviews lies in the conception of the ideal compared to the real, or what can actually be achieved. American icons—the Platonic forms of the ideal man, ideal woman, ideal child, ideal family, ideal community—are reflected in the work of Norman Rockwell, a painter whose enormous popularity resulted from his ability to distill the American ideals of his time and transpose them into concrete images. His images of perfection *à l'américaine* made the artist himself an American icon. These images served as a sort of collective family album, but not of our actual flawed and imperfect families. Rather, we see in Rockwell's paintings a perfection that resonates with what people then—and even today among the nostalgic—would have liked their families to look like, what it was felt they should look like.

While there have been great changes in the American psyche since Rockwell's time, it is still peculiarly American to see these kinds of idealized images as actually achievable. This notion results partially from the American belief that anyone can achieve anything with enough hard work and determination. American mantras such as "Practice makes perfect" and "If you believe and you can conceive, you will achieve" have no equivalent in the French language or culture.

American thinking tends toward the dualistic and the absolutist—perfection itself is an absolute. Most Americans see things as either black or white, good or bad, right or wrong, a success or a failure. What this means is that if anything goes wrong in the quest to achieve the ideal, the *entire enterprise* becomes a failure. Any deviation from the ideal is a major problem and is treated as such, for it has the potential to become catastrophic. A nasty recurrent argument is enough to convince a couple that their marriage is in serious trouble and to compel them to seek professional counseling. A child who does not reach certain developmental milestones properly and on time causes concern and visits with the pediatrician and the child's teacher.

Somehow, despite mountains of statistical evidence to the contrary, despite their own experiences and those of their friends and family, Americans continue to believe that they can achieve the ideal, and that if they do not, it is because they are personally deficient in some way. Everything must be optimized, all the time and forever. An American, then, experiences profound disappointment and distress if the real does not correspond precisely to the ideal.

C'est Comme Ça; La Perfection N'est Pas de ce Monde (That's the Way It Is; Perfection Exists Only in Heaven). The French ideal is seen as a goal to be aimed for but which cannot by its nature be achieved. The real cannot correspond precisely to the ideal. It is not expected to, and the mismatch is simply acknowledged and accepted, with neither great distress nor great disappointment. People are expected to do their best and to achieve as much as they are capable of, but this capacity does not include perfection. The perfect grade of twenty points out of a possible twenty exists, at least *en théorie*, but *en réalité*, no one ever seriously expects to reach it.

From the French perspective, minor problems or deviations from the ideal are quite normal and acceptable and do not necessarily mean total failure—or indeed failure at all. Fate plays a part. Other people are involved, other forces beyond human control. One does what one can, but these things happen. The French meet them with a classic Gallic shrug, a bemused expression of resignation, and a resilient *"C'est comme ça, hein?"* ("That's just the way it is, isn't it?").

By way of illustration, let's look at expectations and preparations for weddings in the two countries. How people approach this important personal, family, and often religious event says a great deal about their cultural values.

American weddings, unless in a strongly traditional ethnic community, are usually expected to shine with perfection. The profession of wedding coordinator must be uniquely American. These planners advise couples that everything must be perfect on this most perfect of days. There should be no surprises on *The Day*; every element must be planned, double-checked, and rehearsed so that nothing unexpected occurs. The planners offer lists and even pocket reminder cards for everyone involved, detailing exactly what each must do, exactly when, and exactly how. There is an element of a performance, something apart from, and better than, real life.

French couples and families also bicker endlessly and energetically about wedding details. But there is no expectation that everything will be or must be perfect. The idea of having a rehearsal is seen as absurd. Who would want to have a mechanical Barbie doll wedding? Most important is a feeling of authenticity, of spontaneity. A French couple attending the wedding of a distant cousin in the United States was astonished by the "show" or "parade" aspect of the event. From their perspective, those in the wedding party were little more than dressed-up marionettes.

An American, then, lives by striving for perfection, refusing to admit the possibility, let alone the virtual certainty, of failure. A French person lives by accepting—perhaps even by enjoying—imperfection. As noted above, what seems to interest the French is deviation from the ideal rather than correspondence with it. The emphasis is on difference—and *vive la différence!* From this emerges the French love of confrontational arguments, of making and valuing friends with whom one does not necessarily agree on important issues.

SEX REARS ITS UGLY HEAD

Most Americans in France notice that French attitudes toward sex and nudity are much more liberal than those in the United States. Whether this is a sign of a refreshing lack of inhibition or an indication of decadence is open to debate. The fact is that even prime-time commercials for soap or towels in France might earn PG-13 or higher ratings in the U.S.

Political sex scandals in the U.S. often torpedo careers, or do irreparable damage at the very least. The Clinton-Lewinsky affair produced rivers of ink on both sides of the Atlantic. For the French, it was largely another amusing story of childish, prudish Americans getting in a tizzy over sex and washing dirty laundry in public. One observer noted, "Yes, we understand that Americans are upset because their president lied. Of course he did! He's a politician! In France—well, in the rest of the world, really—we know politicians lie. We expect it. We also expect them to get on with their jobs."

More recently, Eliot Spitzer, former governor of New York, resigned when his affair was made public. John Edwards, senator and two-time presidential candidate, also kissed his career good-bye after admitting to an affair that produced an illegitimate child. South Carolina Governor Mark Sanford has refused to resign for the moment, despite giving the world a new euphemism for extramarital sex: "He's hiking the Appalachian trail."

David Bonior, Edwards' 2008 presidential campaign manager, highlighted the link that Americans often see between a politician's personal morality and his reliability as a public figure: "You can't lie in politics and expect to have people's confidence."

Contrast this with the spirited defense of Dominique Strauss-Kahn following his confession of an affair, which has not derailed his successful career. He is still seen as the favorite potential candidate of the Socialist party in the 2012 French presidential election.

As noted earlier, Americans' preoccupation with the sexual activities of politicians and celebrities fuels "sensational news" revelations and endless talk-show chatter. Sex appeal sells in France as well as anywhere else, but Americans' insatiable appetite for peek-a-boo titillation does not translate well in a country where topless beaches are common.

Part of this difference may be explained by American puritanism and prudery. This is, in fact, how many French understand it, and they find American attitudes childish and utterly hilarious. In a wider sense, however, what shocks Americans is the opposition of the ideal and the real—or at least in its becoming common knowledge. The ideal American marriage involves two people who are faithful to each other forever: "Cheating on one's wife or husband is unforgivable" (Vitiello-Yewell and Nacher 1991, 37). It happens, but it is unforgivable, and once it becomes common knowledge, divorce is the most likely result.

Badinter notes that the puritan ideal of purity implies control of the body and utter clarity of the soul, both of which are violated in an affair (1995). She goes on to say, however, that the French do not demand utter truth and clarity, but rather negotiate between truth and lies. Ultimately, lies may be better than a harsh truth and its consequences; peace may be more important than truth. We see here, as well as in many other areas of French life, the importance of context and subjectivity on one end, as opposed to black and white, objective truth on the other.

Although Americans talk about "little white lies" and often recognize their necessity, their conception of truth is generally an either-or proposition. Either something is true or it isn't, and that's all there is to it. Strongly associated with this is the idea that "honesty is the best policy." In France, a person may have *péchés mignons*, literally "cute sins," such as a weakness for temptations like rich pastries. And while lying is a sin in the Catholic religion, French proverbial wisdom teaches that *toute vérité n'est pas bonne à dire* (all truths need not be spoken).

American culture encourages people to "open up" about their problems. Discussing one's problems with others is the best way to find a solution or to cope with them. The opposite is usually true in a group in France, where silence is often the preferred way to address a problem. The expression *mettre sous silence* (to place under silence) is revealing here. Something is wrong and everyone in the family, for example, knows about it. Since they already know, they do not need to talk about it but simply live with the situation. It is a fact of life, not a problem that must be solved before life can go on.

MONEY MAKES THE WORLD GO 'ROUND

A 2003 study asked respondents about the most important changes in the last ten years about French attitudes toward money. Forty-eight percent of the respondents mentioned lack of concern for the disadvantaged; 35 percent said greater financial independence for women; 29 percent said that more and more French people were finding out about the stock market; 21 percent said an increase in family solidarity; and 19 percent mentioned that people no longer had qualms about revealing their wealth.[28]

These findings underline the social and familial aspects of money in France. The relative ease with which people talk about money and possessions represents a shift from tradition. One French manager, after working in the United States for some time, compared sensitive subjects in the two countries: "In the U.S., a businessman shows his company's financial statements but hides his mistress. In France, a businessman shows his mistress but hides the financial statements" (Bull Worldwide Information Systems 1992). He may have been exaggerating for effect, but money in France is surrounded by almost the same secrecy and vague sense of guilt as sex is in the U.S.

Although the gap between the highest and lowest wages is less pronounced in France—and for that matter, in most of Europe—than in the United States, making a lot of money is something that one does not talk about, and certainly does not brag about. Revelations by the satirical newspaper *Le Canard Enchaîné* of the generous annual salary, about $600,000, received by former Peugeot CEO Jacques Calvet in the late 1980s were greeted with hoots of derision directed at him and accusations of scandal. True, he had turned the company around from

---

[28] *www.csa.eu*

the brink of bankruptcy, but many French people saw it as personal enrichment on the backs of exploited workers. Similarly, when Philippe Jaffré, former CEO of ELF, left the company following its 1999 acquisition by TOTAL, he received a "thank you" bonus of 60 million francs. Such a generous French severance package provoked an angry reaction, even from the right wing.

Inflation has obviously taken its toll on the French economy in the case of Henri Proglio, the newly appointed CEO of EDF. Henri Proglio was hand-picked by the French government to head EDF while at the same time keeping his position as chairman of the board of VEOLIA, a private water treatment and waste management company. A graduate of HEC, he had been working for VEOLIA for a record thirty-seven years and ascended the corporate ladder to become its CEO in 2003. Henri Proglio was offered a salary of €1.6 million by the French government for his civil service post at EDF and kept a compensation of €450,000 for his responsibilities at VEOLIA. In addition to what many people considered an "indecent level of compensation," some wondered how superhuman this person must be to lead simultaneously two of the largest French companies!

Due to public pressure and strong Socialist opposition during debates in the National Assembly, Henri Proglio gave up the compensation for his VEOLIA job, but kept the position. Interviewed on public TV during a panel discussion with eleven ordinary French people, Nicolas Sarkozy justified his government's decision by saying, "I prefer to have a great president getting a high salary rather than a mediocre president getting average pay." It's very doubtful that the 2.9 million unemployed French people bought into this rationale; one of them, a 26-year-old woman unable to find a job with a master's in marketing, was part of the panel that evening.

In contrast, when American employees of a Philadelphia-based company learned that their CEO was ranked only number nineteen on the list of the region's highest salaries, they were disappointed that he hadn't placed higher. This reflects the pride American workers take in being employed by the company with the most "successful" (i.e., highest paid) CEO.

The French attitude toward money was shaped by many factors. Catholic ideology calls for disregard of earthly riches in hopes of heavenly reward, and despite the Church's much reduced contemporary role, there remains a general feeling that rapidly acquired wealth is suspect. A spectacular financial ascent is assumed to be based on shady dealings or outright exploitation.

In addition, the *nouveau riche* ("new rich" in literal translation, "crude rich" in cultural translation) is a traditional butt of jokes and satire. Conversely, classic and popular French literature contains many stories about poor but brave and honest figures like Jacquou le Croquant and Cyrano de Bergerac who set out, like d'Artagnan, *sans un sou vaillant* (penniless), and are held in high regard.

Although younger French generations are perhaps more eager to obtain lucrative jobs than their parents, there is still a sharp contrast between the way French and Americans relate to money and material possessions.

L'AUTORITÉ EN CRISE
(AUTHORITY IN CRISIS)

Due to the hierarchical nature of French society, there is one (fairly non-American) phenomenon that deserves attention: *Autorité* (Authority), a characteristic of French society that is being challenged every day in many areas such as home, school, church, and corporate life, not to mention the media and the police.

French society has significantly evolved since the beginning of the twentieth century, when authoritarian models of governing and raising children were much more common and has emerged as a so-called "modern society." General de Gaulle, an emblematic French figure, might very well illustrate the perfect image of the WWII French leader (read, Authority), one who is not questioned, and indeed cannot be questioned.

The fact that Authority is now being challenged at every level might be a healthy sign of a people finally throwing off the remnants of pre-Revolution, archaic modes of living and working, where *responsables* (leaders) at the top decide for the "servants" at the bottom.

In March 2006, *Enjeux*, a monthly economic magazine, devoted a special issue to "Authority in Crisis" and analyzed its implications in various areas of French society. They interviewed "authority figures" such as parents, school teachers, managers, priests, police officers, and other leaders to determine the depth of the syndrome—a syndrome that has not diminished in the years since this issue was published and as French society continues its evolution.

Comments from interviewees show the extent to which Authority is an intricate part of French culture and history. From a father: "Authority seems understood, although, at thirteen, it is not always accepted." In the school system: "We went from *une autorité allant de soi* (an authority that is not called into question) to *une situation où tout le monde revendique des droits* (a challenged authority where everyone claims his or her rights)." In the corporate arena, where "employees do not listen as they used to," programs offered by private training companies run from *"Exercer son autorité avec diplomatie"* (using authority diplomatically) to *"leadership et autorité"* (leadership and authority). In the religious sphere, where the Catholic Church is experiencing a sharp decline in the number of young people choosing a religious vocation, more laypeople are involved in the preparation of baptisms, funerals, and catechism: "More personalized authority requires a capacity to initiate dialogue, to negotiate, or more personal charisma." The cherry on the top came from a police superintendent: "In the end, even though we are the only authority that remains [in the country], we get the feeling that our uniform is less respected than before."

Overall, people polled for this special issue describe a person with authority as someone who:

- knows how to get respect (80 percent)
- is accountable (70 percent)
- is competent (65 percent)
- is experienced (58 percent)
- is a role model (55 percent)
- has power (38 percent)
- knows how to be feared (32 percent)

A French expression sums up a person whose authority is respected: he or she knows *comment exercer son autorité* (how to use his/her authority). Authority might be construed as something that you exert upon others to get things done or to restore order, for instance, in the case of a protest or an employee challenging your authority.

Another result of the *Enjeux* research showed that the three top institutions or people that respondents feel should be granted more importance are parents (90 percent), school (89 percent), and scientists (77 percent).

In relation to this Authority phenomenon, the following diagrams show the roles and responsibilities of the different stakeholders involved in the *éducation* (upbringing) or socialization of a child, comparing U.S. and French modes of operating in three realms: family, school, and workplace.

The reader needs to keep in mind that these modes are contextual and therefore may vary depending on the family, school environment, or workplace where the individual is shaped. Yet they provide an interesting comparison, knowing that this French phenomenon of challenging authority would tend to move French patterns toward the U.S. default mode—which is obviously not shared and not practiced by every American parent, school teacher, or manager.

An evolution of these upbringing patterns in France toward more empowerment and autonomy is illustrated by the fact that parents may become partners with whom their children can negotiate, but the concept of parents as buddies (*copains*) hasn't quite penetrated French society.

Egalitarian Patterns
(U.S. default mode)

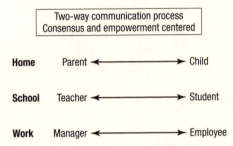

The egalitarian pattern does not necessarily mean that both partners are equal and, in general, the parent, teacher, and manager have more power and the final word. But in this pattern, the expectation is that each partner will have some input, and that the input of both partners is considered and taken seriously. For example, an elementary school teacher clearly doesn't ask her students what they think they should learn, but does give them some autonomy and responsibility for directing their own work. He or she might say, "For our lesson on the Middle Ages, we're going to divide into groups and each group will decide what project to work on and present to the entire class." The groups will then decide to build a model castle or produce a poster explaining details of a suit of armor and, with the teacher's help, split the project into smaller tasks for each pupil. The teacher can make suggestions or veto students' ideas to ensure the work is up to standard. This egalitarian pattern tends to result in the following "Growth and Development" outcomes, as the child grows toward an "ideal" that may be different for each individual, influenced by any number of factors in addition to parents and school. The idea is to encourage the individual's freedom of choice and action and develop his or her self-esteem, self-reliance, and ability to venture out and try new things.

By contrast, French parents and schools still play, to a large extent, the role of a *tuteur* (a stake) that provides the child with boundaries concerning what can be done and what cannot, and the direction in which he or she can grow. In this model, the teacher is by definition the expert, so that knowledge flows essentially in one direction. Teachers assign work to students and, particularly in the elementary grades, structure the work in specific, methodical ways to ensure that knowledge and critical thinking skills are understood and utilized. Other influences have effect as the child grows, but parents, who educate, and the school, that instructs, play the primary roles. Consistent with what Lawrence Wylie described

Growth and Development

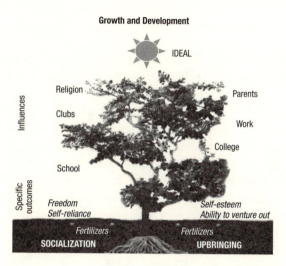

earlier, the idea here is to develop an individual who has internalized the structure, discipline, restraint, and manners that are essential to living in society.

Interestingly, the concept of psychological growth is not appealing to the French, and they would rather speak of development and enrichment, resulting—as the open flower illustrates—in the child's blossoming to maturity.

In contrast, the French patterns that produce these outcomes might appear as in the following figure. There is a tendency in French society to put the expert

Enrichment and Blossoming

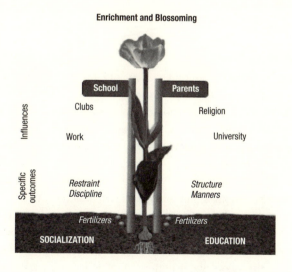

(be it the teacher, boss, or possibly parents) above the non-expert, because of her level of knowledge or at times for fear of disturbing the person or putting her in a bad light. One wouldn't want to *déranger* (disturb) one's boss by asking him to do something out of the ordinary; or ask a question of a teacher, as it may be perceived as challenging the person's authority. Just as we do not intend to present a fixed U.S. model, our approach to French patterns should not be seen as carved in stone. But our analysis is consistent with American university professors who come to teach in France for a semester or two and can't get a question out of their French students' mouths—education indeed tends to be unidirectional in France. Similarly, it is well known that the purpose of a business meeting in France when different hierarchical levels are present is often *not* to make a decision but rather to collect information and feedback so that the person in charge can make the appropriate decision with all the cards in his or her hands.

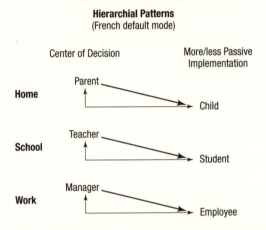

Hierarchial Patterns
(French default mode)

Again, the reaction of the child, student, or employee will vary according to his or her personality and the family, school, or organizational culture in which he or she is involved. Yet this phenomenon of challenging authority pervading French society is clearly a challenge of or protest against the "center of decision" described above—a practice that is still very common in many French families, schools, and corporations.

Fighting Authority. Fighting Authority is a popular activity in France that may not have any equivalent, or at least not enjoy the same popularity, in other societies. It shows up in the streets during a protest, the sequestration of the boss at a plant where employees are threatened with layoffs as their jobs are moved elsewhere, or in the school where notions of respect for classmates and teachers alike have dwindled in recent years—to the point that teachers have been physically threatened and even occasionally attacked.

Yet, fighting Authority has its dangers, and French people generally assess the stakes, the context, and the measures to be used. Solidarity plays a role here, especially when it comes to unionized movements, and it is usually wiser to undertake these actions as a group.

Solitary challenges may be faced with repression, as well as possible popular support, as the following example shows.

Alain Refalo, an elementary school teacher in Colomiers (Haute-Garonne, near Toulouse), wrote an open letter in November of 2008 stating his opposition to reforms from the Education Ministry regarding "personalized assistance to students with difficulties" on the grounds that it would go against the students' interests. His refusal to apply the new measures sent a strong signal that was well received among the teaching community. As a result of his *désobéissance* (disobedience), he was first sanctioned with a nineteen-day pay cut. After the disciplinary commission examined his case, he was demoted, although he received high marks in his evaluations by inspectors of the academy (regional school district).

His reaction to the sanctions highlights a pattern—repression from the top—which doesn't promote empowerment and consensus building. In Alain Refalo's words, "The new minister hopes with this measure [against me] to crush any hints of opposition during the back-to-school period. He is wrong, and authorities isolate themselves in a repressive attitude that can only generate regrettable tensions in the future." Such a position may seem odd in a hierarchical culture, but standing up to authority in this way is an important feature—and safety valve—in French society.

TRUST AND DISTRUST

In 2007, two researchers, Yann Algan and Pierre Cahuc, published an explosive ninety-nine-page pamphlet under the title, *La Société de Défiance–Comment le modèle social français s'autodétruit* (Distrust Society: How the French social model self-destructs). They reviewed social research conducted over the past twenty-five years in Europe and North America and highlighted the fact that the French, more than people in most developed countries, do not trust their fellow citizens, the State (*les pouvoirs publics*), or the market. Their conclusion shows a French "trust deficit" as well as a "civility deficit," neither of which, they say, is irreversible. By going even further back in their analyses, they also noticed that this double deficit started after World War II.

The main factor behind these troubling matters, they report, is the role of the State, which made French post-war society dependent on corporatism and state intervention (*étatisme*). They define corporatism as "a practice which allows specific social rights based on status and profession," and which "segments society, hinders social relationships, which in turn favors the development of unearned income, sustains mutual suspicion and destroys solidarity."

The French form of étatisme "regulates every detail in each and every domain of civil society, empties social dialogue of its meaning [since the state does not rely on or empower independent third parties], hampers competition and enhances corruption."

In turn, they assert, these practices of corporatism and excessive state intervention lead to more distrust and more incivility with, at the same time, more reliance on what the French call *l'Etat-providence* (the providence-state). This vicious circle paralyzes French economy and society.

While our purpose is not to delve into the macro or micro details of the researchers' study, it is easy for any visitor to observe that French society is not built on a "Trust Default Mode." One small example, among many others, follows.

In virtually every large supermarket in France, you find shopping carts with a coin-operated security system. Putting a one- or two-euro coin into a slot on top of the handle allows you to unlock it. If you do not return the caddy, you simply do not get your money back. Experience has shown long ago that carts not protected by this deposit tend to end up in people's homes or gardens.

French expats in the U.S. have told us of their amazement at the basic trust shown in everyday American life, as it is such a contrast to what they are used to. An expat in Dallas could hardly believe that the mail carrier often left parcels on people's front porches if no one was home, and that they weren't stolen. "One time, my wife even forgot to close the garage door when she drove home. It was open all night long, and nothing was touched!" Another told us of his first visit to a self-service doughnut shop. "I picked out a dozen doughnuts and took the closed box to the cashier. She asked, 'How many have you got?' and didn't even check! A shop that did that in France would be out of business fast, especially once word got out that they were too stupid or lazy to check quantities!" The idea that the shop didn't check quantities because they trusted customers to be honest, and the concept that customers might not try to take more than they paid for, didn't seem to be on his radar.

This lack of civility and trust, reinforced by a fiercely competitive, corporatist educational system (see section about the grandes écoles in chapter 7) is certainly not conducive to cooperation and teamwork. No wonder then, as our two researchers assert, that this state of affairs affects labor market conditions and employment, France's competiveness in the world, as well as French people's happiness—the more people distrust their neighbors or people in general, the less happy they are, according to studies they reviewed.

There is one additional explanation we would like to offer, and this has to do with the French tendency to oppose—to oppose virtually everything. Opposition creates friction, discussion, debates, even fights, and possibly value, but generally hard-won value. As we mentioned in the "With Politics" chapter, the minority parties in the French parliament are called "opposition." This term is a clear indication of an environment where those parties' job is to fight and not to cooperate in the creation of a healthier society.

Similarly, the pattern of "opposition to the system" we find in pre-1789 France is still potent in labor relations today, as well as other areas of French society. The triad Nobility/Church/Third State is now mirrored in the work environment by another triad, Employees (and their unions, if involved), the State, and the *Patronat*, owners of capital or bosses. Often, we see the workers opposing the State's decisions or actions, as in the case of strikes or lockouts for safeguarding *certains acquis sociaux* (social benefits), or the State restricting employer and market freedom by instituting new laws and regulations. These tend to be win-lose situations, so that what the employees gain, the employers lose, and vice-versa. The 35-hour week is an example. Rarely do we witness a situation where all stakeholders cooperate for everyone's benefit, as well as for the good of society at large. Indeed it might take yet another century or so for these "revolutionary patterns" of expression and *lutte des classes* (class struggle) mentalities to subside in France.

As a way to close this section, we would like to offer some "food for thought," both to the non-French observer and to the French reader as a way to reflect on his or her own environment. In the introduction to their book, Algan and Cahuc use a quotation from Alain Peyrefitte:

> Distrust society is a cautious society, win-lose: a society where living together ends up being a zero sum game, sometimes even a negative sum game (if you win, I lose); it is a society that sustains class struggle, unhappy living—both nationally and internationally—social jealousy, "closedness," the aggression of mutual surveillance. Trust society is an expanding society, win-win, a society of solidarity, of common projects, of openness, exchange, communication.

FIFTEEN

Dialogue between Two Worlds

Interculturalists use the "sunglasses" or "colored lens" analogy to explain how our worldview is filtered through the perspective of our deep culture—the hidden part of our cultural iceberg—embedded within us. Imagine for a moment that all Americans are provided with yellow sunglasses. No one notices them as anything special because everyone has them. What makes the sunglasses yellow is the unique set of values, attitudes, beliefs, and assumptions that Americans have in common. The yellow lens thus represents "American-ness." In France, everyone is also provided with sunglasses, but the sunglasses are blue.

More and more people are aware of these kinds of dissimilarities in perception and mindset between people from different cultures. But often, when Americans are traveling to France, for instance, they believe all they have to do is acquire some blue sunglasses in order to learn about French culture, to see and understand the "real" France. They are then convinced when they come back that they *do* know French culture—and it's green!

The moral of this fable is this:

Before we are open and free to learn about another culture (and put on their sunglasses) we have to remove our own, so that our interpretation of the new culture will not be "colored" or filtered by our own values, attitudes, and beliefs. We are not here to judge another culture, but to learn about it. We need to develop "double vision" or the ability to see more than one side of an idea. (Mercil 1984)

We will need both pairs of sunglasses handy as we examine points of similarity and difference in the worldviews of French and American people. Things that make sense in one context do not always make sense in another. Understanding and making sense of a new environment, seeing the positive and the inherent logic in it, require time and patience. As we look for the "why" behind the behavior we observe, we find we cannot simply make snap judgments from our own set of values and beliefs.

WHO DO YOU THINK YOU ARE?

I Think How I Think, Therefore I Am What I Am. Intellectual mastery of an issue is very important in France; results are what matter in the United States. The French must have the proper *démarche*, the right intellectual approach to a problem. Démarche refers to the way people reason and think before acting. It involves a lot of back-and-forth questioning of the nature and scope of the problem itself and requires consideration of all aspects and ramifications of potential solutions. Not surprisingly, the word *démarche* is hard to translate into English. It means, loosely, "approach," but includes notions around the approach itself: how and why something is done, not just the steps involved in doing it.

This intellectual questioning in practice works like this: if a normally closed door is left open in the United States, a person will simply walk in. In France, a person will first wonder who opened the door or left it open, and why, before going through. *Why* is always a very important question, and people love to argue and debate just for the sake of the enjoyment they get out of arguing.

At least as crucial as the *why* in the French thinking process is the *how*: how do I think about what I think about? Rational thought is the highest expression of French intelligence, and thinking about something rationally can be an end in itself. This brings us to René Descartes, as most discussions of French thinking inevitably do.

Descartes (1596–1650) was a philosopher and mathematician whose *Discours de la Méthode* (*A Discourse on Method*) became the ultimate *"art de,"* or "how to," guide for reasoning. His approach is summed up in the famous quotation *"Cogito ergo sum"* ("I think, therefore I am"), and his influence on French thinking can be felt to this day. "Descartes affirms the rational character of natural law. Everything in nature can be explained in terms of cause and effect, and if certain mysteries remain, it is only because of our ignorance. They have no reality in and of themselves" (Ferry 1995, 59).

The method requires a person to think in a rational way. It does not require the thinker to actually experience the object of thought, nor does it require practicality, which often means that "the little cogwheel that should connect grand conceptual thinking to reality is missing" (Dale 1998, 11).

Virtually all of Descartes' scientific conclusions, reached without leaving the comfort of his study, were wrong, but he is not revered as a scientist.

> It does not matter that his findings were inaccurate, as long as the method was convincing. Descartes is the intellectual father of French preoccupation with form. A general who devises a perfect battle plan with incomplete information about enemy capacity, and goes on to elegant defeat, is Cartesian. An engineer for the ministry of Ponts et Chaussées who designs a bridge for a town on the Drôme which he has never visited, on the basis of topographical maps, is Cartesian. When he is told that the bridge has been washed away by floods, he merely says, "That is impossible!" (de Gramont 1969, 304)

In typically French fashion, the French debate Cartesianism itself: Are we still Cartesian? Were we ever truly Cartesian? What is the legacy of Cartesianism in the twenty-first century? One writer suggests that the reason for Descartes' quasi-deification in French culture is that his ideas correspond with three profoundly French characteristics: "the inability to learn from experience, the inability to tolerate contradiction, and the refusal to change one's opinion in the face of a valid objection" (Revel 1995, 63).

The Cartesian method also requires that all elements of a problem and its solution be thoroughly mapped out before any action is taken. Intellectual mastery of the situation is what matters. Americans faced with such a purely intellectual approach—and a corresponding disregard for practicality and results—can rapidly be driven to distraction. In the United States people prefer to take action as quickly as possible and make adjustments as needed. They need to understand in general where they are going but prefer to deal with details as they crop up. One American company used the term "directionally correct" to describe its corporate philosophy. As long as things were moving toward the desired goal, the details could be worked out as things went along.

Americans pride themselves on their pragmatic approach to thinking about and solving problems. They want to get down to business as soon as possible, get the problem solved, the work accomplished, the goal achieved. Devising elegant theoretical frameworks is a waste of time, since it doesn't resolve the problem. French scientists about to test a new drug may speculate on and discuss the likely results of clinical tests, while the more practical American will do the tests first and discuss the results later.

American rationalism is more likely to be technical in nature—something objective that we can synthesize into a flowchart with bullet points or restate as a logic tree that will eliminate unreliable elements such as intuition, personal preferences, and bias. This type of thinking allows for clear and rapid decision-making based on objective facts. A step-by-step decision matrix can be drawn up to determine the choice of new accounting software, for example. By matching the company's needs to the features offered by various packages, this kind of tool helps people concentrate on the essential points rather than spending time on abstract and theoretical issues. Can the software consolidate budgets across departments? If Package A cannot but Package B can, then B is the better choice. The process continues with other constraints such as price, compatibility, and so on.

In the holistic, rational French mind, there is little room for dualistic thinking that seeks to reduce every question to yes or no, black or white, true or false. The two extremes of a continuum do not represent the entire spectrum of opinions or results. Here again, the French normally see things in shades of grey. Pointing out a hitherto unremarked aspect of the situation or presenting an original line of reasoning also gives the French a chance to shine intellectually—something they always appreciate.

Despite their Cartesian passion for classification and definition, the French do not conceive of the world as being restricted to a few boxes, whatever their content or format, and resent being pigeonholed. It is all very well for other people and things to be put into specific categories, but certainly not the French. How, they wonder, can such a people be confined in such a way? Remember that the French defy classification, even their own.

Elementary, My Dear Watson. Another important difference between French and American thinking patterns pertains to the logical progression of the thought process. Thinking and reasoning patterns affect how we discuss, present, and try to persuade others. What is a "convincing" argument? Recall the discussion on deductive and inductive lesson plans in elementary school: how we learn as children formats our brains and sets up our expectations for how knowledge is presented and absorbed.

In the French higher education system, students learn to think through a problem using the "thesis-antithesis-synthesis" method. When addressing a question—for example, should immigrants who are not citizens be allowed to vote in France?—one begins by presenting arguments in favor of the position, then by providing counterarguments. Finally, one integrates both arguments to determine which has the stronger claim. So, like French textbooks, French presentations often begin with the equivalent of *Je retiens* (I memorize): theory, abstraction, and context of the problem and attendant issues show that the speaker has mastered the subject in all its complexity. Then the speaker essentially tries to poke holes in his or her own argument to show that all possibilities have been foreseen and addressed. This also demonstrates objectivity. Out of these emerges the best (most logical) conclusion. The point does not need to be hammered home, as the speaker assumes his or her audience is intelligent enough to get it by themselves. They do not need to be insulted by hearing it again.

The French tend to proceed deductively in the thesis-antithesis-synthesis process. Like the French CEO who described the medieval battle that took place on the site of his company's planned high-tech manufacturing facility, they need to consider the background of current issues. Next, in order to *planter le décor* (set the scene), they begin by building the contextual framework of the problem, establishing which elements are relevant to the question and which are not. From this process of definition and clarification, they then work their way down to specific examples and illustrations to make their point and reach a conclusion. To continue the example on page 178, a French group trying to choose a new accounting software package will probably prepare qualitative arguments for and against Package A and Package B. A choice will be made by comparing these arguments to determine their relative strength.

In describing American and European thinking styles, Edward Stewart and Milton Bennett observe, "[Europeans] have faith and trust in the powers of thought; Americans place faith and trust in methods of empirical observation and measurement" (1991, 41–42). Americans do not feel the need to work from theory. They value systematic observation and experimentation. They are inclined to look at specifics, at what is actually going on: the facts, statistics, research studies, and the evidence from their own eyes and ears. Working inductively, they use these concrete examples to develop a theory or abstraction that accounts for the findings. If further examples contradict their working theories, they easily adapt those theories to reflect what they see as objective reality. Had Descartes been American, he would have risen from his desk, left his office, and gone out to look carefully at things before concluding anything about the nature of the world.

American presentations usually get straight to the point: "Here is the solution I propose." Evidence (preferably "hard facts" and figures) is provided to support the decision, and theory may—or more likely may not—enter unless absolutely necessary. The conclusion reinforces the original point and summarizes it in a memorable or striking way. As the old saying goes, "Tell them what you're going to tell them, tell them what you've got to tell them, tell them what you've told them."

Decision-making is not just a matter of convincing or rational arguments. Elements such as the importance of action, time and resource constraints, time management, and risk assessment also influence the way people in both cultures make decisions.

In geometry, the shortest route between two points is a straight line. In American thinking patterns, the shortest route to *action* must be the most efficient and the most practical, and therefore the best. Americans make decisions and implement them rapidly, making adjustments as they go. Sometimes, they have to scrap a plan completely and start again from scratch, but this is not considered a problem. By following this linear and segmented pattern, another plan can get off the ground quickly.

The French, on the other hand, take to heart the message, "look before you leap." They are in no hurry to implement a plan and prefer to map things out completely before taking action. The shortest route may not be the most scenic one, and though it will get you to your destination quickly, you might miss something important along the way. French thinking may meander from one solution to another, to a modification of the first, and to all points in between. Only when they have an intellectual control of all aspects of a plan do they feel confident enough to implement it.

The following diagrams show in graphic form the difference between the American and French ways of approaching problems. For the Americans, a "directionally-correct approach" means that they head straight to the goal as soon as possible and adjust along the way as needed. The French prefer to map everything out before doing anything. They step through every possible way of reaching the goal and, only then, move toward it by what they have determined is the best route.

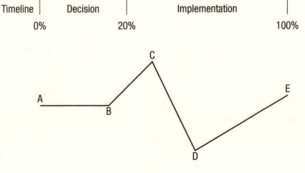

American Way to Approach Problems

French Way to Approach Problems

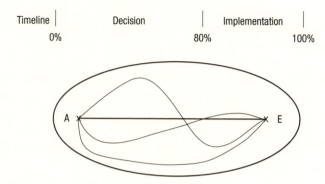

When French and Americans come together, these fundamental yet often hidden differences are likely to lead to misunderstanding and frustration on both sides. Americans may conclude that the French are indecisive or that they simply love to hear themselves talk. From an American perspective, time, energy, and money are being wasted. They cannot see that the problem is in fact being addressed and will eventually be solved. They look for results to come much faster and get frustrated with what they term the French national "analysis paralysis" syndrome.

From the French perspective, Americans' tendency to take action—any action—as soon as possible and make course corrections as needed is risky and amateurish, reflecting a lack of preparation and seriousness. The French see it as a waste of time, energy, and money when Americans start over again if results are unsatisfactory. They may conclude that Americans don't really know what they want or that they don't know what they are doing. In some areas, the more cautious French approach may be better in the long run. For example, in the U.S. pharmaceutical industry, time to market is a key factor pushing decisions to be made quickly so new products can be introduced. Unfortunately, in recent years there have been many cases of new drugs rushed to production that turned out to have disastrous side effects, including patient death.

Objections to Objectivity. The French do not believe that only objective ways of appraising situations and people are valid. They allow more room for human observation and interpretation, thereby giving more weight to subjective measures. In France, objective measurements are generally perceived as too mechanistic and lacking in the human element. Qualitative evaluation through personal assessment is also important. Such tendencies are perceived as at least suspicious, if not dangerous, in the United States. Americans argue that human beings are fallible and make mistakes. Advertisements boasting that a product is "untouched by human hands" imply it is pure and perfect. Accordingly, Americans feel the best and fairest evaluation is an impartial test, an objective measurement, a result that can be quantified.

An excellent example of the personal touch in France is the preference for handwritten rather than typed letters. Most letters of application—to schools or for jobs—must be written by hand in France, preferably with a fountain pen. French students appreciate computers when it comes to schoolwork such as term papers, but even the younger generation finds the idea of sending an e-mail love note simply laughable.

An American HR manager, on receiving a handwritten letter from a French candidate, had a typical American reaction: "Go out and get a PC, buddy!" The personal touch of handwriting is not appreciated in the United States because it is seen as unprofessional and a bit sloppy, and it suggests that the writer is not altogether serious. Americans want the facts in black and white, and they want them legible.

Behind the French preference for handwritten letters of application is the use of graphology (the study of personality traits through handwriting) in hiring decisions. Not all application letters are subjected to handwriting analysis. Generally, once a short list of candidates has been established, a graphologic analysis is carried out to spot any potential problems that might affect job performance. Results are seldom given to applicants but remain part of the employee's personnel file.

Despite the increased use of the Internet for job recruitment, graphology continues to play a crucial role in the French workplace, to the extent that in 2001, the French government established standards for the use of graphology in the recruitment process, recognizing it as "a tool that assists in professional recruitment alongside other techniques." Even those who apply online are required to provide a handwritten letter of application once they have passed the first hurdles.[29]

All of the differences we have discussed so far form the basis for the cultural distance between France and the United States, two Western countries that do not share many perceptual or conceptual similarities and look at the world with different-colored sunglasses. These differing realities are accentuated by the respective roles the two economic and political powers perceive themselves as having in the world.

---

[29] *www.segp-asso.org/*

WORLDS APART

Those who travel outside their own culture wear their country on their sleeve. They become, in effect, representatives of their nation, like it or not, and are often lumped together with their nation's political leaders, social institutions, military actions, sports figures, and movie stars. Americans vacationing in France are sometimes startled when called upon to defend or justify the actions or words of American politicians or celebrities, while more than one French visitor to the United States has been called on the carpet personally for France's lack of support for the Iraq war and perceived anti-Americanism. The individual's position is not taken into account, and it can be very unpleasant to find oneself backed into an ideological corner, forced to explain and defend policies or people one may not personally support.

France on the International Stage. On entering the courtyard of Versailles, you can see the following words engraved at the top of the building to your right: *A Toutes les Gloires de la France* (To All the Glories of France). These glories may have faded since the seventeenth century, but France and her people still love to remind visitors and citizens alike of the nation's greatness and magnificent beauty.

If France were a person, she might be a wise old woman deserving of respect for the gifts she has given humanity through the ages. Many French people maintain that without France, the world (read, "the entire world," including the United States) wouldn't be what it is today. France brought civilization, culture, arts, and knowledge to the planet well before the United States was even created, much less united. French writers have often pointed this out.

The glory of France is one of the world's noblest ornaments.

—Montaigne

O a thousand times happy land and fertile! O pearl of Europe! O this world's paradise! France, I salute you, mother of warriors!

—Guillaume de Bartas

French: the first people in the universe.

—Gustave Flaubert

France, France, the world would be alone without you.

—Victor Hugo

France has always sought to stamp its cultural mark on the world through the work of its most prestigious artists and intellectuals and also through the role of its politicians and state representatives. These are the people who spread France's grandeur throughout the world, and many institutions and monuments attest to their accomplishments.

The duties of politicians and state representatives have evolved over the centuries, but through their actions and words, they provide a good indication of France's attitude toward the rest of the world. Since the end of the Second World War, France has worked toward affirming its identity and independence while at the same time striving to build a strong European community. The 1966 NATO crisis in which France withdrew from the organization's military command and France's search for nuclear power illustrate its need to become a strong and independent nation relying on its own military forces to defend its territories. France and Germany, the sacred tandem, have devoted enormous energy and time to building the European Union into a powerful economic and political bloc that rivals those of North America and Asia. French politicians have acted upon the vision of General de Gaulle, who saw France's best hopes and her future in this ambitious project.

Despite a new world order and globalization trends, official French attitudes have not changed much. Controversies related to nuclear testing in the Pacific, the Middle East peace process, and conflicts in Africa, Lebanon, and the former Yugoslavia, among others, demonstrate France's need to impose its views and set itself apart from the crowd. During a 1995 session of GATT (General Agreement on Tariffs and Trade) negotiations, the French demanded and were accorded a special *exception culturelle* (cultural exception) establishing films as cultural artifacts rather than commercial products. French negotiators and public officials enjoyed a champagne toast to this success. France saw itself as a counterweight to American hegemony in the Iraq war and proudly refused to fall in line with the United States. Such actions typify French individualism as described earlier and often negate or undermine alternate opinions or approaches.

French political leaders are indeed a good model of French individualism, sometimes going against basic principles of cooperation and consensus in favor of drastic and spectacular intervention. Considering the influence of politicians in French social life, it is no surprise that individualistic tendencies are broadly reflected in the French mentality. The French workplace is no exception to the rule; the attitudes of French public officials on the international scene are mirrored in corporate meeting rooms. Whatever the circumstances, the French absolutely must throw in their two *centimes* worth.

A Question of Leadership. As the only remaining superpower, the United States sees itself as the de facto leader of the world. This viewpoint annoys many national leaders and their citizens. When the U.S. assumes its leadership role in a unilateral fashion, other countries often see this as evidence of neo-imperialism. And while the U.S. has managed to rally international support for several of its positions, it would be unwise to assume that other nations—and particularly France—will simply fall into line behind America's lead.

Many French people feel that their nation's often stubborn stance against American international policies acts as an essential counterweight to American hegemony, whether intentional or not.

Both nations share a goal of enlightening the world, and France and the U.S. are among the few nations that see their cultural perspectives as having universal appeal and application. The French and American models are often contrasted in the French press and public discourse: on the one hand, capitalism and Hollywood, and on the other, concern for human values and big C "culture" (the arts, historical treasures, literature, etc.). This is an oversimplification, of course, but it does represent a commonly held French view of the contrast and conflict between the cultures. In the U.S., those who argue for the universalist aspect of American culture stress democracy, freedom, and human rights—areas in which neither country has an unblemished record.

France may eventually express support for an American position (or not, as the 2003 Iraq crisis demonstrated), but only after it has forced a consideration and discussion of alternative or opposing options. The French cannot bear to see American positions adopted simply because the country is so powerful. They must open the debate before agreeing or disagreeing. A good example was the selection of Kofi Annan as secretary general of the United Nations in 1997. Initially, France supported the incumbent, Boutros Boutros-Ghali, for reelection and for some time stood as the only nation opposed to Annan, the American choice. In this position, France was able to force a debate on the merits of the two candidates, preventing a shoo-in for Annan. Finally, having aired their views, the French threw their support behind Annan.

Similarly, when the French oil giant TOTAL broke a U.S.-imposed ban on foreign investments in Iran in 1997, most French people, including politicians, were delighted to thumb their noses—albeit vicariously—at the Americans. The ruling ayatollahs are no more admired in Paris, France than in Paris, Texas, but the essential issue was not so much an expression of support for Iran as a bit of a raspberry for the United States—and a lucrative deal for TOTAL and its Russian and Malaysian associates. These conflicting leadership roles have been analyzed by Richard Kuisel, who offers an American interpretation of France and Frenchness:

The basis of anti-Americanism is cultural and pivots on the notion of protecting and disseminating *civilisation*. Though differences over international relations, trade, and economics will continue to stir criticism of the hegemonic Western power, the core of resistance derives from a sense of French difference, superiority, and universal mission—all bound up in the term *civilisation*. I see little evidence that this sensibility has dulled since the last war. It has spurred every generation . . . to attack America. The criticism may have quieted . . . but the rivalry is latent and potent.

The implied universality of *civilisation* inevitably breeds competition with the United States because America has its own sense of universal mission. Americans like to think they stand for elevating humankind by advancing freedom and prosperity. The French feel culturally superior and destined to enlighten the globe.

The history of Americanization confirms the resilience and absorptive capacity of French *civilisation*. The French seem to have won the struggle of how to change and yet remain the same. The contest and the debate continue. But, as of present, Americanization has transformed France—has made it more like America—without a proportionate loss of identity. France remains France, and the French remain French. (1993, 236)

FRANCE IN THE TWENTY-FIRST CENTURY

A French proverb notes that the more things change, the more they remain the same. As we have seen, certain aspects of French culture are relatively stable through time, although the way in which they are demonstrated at a given point may depend on contemporary circumstances. At the same time, profound changes are taking place within and beyond French borders that will certainly reshape French culture and thought.

This being said, it is important to note that many cultural changes occur initially above the waterline—in the visible part of culture. While some French companies are adopting American management techniques or practices (for example, casual Friday), it would be premature to conclude that deeply embedded assumptions and values are also changing. Despite their evolution, deeply rooted cultural elements such as child-rearing practices, communication patterns, and relationship building are not as easily changed as substituting a pair of jeans for a suit.

Would-be clairvoyants risk making fools of themselves in offering predictions about the future of France. Instead of searching for a crystal ball, we will consider some essential questions that France and her people are facing in the twenty-first century.

French Identity. One of the crucial geopolitical and social issues of the twenty-first century is the definition of nationality and thus of national culture in the European and global contexts. Given the unique history of the United States, it is extremely difficult to say who is a "typical" American at the dawn of the twenty-first century. Even in Europe, however, where national identity has traditionally been a matter of blood and ancestry, it is becoming clear that monolithic national cultures cannot be established, and certainly not imposed. Arbitrarily drawn boundaries, historical accidents, and waves of immigration have made it impossible to draw the portrait of a typical or even representative French citizen—if such a person ever truly existed.

In late 2009, the French government, at the initiative of the Ministry of Immigration, Integration, National Identity and Cooperative Development, launched a project called Le Grand Débat sur l'Identité Nationale (the great debate on national identity) aimed at collecting peoples' opinion on what it means to be French. At times, it seems that more energy is spent arguing about the value of having such a debate on national identity than answering the question itself.

If Pierre Dupont is no longer the national caricature of the beret and baguette, what is he like? And what of Pierrette Dupont? How is "Frenchness" to be defined when, on the one hand, the regions are being given powers that were once unimaginable in the centralized French universe, and, on the other hand, the European Union continues to expand both in number of nations and in power over its member states?

These two poles—regional or provincial identification and pan-European identification—can be imagined as the two ends of an hourglass. The middle of the glass represents French national identity, the transition point between one pole and the other.

Regional identity has traditionally been affirmed through specifics of language, custom, and cuisine. Increased regional power has led to demands for recognition on the national level of these particularities—for example, the use of Basque, Gascon, Breton, Alsatian, and other regional languages in public schools. This demand for cultural recognition has not usually involved corresponding calls for increased political autonomy.

The case of Corsica, an island southeast of France, and one of the twenty-two French regions, is something of an exception to this rule and often a thorn in the government's side. Over the past thirty years, and because of its location, history, and culture, Corsica has enjoyed a degree of autonomy that includes provisions for teaching Corsican and affects areas such as administrative authority, the tax system, and legislative powers. Corsica has its own legislative assembly— l'Assemblée de Corse. Its specific status makes Corsica an entity halfway between a traditional region and an overseas territory—something that is administratively called *une Collectivité Territoriale* (a sort of local government)—and gives Corsica an opportunity to set itself apart from the rest of France. Interestingly enough, though, a public referendum aimed at making Corsica a one-département region (*collectivité territoriale unique*) was rejected by the island's inhabitants in July 2003. Corsica therefore remains a two-département region with no change in the French government's presence and intervention.

At the same time as decentralization moves certain powers to a subnational level, the European Union represents a supranational body whose member states accept that European law, in some areas, supersedes national authority. In both cases the power of the French state is reduced. A lawyer in the Basque country sees the future in this way: "The centralizing French state will not hold up against the construction of Europe" (de Chikoff 2000, 5).

Some French people fear a loss of national identity and security in this dual movement away from the traditional French state. Some other Europeans share these fears, while still others eagerly embrace the changes. The cultural challenge of the twenty-first century may well be in finding some kind of balance between regional and European identities while integrating an increasing immigrant population. Whether we are talking about a threat to the existing national identity or the opportunity to build a new one, the push may come as much from the rest of the world as from the European Union. In light of what Europe experienced during the first decade of the twenty-first century, it is clear that the influx of non-European immigrants is changing the cultural landscape of every European country—far beyond what we would have imagined only twenty years ago.

The French Social Model. Another twenty-first century challenge will be to maintain France's traditionally generous social support structures (e.g., health care and retirement) with an aging population drawing more resources and fewer young workers paying into the system.

In the nineteenth century, the retirement age for railway workers in France was set at age fifty-five in recognition of the intense physical strain of shoveling coal and driving steam locomotives. Even after the TGV (high speed train) had been running for many years via a system of pushing buttons rather than shoveling coal, railway employees still enjoyed early retirement. Employees of other public services such as the EDF (France's largest utility company) and

RATP (Paris public transportation system) could also retire with plenty of time to enjoy life.

In 2008, Nicolas Sarkozy spearheaded legislation to "level the playing field" between the public and private sectors. Retirement with full pension is based on a combination of the employee's age and how many years he or she has paid into the retirement system. Previously, a discrepancy between public and private sectors allowed employees of the former to retire at 55. The 2008 legislation set the same conditions for all employees with a retirement age of 60 and 40 years of paying into the system. In an attempt to reduce the deficit of French pension funds, there are plans and discussions to increase to 41 the number of years a worker must pay into the system while raising the legal retirement age to 61 or even 62.

Globalization and the Role of France in the World. In a 2004 interview, Professor Jacques Barrat defined *Francophonie* and its role in the world as:

> a movement that aims to transform the linguistic, cultural, and histori-
> cal links that bring people together into a larger political and economic
> entity, and which implies the establishment of institutions and multilateral
> cooperation programs.
>
>   Moreover, Francophonie has a unique place in the context of another
> kind of globalization—a more human, caring kind—which rejects tra-
> ditional globalization. It is the only organization in the world today that
> shows the way to listen to one another, which favors above all dialogue,
> the respect of universal values such as human rights, and tries to limit the
> damage of "bottom line" economic growth that is progressively destroying
> our environment.[30]

Barrat echoes the words of then-prime minister Lionel Jospin, who declared in 2000, *"Le français n'est plus une langue de pouvoir mais il pourrait être une langue de contre-pouvoir"* ("French is no longer a language of power, but it could be a language of counterbalance") (National Public Radio, *All Things Considered*, 21 July 2000).

Beyond the question of language, these statements might equally apply to the role of France on the world stage. No longer a major power, France nonetheless has the potential to act as a counterweight to the power of the United States and to be an active player among smaller, regional superpowers. Recall the earlier discussion of the French role in forcing a debate on the choice of Kofi Annan as UN Secretary General and TOTAL's defiance of sanctions against Iran. By refus-

---

[30] *www.ladocumentationfrancaise.fr/dossiers/francophonie/jacques-barrat.shtml*

ing to toe the U.S. line, France can call American decisions and philosophy into question. This can force a debate of the issues and prevent virtually unilateral action on the part of the U.S. Most French people and politicians see this as a useful, even essential, role.

Cultural Diversity. The 1998 World Cup victory of the multiracial and multicultural French national soccer team, while uniting French people in a celebratory euphoria, has not resulted in significant changes in the recognition and inclusion of immigrant minorities in the country's political, social, and cultural landscape. Blacks, Arab immigrants, and *Beurs* (people of Arab descent born in France) have not tried to claim the same type of recognition as Basques and Bretons, for example. Much remains to be done before these groups and others are accepted and integrated into mainstream French society.

At the same time France is showing encouraging signs of openness toward the wider world and other cultures. At the memorial service following the tragic crash of the Concorde in 2000, observers of French culture noted the presence of a Protestant minister, a Jewish rabbi, and an Islamic imam in addition to a Catholic priest. This was a tacit recognition that French and European societies in general are becoming more diverse, and an acknowledgment that—at least in some circumstances—the universalist principle may no longer be appropriate.

The twenty-first century has opened with new challenges and opportunities for France and her people. There is considerable evidence that the French are capable of adapting to the future without abandoning their past, although this is not necessarily an easy process. Over the centuries, they have developed and fine-tuned a capacity to dance on the borderlines without being knocked seriously off balance. As the pace of change increases and borders become more permeable, this talent should serve them well—and provide quite a show for observers.

PART III

Coming Together:
For What—and How?

SIXTEEN

Rhône-Poulenc Rorer:
A Case Study of a Successful
French-American Merger

Horror stories of French-American projects gone wrong abound. Rather than concentrating on these amusing tales of ineptitude and poor decision making, we have chosen to analyze a case where things went right, specifically the merger of Rorer, an American pharmaceutical laboratory, with the health division of Rhône-Poulenc (RP) in 1990 to form Rhône-Poulenc Rorer (RPR).[31] We conducted a series of in-depth interviews in France and the United States with more than thirty French and American managers and employees of the firm, the majority of whom were current or former expatriates in each other's country. These interviews provided illustrations of many cultural differences and ways they were addressed. Other information for this section was gathered from internal and external sources.

---

[31] Toward the end of 1999 Rhône-Poulenc Rorer merged with Hoechst-Marion-Roussel to form Aventis Pharmaceuticals

CORPORATE CULTURE AND
NATIONAL CULTURE

Paul Orleman, an American training and development manager and former expat in France, was a key member of the team that orchestrated the cultural integration of the two entities. He noted that RPR had to address several specific international and intercultural issues that do not normally come up in a domestic merger. One important element was that Rhône-Poulenc in France was a state-owned company. "The mission of a nationalized company is not the same as a publicly held one. Many of the employees of RP viewed themselves as state employees. There was no focus on shareholders or earnings per share. The concept of being entrepreneurial was not part of the RP culture" (1992, 5).

At Rorer, "The portrait of a successful manager was an individual who was entrepreneurial, quick at making decisions, fast, not restricted by bureaucracy, and whose worth was appraised by the results produced" (5). Rorer's philosophy was to be "directionally correct": moving ahead in essentially the right direction, but without worrying too much about details. Direction was adjusted on the fly.

From the American side, the concept of a state-run organization had a very negative cast. It implied entrenched bureaucracies, a "civil servant" mentality, and a general lack of spirit. The French, for their part, were wary of being taken over by "cowboy capitalism" in which everything was secondary to the sacrosanct bottom line.

Added to these differences between corporate cultures was the entire range of national cultural differences. In effect, both RP and Rorer employees had a dual cultural adjustment to make. This was felt most strongly by French managers sent to work in the United States and by American managers assigned to work in France. These people became "double expatriates."

Early on in the merger, Dr. Thierry Soursac, then RPR's corporate vice president for strategic marketing, emphasized that it was not only a question of French and American cultures. The combined company operated in a large number of countries, cultures, and languages; cultural differences had to be considered both in relation to the company's internal functioning and to the markets it served. Thus its focus had to be global, not binational.

> For Rorer, the U.S. was the power—the major source of sales. For Rhône-Poulenc [Health Division], it was the French labs [the sales and marketing divisions located in France] which produced by far the largest percentage of overall sales. What they wanted, they got.

Today, North America is only 25 percent of global sales, and France is only 30 percent. Neither country is the powerhouse it once was. Now, Rhône-Poulenc Rorer has to look at a global marketing strategy. We need to tap into the best ideas from every country, and achieve cross-fertilization.

Globalization will not be achieved in six months; it is a long-term, ongoing process. It is also a way of thinking. (57)

According to a document produced in July 1995, RPR's cultural change mission was "to create a common business culture out of two different business and national cultures; to identify potential company and national culture differences, and help all employees to understand and leverage them" (Orleman and Cohen 1995, 11).

APPRAISING THE SUCCESS
OF THE MERGER

What happened at RPR is unusual for three reasons. First, the company was willing to risk resources for its stated values, committing itself to supporting the cultural change process in concrete ways. Second, the attention to cultural issues permeated all levels of the company and all aspects of its operations; thus, it addressed the whole system and its subsystems. Third, as reflected in the last statement of the quotation above, it was seen as a long-term commitment rather than as a one-shot training program.

Besides looking at the diverse population of RPR expatriates, managers, and employees, one way to appraise the success of the venture is to consider the entities responsible for the ten top-selling RPR pharmaceutical products in the world in 1997. This will give us an idea of the degree of integration and synergy resulting from the merger.[32] Since the time to bring a product to market in this industry is about ten to fifteen years, all but one of the products were developed and launched by premerger entities.

Of the ten best-selling products, six were launched by Rhône-Poulenc, two by Rorer, one by Fisons, and one by RPR. This represents a robust mix, since the health division of Rhône-Poulenc was about twice the size of Rorer in 1990. It indicates that mechanisms and structures in both companies had been integrated to form a unique entity.

---

[32] Note that a major acquisition by RPR of a British pharmaceutical company, Fisons, was completed in 1995

However, in 1998 a top-level RPR manager added a note of caution. While he felt the integration of the two entities had gone relatively well, it was still too early to evaluate the merger's success. In his opinion, complete integration would take at least ten years. At least a decade is needed before the company can be considered to have established itself enough to be widely known by medical personnel and the public.

Managers we interviewed in both countries suggested numerous reasons for the venture's success.

- This was not an "arranged marriage" that happened against all odds. Each company's products were in fact complementary, so that a real synergy emerged from the merger.
- There were no winners or losers: the health division of RP gave its assets to Rorer in return for RPR shares (RP had a 68 percent stake in RPR). Employees in each company were convinced that their own company had acquired the other. It seemed a fair compromise between the two entities.
- The company set up two worldwide headquarters, one in Collegeville, Pennsylvania and one near Paris. Although Rhône-Poulenc, the parent company, was based in Paris, the RPR CEO was working in Collegeville, and the company was incorporated in the United States. This, as well as sharing equal or similar responsibilities between the two countries, demonstrated the company's commitment to make the venture a success. In addition, for the first two years, the position of president of RPR was shared equally by American and French executives, both former employees of Rorer and Rhône-Poulenc respectively.
- The personality and international experience of Rob Cawthorn, RPR's first CEO, helped during the transition years when adequate structures had to be set up between the two countries and in the rest of the world. Being British, he was seen as culturally neutral. Cawthorn also shared a common vision for RPR with the president of Rhône-Poulenc, Jean-René Fourtou. Cawthorn's successor, Michel de Rosen, was French, but had enough global experience and sensitivity to manage successfully the second step of the integration.
- There was a good mix of supporters of French ideas in the United States and of American ideas in France. A lot of atypically rational Americans were brought together with a lot of unusually empiricist French, which led to a nice cultural blend, enabling people to move rapidly into action. This wasn't merely luck or coincidence. RPR deliberately searched internally or recruited people who showed an open mind and a willingness to cross cultural boundaries and live abroad. All of these people demonstrated what

a French expat called "teamwork skills." The potential of both entities was harnessed while creating a hybrid structure. This was one of RPR's major strengths and reasons for success, especially compared with similar operations and mergers in the pharmaceutical industry.

- Implementation of global functions proceeded rapidly, with truly global people. The CEO and his team addressed the challenges of the merger as soon as possible and dismantled monocultural teams in order to form culturally diverse ones. In a few years the company became genuinely global—by choosing the best people around the world. A great deal of autonomy was given to all divisions and departments, and top management didn't favor one side or the other.

- Cultural and language training was offered to people at all levels, which increased their communication skills and cultural awareness. For example, French lessons at the Collegeville facility were offered at no charge and during business hours to any interested employees, demonstrating the company's commitment to the success of the merger.

- Conference rooms at the Collegeville facility were given the names of countries in which the company operated. The general manager of each national office was given an art-buying budget to acquire pieces reflecting that country's culture(s). The chosen art was displayed in the corresponding conference room. This created an atmosphere that affirmed RPR's global commitment and helped draw together the national and corporate cultures in the company.

- In addition to expatriate assignments, the company invested time and money in bringing together employees from different corporate and national cultures. In a relational culture such as France, this kind of face-to-face interaction provides an essential foundation for a good working relationship. The importance of personal contact is difficult to overstate. By sending employees at all levels—including secretarial staff—for short-term overseas assignments, RPR built these foundations. Even for Americans, who are less relationship-oriented, being able to "put a face to a name or a voice on the telephone" was invaluable.

- A global training and development team was created. Its mission was clear from the beginning: forging RPR. It helped RPR become a single company through organizational and professional development, training, and teaching. It also developed common ways of working together across different populations and countries and in building a new corporate culture.

- Special training programs were offered in France and the U.S.: leadership for managers, directors, and vice presidents; "Knowing RPR" for any employee; strategic leadership in the pharmaceutical industry for marketing personnel; and team building and manager assimilation for employees at various levels.

A French expatriate offered a nice metaphor for the success of the venture: *"La mayonnaise a bien pris"* (literally, "the mayonnaise took well"). Making mayonnaise by hand is a delicate operation. It requires the right ingredients at the right time (how much oil and how many egg yolks and how and when to blend them); the right conditions, that is, room temperature; and the right chef, or the person who makes it all happen.

Of course, difficulties and conflicts arose during the merger. Some people left the company because of these conflicts. In spite of this, both internal and external evaluations of the merger were positive.

Studying the success of the cultural blend in the RPR merger can give us some guidelines for how to do it right. However, we believe it would be a mistake to use this success—or any success, for that matter—as a blueprint for any other joint venture. The human, creative side of the project, in our opinion, played a major role in RPR's success.

BLENDING MANAGEMENT PRACTICES AND DECISION-MAKING POWER

As a hybrid French-American structure, RPR retained most of the management techniques commonly used in the United States for meetings, public speaking, presentations, teamwork, performance appraisal, goal setting, coaching, and so on. In this case, these techniques were quite successful across cultures and were widely accepted. Compensation practices also incorporated American elements such as stock options along with plans adapted to each culture's standard practices.

RPR retained its French orientation in terms of corporate politics, high-level decision making, networks of influence, and flow of information, which bear little resemblance to official channels on the organizational chart. American top management adapted quite well and even became expert at operating in the French information system. Top-level French managers on assignment in the United States served as "audiovisual aids" on how the game is played, allowing Americans to experience firsthand the role and importance of personal relationships in information gathering.

Interestingly, RPR acquired the "hard" and tangible elements of American quantitative culture that allowed for objective measurement while incorporating the "soft" elements of French culture based on subjective appraisal and an intangible network of information and influence. It appears that the company has integrated what works best in each culture, what could be considered each country's cultural strengths, creating a subtle combination of hard and soft practices.

CONCLUSIONS

The RPR experience provides valuable guidelines for successfully managing international mergers and other substantial cross-cultural business operations. Our four principal conclusions are as follows:

1. Continuing intercultural training and guidance must be incorporated at every hierarchical level, in every department, and in every functional and operational aspect of the organization as an integral element, not just as a short-term action or add-on.
2. Commitment to creating a truly intercultural organization must come from top-level management, since this is where policy decisions are made, corporate vision and mission are crafted, priorities established, and resources allocated.
3. This commitment must be consistent in tone and content.
4. The creation of a truly intercultural organization requires a sustained effort over a long time. In fact, there is no end point where everyone can relax and say, "We did it!"

In short, RPR was willing to "put its money where its mouth is," not just pay lip service to internationalization. It backed up its commitment in concrete actions. It envisaged intercultural synergy as a mindset and a long-term effort, and it fostered intercultural interactions throughout all levels and areas of the company.

Based on our interviews with RPR personnel, the two chapters that follow describe and analyze in detail critical points of interaction in the context of a French-American work environment. By examining the cultural dimension of managerial situations encountered at RPR, we can comprehend how the cultural elements discussed in Parts I and II emerge in the workplace and influence employees' behavior.

SEVENTEEN

Working across Cultures

ANALYZING INTERCULTURAL INTERACTIONS

On both sides of the Atlantic, it is important to understand the culture-driven values and assumptions that govern what a manager expects from a subordinate, from a team, and from his or her supervisors. There are profound differences between the two countries regarding these expectations, and successful intercultural management requires a clear understanding of what they are, what effect they have, and how they differ from France to the United States. On the other hand, it is also important to recognize that many behaviors depend on personality, life or work environment, and, perhaps, profession. In this case, behaviors do not necessarily trace back to a shared cultural value system but are in fact what makes each person and situation to some degree unique.

Therefore, when problems arise, start by identifying the cause. Are cultural differences behind the problem or misunderstanding? Or is it the environment, the corporate culture, or simply the person you are dealing with? Is it a combination of all these factors? You may be dealing with cultural differences or simply with someone who is difficult. If the problem is of a cultural nature, then you need to have a basic and reciprocal understanding of the frames of reference in which everyone (including you) operates.

Here are some questions to help you analyze intercultural interactions. Not all of these questions will apply in every case, but they provide a good starting point.

- What is going on?
- What are the obvious and not-so-obvious messages being sent and received?
- What assumptions is each person making?
- What information is being taken for granted on the part of each person?
- What information does each lack?
- What are the underlying cultural values behind their behavior or comments? Based on these elements, how do they reach their conclusions?
- Would you do anything differently in such a situation, based on your knowledge of the cultures involved? Why or why not?
- What reaction(s) might you get if you acted differently?

The incident discussed in the following conversation between two American HR specialists, Cathy and Lisa, could reflect a cultural, professional, or personal misunderstanding. Try to use some or all of the questions above to analyze what happened one morning at a software company in California between Cathy and Claude, a newly arrived French expatriate.

CATHY: What a morning! I'm really starting to wonder if this joint venture with France is such a hot idea after all.

LISA: What happened?

CATHY: I had to do the new-employee orientation for Claude, the new product development manager.

LISA: Oh, yeah, I ran into him yesterday. Seemed like a nice guy.

CATHY: Maybe, but I don't know what the deal is. He was *in my face* the whole time. When we sat down to go over the health plan, he moved his chair right up next to me. Then all the time I was talking, he practically had his nose glued to mine.

LISA: What do you think that was all about? Maybe he thinks you're cute.

CATHY: The guy is no fantasy Latin lover, believe me! I got the feeling he was just plain arrogant and pushy. Let's just hope they're not all like that!

Here are some suggestions about using the analysis questions. This is not intended to be a hard-and-fast step-by-step procedure, but rather an indication of how you might reflect on the situation.

- What is going on?
  Cathy is irritated because the Frenchman she helped through new-employee orientation came across as aggressive; possibly in a sexual sense.
- What are the obvious and not-so-obvious messages being sent and received?
  Cathy felt that Claude wanted to sit or stand close to her. All we can say about Claude at this point is that he felt the need or desire to get closer to Cathy as they talked.
- What assumptions is each person making?
  Cathy and Lisa attribute this to personal interest or pushiness.
- What information is being taken for granted on the part of each person?
  We can be fairly confident that Lisa and Cathy know unconsciously what the "correct" physical distance in such a situation is—in their own culture, at least.
- What information does each lack?
  Neither woman has any idea about appropriate conversation distances or physical spacing in the other culture.
- What are the underlying cultural values behind their behavior or comments? Based on these elements, how do they reach their conclusions?
  Cathy and Lisa, based on their American cultural values of privacy and freedom, are accustomed to maintaining a large personal "spatial bubble" around themselves. They conclude that Claude's behavior constitutes an invasion of Cathy's space. Such an invasion in their culture reflects either aggressiveness or flirtatiousness. Claude's culture places much less emphasis on maintaining physical distance, so it is hard to say if he intended to send such a message to Cathy.
- Would those involved have acted differently in such a situation if they had had knowledge of the cultures involved? Why or why not?
  If Cathy had known more about French personal space, she might have been less upset by Claude's physical closeness. If Claude had known about the importance of maintaining physical distance in American culture, he might have made a conscious effort to leave Cathy enough space to make her comfortable.
- What reaction(s) might Cathy have gotten if she had acted differently?

Cultural adaptation involves finding a solution that is acceptable to all parties based on their cultural frames of reference. This will almost never be a fifty-fifty compromise, an ideal midpoint between the two cultures. The solution is more likely to be flexible and will evolve according to the issues at stake and the people involved.

For example, an RPR American manager, fully fluent in French, found that a good mixture of management styles for his department in France was 60 percent U.S. and 40 percent French. Clearly, these proportions will not work for everyone. Your strategy needs to be contextual, taking all elements—people, team, environment, department, and company culture—into consideration. Successfully adapting to another culture means you will need to find an effective hybrid and synergistic style of management.

When we work with people from our own culture, our shared "internal landscape" allows us to take a great deal for granted. We already know what constitutes promptness, efficiency, and productivity, for example, so we certainly don't need to discuss such things before we can begin a planning meeting.

Once we become involved in a bicultural or multicultural environment, though, we need to call into question everything we take for granted. "Abandon all assumptions, ye who enter here" is a good motto. We need to consider and reach agreement about a number of issues we may never have thought about until now.

Five years into the merger, RPR's global training team assembled three lists of questions that needed to be discussed at various points: (1) when we get together, (2) when we run the business, and (3) when we manage our people. These lists appear here in slightly modified form. While they are not comprehensive, they provide a solid framework for preparing people to work in a multicultural environment.

Note that these are not checklists but questions with which to begin your own reflections. In the discussion that follows each list, we address issues we typically see in French-U.S. contexts, some of which do not necessarily appear in the RPR lists. Questions not directly addressed in the following sections are covered in other chapters or left open for the reader to answer in his or her own context. Please keep in mind that the examples we use from RPR and other organizations are applicable to most interactions between French and Americans in the workplace, whether it be corporations or nonprofit agencies. Even after agreements are reached and decisions are made, it may be necessary to reevaluate things as a project evolves and team composition changes. It might be good to preface these questions in a way that helps to keep this in mind, for example, "For *this* project, *this* team, what does 'on time' mean?"

GETTING TOGETHER

Questions Needing Answers

- How will we manage relationships: diving right into business or taking time to establish trust?
- What is trust and how is it earned? To what extent do we value commitments or promises?
- How will we address people? How formal or informal will we be?
- How will we express opinions and emotions?
- How will we communicate?
- What language(s) will we use?
- What does "on time" mean?
- What is the priority of time?
- What is the importance and priority of deadlines?
- What do we do about missed commitments?
- What is an effective presentation?
- What is the purpose, process, and timing of meetings?
- How, where, and when do we make decisions? Who makes them?
- How will information be communicated? To whom? When? Formally or informally?
- How will we present information? Within what framework, and for what purpose (i.e., reflection/thinking, research, action)?
- Will we socialize together? When?

Building a Business Relationship. Building strong relationships between American and French colleagues is one of the most challenging tasks in working effectively together. Generally speaking, in the United States the business drives the relationship, while in France the relationship usually drives the business. If a French person doesn't like you, he or she isn't going to do business with you. An American dealing with an abrasive potential client may reason, "Well, the guy's a real pain, but it's a terrific deal." A French person is more likely to think, "I may lose a good deal, but at least I won't have to work with that boor."

As noted earlier, Americans start out assuming a person is trustworthy until proven otherwise. Things do not always work that way in France. You may encounter an initial barrier of distrust until you prove yourself. The French tend not to involve themselves very rapidly in any endeavor, personal or professional.

Before trust develops, there is always a period of observation that, for Americans, may seem to last forever. An American top manager puts it this way:

> A French businessman mistrusts the very things in which an American business-man has the most confidence. Examples? The Frenchman is innately suspicious of the figures on a balance sheet, of the telephone, of his subordinates, of the law, of journalists, and of what he reads in the press, of investment banks, and, above all else, of what an American tells him in confidence. The American, *au contraire*, has trust in all these things. (Hill 1992, 60)

Then again, in French culture, trust cannot be isolated for analysis. It is part of a bigger and more comprehensive process, the process of knowing someone. In this context, building trust with someone in the United States would be the equivalent of getting to know one another in France. Americans might be more inclined to call it "establishing rapport," which they will admit is a slower process than functioning on a basis of assumed trust.

To make matters more challenging, the task, or achievement, orientation of Americans makes it difficult for them to spend the time needed in building rapport with their French colleagues, especially when the business could be taken care of in minutes in the United States. Yet in French culture, where people place a high value on affiliation and interpersonal bonds (referred to as *atomes crochus*, "atoms hooked together," good vibes), it is important to go through these long observation and discovery stages.

While dealing with your French colleagues, it is important to be pleasant, efficient, and well prepared, as Americans usually are, but these attributes alone might not obtain the results they would in the United States. Veteran American expatriates agree: the time you devote initially to building personal relationships is well spent.

This achievement-affiliation contrast between American and French cul-tures affects other aspects of business and professional relationships as well. Achievement cultures stress the importance of commitments: commitments to things or tasks, to getting something done, or to achieving some desired outcome. Affiliation cultures stress the importance of relationships with and promises to a person. A promise, consequently, carries a much heavier weight in France than a commitment does. In fact, the term *commitment* is difficult to translate into French, as the equivalent word (*engagement*) has other mean-ings than the American notion of commitment. When popular, an orchestra director has many engagements a year. A politician is *engagée* once he or she expresses publicly a set of opinions. Someone *s'engage* (commits himself) in the army when he signs a contract for a few years. All these meanings make the idea of commitment difficult to pin down in French culture, in addition to the fact that committing oneself to something—especially a deadline—might not seem very exciting or very human for French people. Rather, they would go the extra mile to keep a promise to someone they know well and respect, someone they find *sympathique* (friendly, nice) and *attachant* (appealing). In contrast, a U.S. business manager observed, "A 'promise' is not a business concept." Not in the U.S., anyway.

At one point in an intercultural seminar in the U.S., we asked a French participant who understood the notion of commitment but would not commit, "You say you won't commit; is it because you would feel pressured, as if you were constricted in a box with your back against the wall?" He replied, "Yes, exactly!"

Reserve and Formality. Another characteristic of the French is their initial reserve and private character. Recall the peach and coconut metaphor we discussed earlier. Family matters are normally part of a French person's private space and kept quite distinct from the public sphere at work. Personal details concerning spouses, children, and other family members—including boyfriends or girlfriends—tend not to be discussed openly in the workplace.

In contrast, Americans often decorate their offices with family photos, diplomas, certificates of achievement, vacation souvenirs, children's artwork, or other personal items in order to feel "at home." These personal touches also serve as clues about the employee: family status, university affiliation, hobbies, sports, and so on. They are good "conversation starters" for getting to know colleagues: "Your son is a Boy Scout? Oh, he's going to Scout camp this summer? Brandon would love that; maybe you can give me some info." This is a common American way of making connections through sharing personal information.

On the other hand, you often hear French people asking about each other's family origins and regional roots, especially in Paris, where people or their parents or grandparents moved "up" to the capital from some other part of France. "I was born in Paris, but my family is from Auvergne" is a way for a French person to give information about his or her background without entering the personal sphere. The conversation may involve regional accents, food and wines, vacation spots, and other details.

In addition to the hierarchical distance created by status and power, French reluctance to share private matters in the workplace makes them appear cold, distant, or aloof to American eyes. But don't forget that what seems "obvious" from an American perspective isn't necessarily the same from a French point of view—or a Japanese or British one, for that matter. Perhaps only a Japanese person could characterize his or her British colleagues as extroverted and boisterous.

As you develop your relationship with your French colleagues, you will have access to more information about their private domain. Consider this change a mark of goodwill and good relationship and be ready to reciprocate with similar information. If in doubt about when to provide this kind of personal information, simply let your host take the initiative, either by asking you questions or by sharing information, thus opening the door to a closer relationship.

You'll know you've been admitted to a French person's inner circle when you are invited to share a family dinner at your colleague's home. This may happen fairly quickly among younger people of similar status; it may happen after a year or two; or it may simply never happen even though you think you've reached a high level of trust in your relationship. If you don't succeed in receiving such an invitation to a closer relationship, don't take it personally. The French might never develop a friendship with some of their colleagues, even after five or ten years.

Formality is a constant in social and professional life in France. The French distinguish among their family, friends, and close work colleagues, whom they address with the casual *tu*, and strangers, acquaintances, and those with whom they have hierarchical and formal relations and therefore call the more distant *vous*. This distinction is important, because you will most likely be included in the second category for a long time, regardless of the language you are using.

This formal distance may seem a bit chilly after all the commentary on the importance of relationships in France, but it's the result of hundreds of years of social stratification. Formality also appears in the respect and deference with which the French greet each other. Greet people with a light (one pump) handshake and a *"Bonjour Monsieur/Madame,"* plus your name and *"Enchanté(e)"* ("Nice to meet you"). Relationships might become more casual as time goes on and a simple "Bonjour" might be enough. But even fairly good friends may still use the formal *vous*. However, use of first names may evolve quite rapidly among persons of similar age and social status.

French posture and body attitudes may appear stiff and restrained to Americans, while Americans' casual posture and stance appear sloppy and uncultured to the French. French mothers remind their children to stand up straight and stop dragging their feet. People who swing their arms when walking, speak to someone with their hands in their pockets or while chewing gum, tip back their chair, or put their feet on desks or chairs are considered to be lacking in respectfulness and good manners in France.

Formal politeness of this sort, in contrast to the extremely informal politeness of Americans, is an everyday rule that opens (or closes) a lot of doors. *Galanterie* (gallantry) toward women is the rule for men and is considered proper.
Men generally hold doors open for women and let them through first: *"Après
vous, je vous en prie"* ("After you, please"). Gallantry is still very much appreciated
and is a proof of good upbringing, education, and *savoir-vivre*.

French people usually shake hands the first time they see someone each day
but not always when they see the person again the same day; they are more likely
to say, "rebonjour" then. Kisses on the cheeks (*la bise, se faire la bise*) are common
in social settings between women, between men and women, and between adults
and children, but rarely between men (except for close relatives). This custom
of kissing is also practiced in the French workplace, for example, the first time
colleagues see each other in the New Year, but don't be disappointed if you don't
experience it yourself on your first trip to France.

Expressing Opinions and Emotions.   Compared with Americans, the French tend
to display their emotions more openly in the workplace, particularly if these
emotions are negative. Emotional outbursts in most French workplaces, while
not encouraged, are normally accepted as part of everyday life. They allow people
to blow off steam in a harmless way and rarely escalate to physical violence. An
American employee, on the other hand, who breaks down in tears or pounds on
the table and yells in anger is seen as "over the edge" and may be encouraged (or
told) to leave the room for a few minutes to "get a grip." To lose control of one's
emotions at work may be seen as a sign of weakness. A person who cannot keep
his or her impulses in check may not be completely reliable in a crisis.

One Friday afternoon an RPR expat manager in France told his secretary she
would have to work late that evening to meet a deadline. He was not prepared
for her reaction, which was to burst into tears; but once she'd had a good cry, she
was able to go back and finish the job. In another instance at RPR, the French
male subordinate of a female American manager expressed his frustration and
anger at a difficult situation by flinging a binder at a wall. The manager recalls
being appalled and frightened because a similar action by an American employee
would be wholly unacceptable and possibly signal danger.

At work, as in friendship and love, the French are usually not afraid of
confrontation and are ready to voice their opinion, sometimes bluntly. To them,
confrontation can be a positive way to bridge differences between people and
does not necessarily alter their relationship. Sometimes, it is even clarifying
and may foster a renewed peace of mind. In any case, try not to lose your com-

posure; confrontation is inherent in the "hot-blooded" French character. Even after repeated confrontations, the French tend not to bear grudges or start a feud (at least outside the family circle). They use the expression *soupe au lait* (milk soup) to mean a flash of anger that erupts suddenly but then dissipates just as quickly.

In a society where people rarely hesitate to assert their rights—in the streets if necessary—methods of resolving conflict depend on the situation, stakes, and parties involved. Minor conflicts are usually best resolved by sitting down privately with the persons involved, provided that they are more or less on the same hierarchical level. Often, people will do this on their own, but they may need a little push in the right direction from a manager or another employee. However, all conflicts in French culture do not necessarily require resolution. It may well be common knowledge that M. Ducros and Mme. Legrand can't even look at pictures of one another, or just can't stand each other and, if at all possible, should not be assigned to projects together. In other cases, people can work together without really getting along.

More serious conflicts, or those between people at very unequal levels, may require the intervention of a mediator or go-between. In this case, the mediator may speak privately with each individual and bring them together later. In any case, the French tend to resist conflict solutions imposed by authority alone— particularly the authority of a foreigner. Here again, they need to participate and express themselves.

Communication Patterns. French people use words and sentences in a very precise manner and in a specific place. The French language has a smaller vocabulary than English. The meaning of a specific word in French is therefore more context-based than in English. Unless they are fluent in English, the French will not be able to express nuances or shades of meaning, which will most likely create frustration and discomfort. This lack is a real handicap for many French people. Imagine trying to "push a wheelbarrow with one arm" (Bull Worldwide Information Systems 1992).

Americans, on the other hand, tend not to be as picky about vocabulary and the elegant turn of a phrase. The American communication style is basically to convey a message in as concise and straightforward a manner as possible. Obliqueness is not considered an asset; the goal is simply to get the point across. When French people are on the receiving end of such uncomplicated communication, they tend to assume there is something more there than meets the eye or ear and are likely to overanalyze, trying to read between the lines and figure out the "hidden message."

In large international meetings, French employees, in contrast to their usual energetic participation in smaller groups, have a tendency to be reserved and are hesitant to express their ideas and opinions. From an American perspective, they limit the effectiveness of the meeting by withholding input that might be vital to coming to grips with the issues. This reluctance to speak up in large meetings may come from feeling intimidated by the hierarchy, a lack of public speaking skills (not taught in French schools), and low self-confidence in speaking a foreign language in public. Consequently, when French people are involved, a meeting is not over when it actually breaks up; much important feedback may come informally afterward, when the French participants have had an opportunity to have a discussion with their colleagues or with the presenter or team leader in private.

Communicating in a foreign language can be very challenging. In your mother tongue, you are a competent, intelligent professional. When you speak a foreign language, you are reduced to the level of a babbling two-year-old, but two-year-olds are not conscious of their lack of eloquence as adults are. It is crucial to the French to be able to conceptualize, not just express basic concrete needs such as hunger or thirst. For many French people, their English language skills are inadequate to the level of conceptualization they are comfortable with, and this can be immensely frustrating for them. Discussions in English (especially technical ones) may move too fast for them, so that by the time they have understood the conversation and mentally conceptualized a response (often requiring translation in both directions), the native speakers have already moved on.

It is physically exhausting, to the point where more than one expat has reported needing a nap immediately when getting home after work. One American former RPR expatriate often used what he defined as the "native language safety valve." In case of frustration or fatigue, switch briefly to your own language, whether your colleagues understand it or not. It's so refreshing that after just a few minutes, you can switch back to the foreign language with renewed energy.

Nonverbal communication can also complicate relations. Gestures, facial expression, body movements, and other nonverbal elements that are meaningful in one culture may not even be noticed by outsiders. In France, the nonverbal aspect of communication is vital and goes hand in hand with a more indirect style—another reason why French people find distance communication somewhat difficult, even in their native language.

The French tend to scan each situation intensely, looking for any clue that might help them to understand everything that is going on. A look that passes between two people at a meeting can indicate to other participants that they have already dealt with a particular issue behind the scenes and that nothing more need be said about it. In a similar manner, a slight pass of the fingernails over the cheek can communicate to a colleague, "I'm about to pass out from boredom here!"

A French-American couple was invited to a business dinner in France that eventually became tedious. The French husband made a discreet gesture under the table to indicate to his American wife beside him that he wanted to leave, and fast. Not understanding, she repeated the gesture above the table and asked him, "What the hell is *this*? What do you want?"

Even the meaning of a closed office door differs among cultures. In the United States, a closed door indicates that those inside should not be disturbed because something serious, important, and possibly secret is going on inside. People in a "closed-door meeting"—a revealing American expression—should not be interrupted unless it is absolutely essential. The correct way to do this is to knock on the door, wait for an answer, then enter. In the French workplace a closed door may signify nothing more than a need for privacy and tranquility. Interruptions are almost always welcome, and one need only knock on the door before going right in.

In addition to the different ways people use language, communication problems are increased by high- and low-context communication patterns. Earlier, we described the French web of relationships as a family. Explicit communication in a family may be minimal, since all family members know the background information that allows them to interpret the meaning of what they hear in order to fill in the blanks. Two or three words, undecipherable to the outsider, are enough to make insiders nod with understanding or roar with laughter. This type of communication is referred to as *high context*; the rich context of shared experience and knowledge allows participants to understand the message with minimal overt communication. French culture tends to be high context: much of the communication is implicit, so people need to have certain shared knowledge and assumptions to understand what is not specified—which explains the importance of strong, time-tested relationships.

Low-context communication means that all necessary information is provided in the linguistic message: everything is spelled out in detail. In this style, we do not assume or take for granted that people have the details they need to fill in the blanks, so we don't leave any blanks. American culture tends to be quite low context. Edward T. Hall and Mildred Reed Hall describe the differences.

A high-context (HC) communication or message is one in which *most* of the information is already in the person, while very little is in the coded, explicit, transmitted part of the message. A low-context (LC) communication is just the opposite; i.e., the mass of the information is vested in the explicit code. Twins who have grown up together can and do communicate more economically (HC) than two lawyers in a courtroom during a trial (LC), a mathematician programming a computer, two politicians drafting legislation, two administrators writing a regulation. (1990, 6)

What happens when the high-context French and low-context Americans work together? When Americans provide clear and detailed explanations or instructions, the French may feel they are being treated like children. In a high-context culture, most low-context interactions take place with children, who need to have things spelled out precisely because they do not have all the background. For an adult to be treated in this way is an insult.

A French employee who receives "too much" information from colleagues and superiors may feel that he or she is considered incompetent or untrustworthy. This type of detailed information strikes the French as spoon-feeding. A sign posted over the sink in the coffee area at an American RPR training facility reads: "Please do not put anything other than liquids into the sink. This means no coffee grounds, plastic stirrers and cups, sugar packets, etc." Specifying in detail exactly what is and is not a liquid is a very low-context message indeed.

One Frenchman who adores trying out traditional American recipes quickly lost patience with American low-context cookbooks: "It said, 'Cover dough with clean cloth to rise.' Do they think I just crawled out of a cave? Do they think I am stupid? Do they think I might decide to use a greasy rag from my garage if they don't tell me the cloth should be clean?"

In the other direction, low-context Americans might feel that they are being kept in the dark and that their French colleagues are hiding something from them, or that they simply do not know what they want.

An American who had just been hired to work for a French corporate attorney met with his new French boss to go over his job responsibilities: "He handed me a letter from Company X announcing their change of address and said, 'We've had litigation pending with this company for years, you can take care of this.' I noted the address change on my Rolodex and brought the letter back. It turned out that he meant I should take care of the whole case. I felt like a complete jerk. Why didn't he tell me what he wanted me to do?" The French response, of course, would be, "He did," but he did so in a high-context way that was not at all clear to the American.

Distance Communication. Nothing can replace a face-to-face meeting for building relationships and making critical decisions. It is preferable for people to meet on a regular basis, though obviously it is not always possible. One RPR American manager who worked regularly with the Paris office suggested that a minimum of two face-to-face meetings a year was essential for maintaining a good working relationship with the French. Every company or organization will have to make its own decisions on which employees are brought together, for how long, and under what circumstances, but those who will be interacting on a regular basis can generally benefit from personal encounters. Recall that at RPR, even clerical staff participated in short-term intercultural exchanges.

The situation becomes more challenging when communication is not face-to-face. Phone, fax, e-mail, teleconferencing, and videoconferencing are useful, but each technology has its limitations, especially in the loss of nonverbal cues and messages. As the experts tell us, 80 percent of all communication is nonverbal.

E-mail might be an efficient way to speed up communication and reduce costs. However, keep in mind that such a communication tool will sometimes rub the French the wrong way because of its casualness and absence of proper form. It should not take the place of a personal call; if possible, try to avoid e-mail until after a good relationship has been established. And even then, don't let it overshadow personal relationships. Employees at the French office of a large American electronics firm frequently checked in with one another via e-mail to decide where and when they would go for lunch, even though their offices were just a short distance down the hall. The Italian CEO became concerned that the quality of human relationships might suffer if people used e-mail to maintain personal connections instead of getting up and chatting with one another. As in any situation that requires the use of technology, it is a good idea to define ahead of time what is acceptable and what is not. While the use of the Blackberry is spreading rapidly in the U.S. at every level in organizations, it is still very common in France to find the Blackberry reserved for the upper echelons of a company.

In addition, many French people do not agree with the American tendency to allow newer communication technologies to eliminate polite frills such as greetings and salutations in virtual conversations. Brutally getting down to business in a virtual situation is likely to frustrate the French, at the very minimum. And in most cases, *silence radio* (no response) will be the answer.

An example of a typical French reaction to the "nuts and bolts" U.S. style was recounted to us by a Frenchman who emailed an American expat in France. They knew each other well, having worked together a couple of years earlier and kept in touch professionally. Since she had just spent a week skiing in the Alps, he asked her about her vacation before addressing a work issue and suggesting a conference call. The response was brief—two lines about the business at hand—and to the Frenchman, quite curt.

"I know that from her cultural standpoint, she's showing respect for me by answering my question and not wasting my time, but I still can't get used to it. But for someone that doesn't know American culture, it could really confirm the stereotype that Americans care about business more than they care about people. They might even think, 'If Americans care so little about people, and care so little about me, why should I bother to respond to them and address their requests?'"

Finally, it's always good to put things in writing. French people love the written word, and memos are usually well accepted and less formal than a letter. When calling a French colleague to confirm a meeting date, an appointment, or some other important matter, it's generally a good idea to follow up with a fax, memo, or e-mail. Especially while discussing technical details on the phone, which often requires knowledge of a specific jargon, give your colleagues a chance to process the information by letting them read what you mean or want as well as hearing it.

In situations where employees are not able to meet their colleagues, it is a good idea to establish ground rules for distance communication. Here are some recommendations:

- Find compromises that are acceptable to everyone in such areas as communication patterns, amounts of information, formality, and so on. It may be necessary to make these compromises explicit.
- Be clear about deadlines and notions of urgency. When requesting information or assigning tasks, don't just announce deadlines. Explain why the document is needed by that date, how it fits into the overall project sequence, and what the consequences of missing the deadline will be.
- Rephrase or reword key terms or sentences to ensure understanding, particularly when you are using technical vocabulary.
- When in doubt, err on the side of low context (i.e., include as much information as you reasonably can), at least until you are sure that your message is getting across. It's easier to start low and go high than the other way around.
- On the phone, speak slowly and avoid jargon and colloquialisms. Give your colleagues enough time to process the information.
- As much as you can, involve your colleagues in what's happening. Tell them and let them feel that they share responsibility for the project.

- Before discussing business or technical matters, establish rapport by spending a moment on nonbusiness subjects.
- Think of distance communication as something beyond a simple request for information. Use it as a means of building a relationship at the same time. Think long term.

Empathize and be patient with foreign colleagues or employees who are not speaking their native language. People often lack sufficient appreciation of this issue. Speaking in a foreign language is mentally and physically exhausting, especially when you consider the challenge of communicating via telephone or e-mail without nonverbal cues, such as body language, gestures, and facial expressions.

Monochronic and Polychronic Time. "Just take it one thing at a time," Americans often advise colleagues who are "swamped" with too many projects and assignments. And in American culture, this is excellent advice. American and other Anglo-Saxon cultures tend to be *monochronic*: people focus on one thing at a time and concentrate exclusively on the task at hand. Ringing phones, visitors, e-mail, and so on are distractions that prevent work from getting done. A busy executive going into an important meeting often sets phone calls to go straight through to voicemail to avoid distractions and focus on the meeting.

Time is a commodity that must not be wasted. Instead, it should be managed and used optimally. Monochronic people usually work in a linear fashion, making to-do lists and schedules to which they normally adhere. This is seen as the most efficient and well-organized way to work. A monochronic person's schedule might look like this:

9:00–9:30	Budget meeting
9:30–9:45	Conference call with regional managers
9:45–10:45	Prepare memo re: marketing plan for headquarters

A French person observing an American working in this way would be amazed by how mechanical and possibly inefficient it all is, plodding along regardless of what changes come up and rigidly ignoring everything else. The cliché image of the overburdened admin, typing, talking on the speakerphone, and shutting a file cabinet with a deft foot all at the same time is a perfect illustration of a *polychronic* individual. French people tend to be polychronic. They do many things at once, hop back and forth from task to task, are easily distracted and interrupted without necessarily being irritated, and look at a schedule as a flexible guideline concerning what might happen. The polychronic person may

216

start the day with the schedule shown above but without the expectation that it will be adhered to.

Living and working in a polychronic mode may look like multitasking, and many people from monochronic cultures certainly see it that way. "Sure, I'd love to stick to a schedule, but my job just doesn't allow it. I have to run around and put out fires all the time. That's just the way it is nowadays."

It's true that the structure of many jobs, coupled with technologies that allow us to be reached anywhere and anytime, may require us to multitask. If you would rather stick to a schedule but have learned to juggle several balls at once, then you have proof that you can adapt to a different style. But the difference between being polychronic and behaving in a polychronic way lies in how you react to doing so. If you are a true monochronic person, you may be able to keep all those balls in the air very well, but you will probably find it stressful. You'll feel like you've been thrown off schedule, and want to get back on track as soon as you can—assuming that you can at all!

Polychronic people generally don't experience that kind of stress as they juggle. That's what feels normal and comfortable to them. If you are a natural polychronic, you may be required to behave in a more monochronic way due to the nature of your job or environment, but you'll probably feel constrained and stressed. One French woman said, "When I do a project in Germany, for example, I am never late for a meeting or even dinner with my colleagues, because I know that if I arrive at 7-ish, as I normally do at home, they'll have the impression that I don't respect them or don't take the project seriously, and I can lose a lot of credibility. It's a huge effort not to be late and it seems silly to me to attach that much importance to time. But I make the effort because I don't want to send the message that I'm disrespectful or unprofessional."

In fact, what often startles Americans working with the French is their lack of concern when schedules are thrown off and tasks postponed. They jump around from one thing to another and are so easily distracted, it looks cavalier and disorganized.

The clash between monochronic and polychronic styles was played out in one incident at RPR's office in Paris, where an American woman who had recently arrived in France was meeting with a colleague in his office. Another French colleague stuck his head in the door just to say hello, and the two started chatting. Annoyed and offended by such rudeness, the expat eventually discreetly left the office and later called the colleague she had been meeting with to explain her behavior. A polychronic French person would have understood and waited for the side conversation to be over, but for a monochronic American, the meeting was over, since another activity had begun.

The effect of a different sense of time is perhaps the most common source of conflict in French-American workplace interactions, at least according to our RPR informants. Paul Orleman quotes an American expat in Paris: "The French are not deadline-conscious like we are in the U.S. If I say to someone 'I need this within two hours,' it's like asking them to crucify their mother" (1992, 25).

On the other hand, a French expat in the United States observed that in France, "A deadline has no meaning in and of itself. If a report is due January 1, and I decide no one needs the report until January 31, the deadline is meaningless. I can reprioritize. Americans don't do this; the *deadline* itself is important" (20).

In fact, a good way to find common ground on deadline issues might be to examine why and how the time frame has been established and what the consequences might be if a deadline is missed. In some cases, deadlines are set arbitrarily, based on established routine. For example, do regional reports really need to arrive at the manager's office exactly one week before the monthly summary is issued, or can more flexibility be built in? The French usually need a logical reason to do something, and "it's due on October eighth" may not in itself be enough. The notion of urgency resonates better with the French when it is associated with the urgent need of a colleague rather than a vague urgency around a particular date. If a French person understands that a missed deadline will result in negative personal consequences for a colleague, he or she will be reluctant to put someone in such a position.

The U.S. manager quoted above had another suggestion: "The French need to learn to understand [the American sense of] 'urgency,' and we [Americans] need [to learn] to not make everything an instant, unstructured need to be satisfied" (25).

Meetings and Presentation Styles. To the purist's horror, the French often speak of *le meeting*. But if the word is understood in both languages, the American concept is not, and many cultural differences are played out in the setting of le meeting. What is a "productive" or even a "good" meeting? It all depends.

From the American perspective, "The French are huge fans of committees and meetings where nothing gets done. It's rare to have a good agenda, purpose, and action plans resulting from a meeting"(18). All very true, the French will agree, but is there a problem with that? A French RPR manager explained, "The point of a meeting is not to get through the agenda. The point of a meeting is to find out who feels what. It is not the place to make decisions"(19).

Much of the emotional temperature taking that occurs in French meetings is high context. Look around; a lot of things are happening. Certain latecomers will be briefed on what they missed, while others will not. The tone of the briefing itself can indicate if the person is important or just being teased. Certain people may always come in late, others might always sit next to each other, power blocs coalesce and dissolve, and side conversations or comments might even take place during a presentation. For the polychronic French, of course, this is not considered an interruption of the meeting or rude at all. It can be very difficult for them to focus, American-style, on one speaker at a time. A French manager in the United States revealed, "I was feeling very French at the meeting; I wanted to have a side conversation. It was driving me crazy"(19). For more monochronic Americans, one pays attention to the speaker while he or she is talking. Chatting with the person sitting next to you is disrespectful; it sends the message that the presenter has nothing interesting or worthwhile to say.

The French use meetings as an open forum for discussions of all kinds. It is difficult for them to function without such intense communication networks, and they feel almost bound and gagged if they are not given the time to express themselves. Here again, building some time flexibility into meeting schedules can help accommodate this. At the same time, limits can be established to prevent a meeting from turning into a cocktail party. It is often possible to combine elements that French and American participants feel are essential for an interculturally productive and successful meeting.

One French manager in the United States appreciated American presentation politeness, contrasting it with the "veritable knife fight" that goes on in France. "When you begin a presentation in the U.S.," he noted, "you know that you will be able to go through your material point by point right to the end. In France you scarcely have time to begin before somebody interrupts you; you can't even get to your third slide" (Bull Worldwide Information Systems 1992).

The typical American presentation starts out with a story or a joke. In France such icebreakers are not necessary and you can get straight to the point more rapidly. People might not understand the point of a story, especially if its purpose is just to engage the participants and it doesn't relate to what follows. In fact, humor is an important element in all but the most formal meetings and presentations in the United States. A few well-placed jokes or comments can lighten things up and even make a difficult discussion go more smoothly. Humor is certainly appreciated in France but is less appropriate in a business setting, where a more serious tone is usually expected. At one RPR meeting between French and American managers, an American joked, "Oops! There goes our annual bonus!" He meant that if a particular task was not accomplished, the year-end bonus might not be paid. The French top manager did not get the comic, throw-away nature of the remark, and replied, "We are not going to worry about the bonus" (Orleman, 20).

The substance and conclusions (*le fond*) of a presentation are far more important to the French than the materials (*la forme*) you use. While clear and legible slides or documents are helpful, audiences will not necessarily be impressed with state-of-the-art technology. The French tend to suspect that slick or razzle-dazzle presentations are trying to cover up a lack of substance.

PRESENTING ACROSS FRENCH AND AMERICAN CULTURES: A BUSINESS CASE STUDY

We would like to share additional insights about French and American presentation styles that we gained from the training trenches. This account is an example of what we discuss about reasoning styles in the section "Who Do You Think You Are?" (see chapter 15). Ways of processing information, approaching a problem, and planning a presentation in terms of goals, format, and sequence, all affect the content and style of the presentation.

As part of a joint French-American effort in one of our client companies, engineers from both countries were brought together in the U.S. to work on the design and construction of a large industrial plant. Both parties' technical presentations were conducted in English, with pauses to allow French people to consult and confirm understanding.

These presentations were part of a session in which the group took a step back to analyze the philosophy and style of their presentations, and how to make them more effective in an intercultural environment. First, participants from each culture determined what makes for a good, effective, and useful presentation according to their own norms and standards, and why. Then the groups worked together to develop guidelines for bridging the gaps and giving presentations that would be well received and understood by the whole team.

While reading these notes, please keep in mind that these are general elements which may vary from industry to industry and from company to company. In fact, it's often helpful to rehearse a presentation with a colleague from the other culture to get criticism and suggestions.

French Presentation Style

General Approach

- Presentation goal is to *inform*
- Presenter must prove validity of his/her approach and understanding of the problem, which means that he/she:
  A. Provides ample background information
  B. Shows how she/he arrived at results; justifies hypotheses and progression of logic

C.   Analyzes various solutions (pros/cons), problems encountered

D.   Offers conclusion and recommendations at the end only

Way to proceed/development

- Presenter relies on technical documents, highlights main points, and focuses on what he/she thinks is important (may not spend time on items deemed unimportant)
- Obtains validation/buy-in from peers/hierarchy before presentation by distributing notes/handouts and analyzing feedback
- Knows audience and usually assesses amount of opposition to expect, depending on topic and decision to be made
- Slides tend to be text- or diagram-heavy with full sentences
- Substance is important in France—possibly at the expense of form
- Reading slides or documents aloud is acceptable, especially if in English
- Slides and information they contain work as a safety net for presentations in English
- No need to question/engage audience; participants will ask questions if they want
- No questioning usually means agreement
- Time is usually not of the essence, as long as there is a good discussion/debate

Summary:

1. Don't use a hard-sell approach to convince a French audience of something; don't use superlatives (*"I've got great results"*), as listeners will most likely be suspicious.
2. Stating that something is so is not enough to convince (*"These are the results I got"*); you must explain your reasoning as well as the choices you made, why you discarded alternative solutions, etc.
3. Be ready to answer questions and do some research to anticipate what questions may come up; your presentation may be in jeopardy if you cannot answer the first question.

American Presentation Style

General Approach

- Presentation goal is to *convince, sell, persuade*
- Presenter is perceived as expert—doesn't need to prove himself/herself or justify results. Results matter more than details of how they were obtained

- Depending on context and purpose of the presentation, presenter builds credibility by suggesting actions that need to be taken; allowing people to make quick decisions is important
- Presenter makes recommendations on decisions desired by audience

Way to proceed/development

- Presenter adapts presentation to hierarchical level of audience, decision-makers (finance, management, etc.)
- Presentation should be "light"; use humor
- Slides provide executive summary first; intro slide may also be conclusion slide
- Presentation more conclusive than French style, less open-ended
- Knows audience and knows that audience is open to listening; audience's goal is usually not to test the presenter's knowledge but to support him/her
- Slides are concise, uncluttered, and show only key information; explanations elaborated orally
- Consistency in fonts, text, punctuation
- Presenter may bring experts from team to support presentation
- Presenter does not read slides but elaborates on all or most points in a slide
- Very time conscious, proper pacing
- Presenter engages audience through Q & A; checks for understanding; can show emotion
- Presenter shows confidence through eye contact and relaxed body language
- It is acceptable to say "I'll get back to you" on occasion

Summary:

1. U.S. presentation should be succinct, precise, and well-timed, and allow decision-makers to make quick, informed decisions.
2. Engaging audience with lively presentation is very important; getting audience's feedback assures success of presentation.
3. Stating objectives/desired outcomes at the beginning, then revisiting them at the end assures audience presenter is focused and not wasting time.

An American engineer commented on his French colleague's presentation: "I would have taken Michel's last slide and made it my intro slide. Then I would have used his appendices slides to develop my reasoning, in the core of my presentation." French people, on the other hand, given so little in-depth reasoning or analysis of different solutions, are likely to ask, "How can we make a decision with so little information?" They may even wonder if their American colleagues are hiding something from them.

Such differences in presentation styles are significant and reflect the way students' brains are formatted in each country. These differences are related to internal logic, reasoning, and, primarily, to what makes sense to us and what we often take for granted—our worldview. The following diagrams, sketched out by Natalie Lutz, capture French and American reasoning and presentation styles.

The French style, based on the *thèse, anti-thèse, synthèse* approach taught in schools, strives to eliminate solutions that do not meet the criteria established in the problem definition. The essential initial phase (thèse) proves the presenter *maîtrise son sujet* (masters the topic). Once this work has been done thoroughly, and different iterations run to eliminate inappropriate ones, *la solution coule de source* (the solution flows by itself, as if from a spring) and is obvious to anyone who understands the context. It may even insult listeners to provide details of *why* this is the best solution, since they can see for themselves.

France

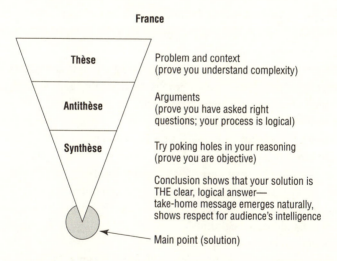

Thèse — Problem and context (prove you understand complexity)

Antithèse — Arguments (prove you have asked right questions; your process is logical)

Synthèse — Try poking holes in your reasoning (prove you are objective)

Conclusion shows that your solution is THE clear, logical answer— take-home message emerges naturally, shows respect for audience's intelligence

Main point (solution)

The American presentation is conceived as a sales pitch that usually starts with the solution itself. Alternate approaches may be mentioned, but only briefly. The focus will be on the best solution, which the presenter is trying to sell. The presenter will then show why this is the best solution. Often, research data that appears at the very beginning of the presentation is summarized again at the end. An American presentation is an interactive juggling exercise where the presenter has to be convincing all the way to the end, and land on her feet.

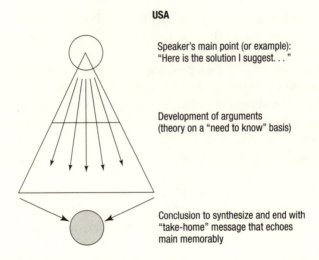

USA

Speaker's main point (or example): "Here is the solution I suggest. . . "

Development of arguments (theory on a "need to know" basis)

Conclusion to synthesize and end with "take-home" message that echoes main memorably

Guidelines for Effective Presentations across French and American Cultures

- Explicitly set goals/objectives of the presentation at the beginning
- Determine level of detail and analysis to provide (including technical information)—and why
- Determine presentation structure, depending on topic and audience (e.g. expectations and desired outcomes first or reasoning and research leading to results; executive summary before/after/both)
- Amount of information:
  - How much is enough to make a decision and proceed?
  - How much background and context to provide (e.g., justification of results, discussion of unsuccessful approaches)?
- Ensure consistency in text formatting, fonts, punctuation
- Send presentation to selected colleagues beforehand and request feedback
- Provide handouts at beginning
- Presenter's interaction with audience:
  - What are appropriate attitude, dress, and demeanor?
  - Move around, approach audience—don't stand behind podium
  - Make eye contact, don't look at slides or notes; don't read word-for-word
  - Determine how to handle questions and interruptions (side conversations, phone calls, texts)
  - How can we make sure everyone understands?
  - Invite open discussion if appropriate and desired

- How much time do we need, and what if we go over?
- Use of English
  - Simple, plain English—avoid acronyms, slang, and sports metaphors
  - Write down large numbers
  - Presenter: check frequently for understanding
  - Audience: ask for clarification if necessary
  - Allow pauses for translation or consultation to establish common meaning

Decision Making. So, if the French don't make decisions during meetings, where do they make them? And for that matter, who makes them? Here again, hierarchy plays a role. Decisions tend to come from on high, and consensus building is rarely an important part of making a decision. French managers take into account individual ideas and contributions from meetings and other discussions but do not necessarily include them in the final decision. And, of course, the discussion does not always end just because a decision has been announced.

In France's risk-averse culture, the decision-making process is generally much longer than in the United States, with a greater need for information exchange in some contravention of their high-context inclinations. The French need to explore every avenue intellectually and practically before they can fill in the gaps. They try to gather as much information as possible before making an important decision. Compared with American practices, the process is much more comprehensive and not so sequential. When trying to solve a problem, Americans tend to look immediately for solutions. The French, on the other hand, try first to understand the causes of the problem. Only when they feel sure they understand why and how the problem occurred do they feel prepared to solve it.

As we discussed, time is much more fluid in France than it is in the United States, and this also influences the outcome and timing of decisions. The French do not necessarily feel they are wasting time when the process slows down or even when they are not working toward a specific goal.

Power and Information. The number of U.S. companies practicing "open-book" management—that is, giving all employees access to company information—is small, but the very idea is enough to send a French manager into shock. In principle, at least, Americans believe that the sharing of information is key to efficiency. People tend to share information freely through both official and informal channels. Long distribution lists and "FYI" e-mails and memos are common.

What happens if an American receives a misdirected e-mail addressed to a colleague but containing useful information? This can happen, for example, if someone hits "Reply All" rather than "Reply." The chances are, he or she will simply go to the person who sent the memo and say, "That kind of info can really help me out in the advertising forecast. Could you add me to the distribution list?" A French person in a similar situation would most likely begin reading between the lines, noting who sent the e-mail, who is and who is not on the distribution list, what being omitted from the list might imply, and, above all, how to get such information in the future without going to the sender. Knowledge of who gets what information, and from whom, is vital to understanding what power blocs and coalitions might be forming or falling apart, or even just how people are getting along.

An American RPR expat described the different conceptions of information: "In France, information is used as a source of power and control much more than in the United States. Managers and team members may withhold information to bestow on an individual rather than share openly with the team" (Orleman, 37). Being "out of the loop" in the U.S. may be an oversight or an inconvenience, but in France, it can be quite deliberate and potentially fatal.

In egalitarian American culture, power is almost a dirty word, and while people acknowledge the existence of office politics, they regard such maneuvering as slightly distasteful. Companies talk of the participative workplace, where employees are empowered to control their own jobs and destinies. The idea of having power over someone or, worse yet, being under someone's power, makes most Americans vaguely uncomfortable if not quite suspicious. In France and other Latin cultures, power is acknowledged and spoken of openly. High-level people use their power freely, usually to their own advantage, and are respectfully deferred to by those they control.

Like personal information about family and friends, professional information is also shared only with those in the appropriate *cercle*. If everybody gets it, it can't be important or the person giving it out so freely is not very clever or discerning. A French RPR expat explains, "Information which is widely distributed is obviously useless information. If I get a memo with a huge distribution list attached, I don't bother to read the memo because I know that it will be of no value for me" (37). Though Americans also appreciate getting "the inside track," the sharing of information is nowhere near as heavily charged as it is in France.

RUNNING THE BUSINESS

Questions Needing Answers

- What is the appropriate time horizon for the business?
- What does *strategic* mean? What is our strategy?

- What are appropriate controls?
- What does *centralized* or *decentralized* mean, and what do we want?
- What processes are involved (planning, controlling, etc.)? How will they be implemented?
- What does *planning* mean? Who plans? How is a plan documented? How is it communicated and to whom?
- What do we mean when we talk of teamwork? What is a team? A collection of people working individually, a consensual group working together, or something else?
- What should be delegated and to whom?
- What is the balance between the individual and the group?
- What is the value of being entrepreneurial?
- What is appropriate risk? How do you approach it?
- What does *ethical* mean?
- How do you negotiate?
- What is the definition of quality? Can it be achieved quickly?
- What is good customer service, and who is responsible for it?
- What is the value of acting versus thinking?

Go, Team! Here again, similar words conceal different meanings. Both French and American businesses consider teams and teamwork important, but that's about as far as the agreement goes. The American value of egalitarianism underlies the expectation that a team functions as a unit where everyone works together. Achievement orientation requires that individual personalities take a backseat to the task or project at hand. Ideally, the team as a whole is more important than any one person. When star players emerge, they increase effectiveness and team cohesiveness by pumping up morale and focusing attention on the successful team while providing positive role models. However, even the stars have to fit in, and big egos do not make for good team players. While there may be a team leader, he or she is expected to provide guidance and leadership rather than to issue orders.

Part of the worldwide amazement that the French won the World Cup in 1998 was because the French are traditionally considered too undisciplined and egotistical to be good team players and provide a united effort. It's true that being a team player American-style may require the French to abandon a bit of their cherished individuality, and, for this reason, making a French team work together can be a bit like herding cats. An English writer notes,

> Getting a group of French people to work together virtually defies the law of dynamics: each of them runs his or her own fiefdom and the operating principle

(from the top down, which is the only way French business works) appears to be "management by information retention." (Hill 1994, 70)

Contrary to popular belief, French teams *can* work together. They just don't look like anybody else's team when they do. The team leader in France has an explicitly directive role, which is mainly to match assignments to people and to ensure that everything runs smoothly. After everyone has enjoyed a thorough exchange of ideas and conversation—in other words, a French meeting—each team member is given a particular task, which he or she then goes off to complete. Eventually, the team leader assembles all the bits into the finished product.

Interestingly, the finished product may look just about the same as the one produced by an American team—or a British or German one for that matter. But the team's process, how it works together, how roles and responsibilities are established and carried out are totally different. Which team is more productive or more effective? It all depends on whom you ask, where, and when.

An American member of a French team may say, "Well, the final result was okay, but what a pain in the neck it was to get there." Since team members are off working on their individual pieces, the American has a hard time seeing that they are working together at all. A team whose members work independently is just not a team. A French participant on an American team might say, "It's a miracle we got such a good result with all the nonsense that went on." The frequent status meetings that ensure everyone is "on board" and "up to speed" appear to be a waste of time. Why doesn't the leader just tell us what to do, so we can get on with it? And expecting us to design a team logo coffee mug. What a joke!

In order to get intercultural teams off the ground, everyone must share the same definition of *team*. While this seems obvious, in practice time is rarely taken to forge a mutual agreement on what *team* means. One French-American sporting goods manufacturer held biannual international product development meetings that included research and development and marketing teams from both countries. At one such meeting, the teams were given the task of developing a new squash racquet. Each group went home with its list of "action items" and worked on the project for six months. During that time, they communicated regularly about their progress and their plans. At the next international meeting, everyone made the unpleasant discovery that the two teams had essentially developed two different products.

Assumptions and expectations about teams and teamwork need to be articulated, examined, and discussed and working agreements reached. There is no "one-size-fits-all" way to create a good intercultural team. Each group needs to determine people issues, process issues, and task issues according to the project, the team members and their competencies, the logistics, the budget and schedule, and hundreds of other variables. When unconscious assumptions are imposed on a multicultural team by default, someone is bound to feel that things just aren't right. It is important to acknowledge that our norms and assumptions are not carved in stone. Successful international teams will need to craft their own rules, taking into account what will be most suitable to everyone.

Competition and Risk. American and French cultures present an interesting contrast when it comes to the competitive drive. As you have read, the French educational system is highly competitive and treacherous. Your performance in school primarily determines what you will be doing the rest of your life. Career shifts are relatively rare in France, especially as one approaches the mid-forties, and economic conditions tighten up. Going back to school full-time at this age would be difficult and uncomfortable, simply because mainstream French society reserves higher learning institutions for younger people. The exception in this case would be attending professional classes to start one's own company—a noble aim, but that will not bring as much prestige as coming out of a *grande école* as a fresh, young graduate. Even the development of online courses will never challenge the sacrosanct institutions that are so well preserved by French elites.

When it comes to the French business environment, the situation is just the reverse, and the French competitive drive appears much weaker than it is among Americans, in whom it has been nurtured by an adventurous and entrepreneurial spirit and a powerful achievement motivation.

Most probably, one of the reasons for this French behavior is the absence of a strong drive to win. As expressed by Baron Pierre de Coubertin, founder of the modern Olympic movement, it is more worthwhile in the eyes of the French public to participate than to win. It is more important for the French to lose with panache than to win without class and style. Quite a few second-place athletes have become extremely popular in France; for instance, Raymond Poulidor, a cyclist who always finished second.

The structure of French society, with its vestiges of pre-Revolution social hierarchies, does not encourage people to move up the ladder. Compared with the United States, the government offers little support for personal initiatives. While jobs in the private sector tend to pay more, French people attach more prestige to working in large state-owned companies and in public administration. The public sector also offers more job security, an important consideration in a risk-averse country with a chronic unemployment problem. The amounts of paperwork, legal formalities, and time needed to start a new business reflect the cultural preference for the status quo and control over unbridled capitalism and individual initiative.

Concomitant with this preference for the status quo is the structural rigidity of traditional French companies. Multiple layers of management along vertical lines of reporting do not favor initiatives or the flow of useful information. People get used to their positions and responsibilities and rarely challenge the established order and pace of doing things. International companies may be more progressive, but most traditional French companies tend to abide by a set of rigid organizational rules.

American motivational techniques are often based on the concept of "friendly" or "healthy" competition. Teams may compete for a special award based on productivity improvement, or individual employees are singled out for public recognition when they surpass their sales goals. Americans love a good competition. They feel that competition brings out the best in people, encouraging everyone to make their best efforts. Corporate programs to recognize the "Number 1 Team" or the "Employee of the Month" strike the French as excessive, silly, and serving to reinforce the shallow side of American incentive or reward management. Such practices are likely to backfire with French employees, who tend to prefer a more personal form of recognition, such as being invited to lunch by their manager or a low-key recognition in the context of a smaller group, rather than appearing in the limelight.

Risk-taking and its potential positive results are an important feature of American culture while, consistent with their noncompetitive attitude, the French tend to be risk-averse. Before taking a risk, French employees will carefully assess the possible effects of failure on their reputation and career, and they often conclude that the risk is not worth it—which leads to the perpetuation of an unchallenged status quo. A common French saying is, *"On n'a pas le droit à l'erreur."* ("You have no right to make a mistake.") If you make a mistake, you generally try to prevent people from finding out, as this would cause you to lose face—and possibly your position, depending on the severity of the mistake or failure.

In the more flexible and mobile American society, negative consequences of failure are usually far less damaging. If someone fails, he or she may be out of a job in the very worst of cases, but chances are that another opportunity will rapidly open up. And in case of success, the person will reap the honors and material rewards that such a bold attitude deserves. On the other hand, Americans often talk about the need to "CYA" (cover your ass), to protect oneself from negative consequences, and the risk of litigation in the lawsuit-happy U.S. culture is generally much higher. Both factors can deter risk-taking.

A 2006 *BusinessWeek* cover headline read, "Eureka, We Failed! How Smart Companies Learn from Their Flops," and the magazine featured interviews with CEOs on "My Favorite Mistake." The idea is that we learn from our mistakes, as summarized by President Obama, who appeared on national television to say, "I'm here on television saying I screwed up, and that's part of the era of responsibility. It's not never making mistakes; it's owning up to them and trying to make sure you never repeat them, and that's what we intend to do."

Nicolas Sarkozy, again breaking the traditional mold, has also admitted openly to making mistakes. In an interview with the *Nouvel Observateur* in mid-2009, he recognized that he had made some mistakes, which he attributed to the learning curve and the importance of the presidential role: *"J'écoute, j'apprends, peut-être même je progresse"* ("I'm listening, I'm learning, maybe I'm even making progress.")

A typical American approach to risk was illustrated by George Simons, an American consultant based in Europe. While discussing an upcoming program with a French colleague, George proposed using a training tool that was in the final testing phase. Despite the suggestion and George's offer to assist in the process, the French trainer decided to use an established tool that had already proved successful. George summed up their cultural difference by saying,

> I think that part of the culture thing may be that I am an American who tries to set off little fires and expects people to contribute fuel to them until we get a good bonfire going and decide what we are going to cook with it. I realize that I have made this mistake before with people who really want to decide on the menu before starting the fire. (Simons 1996)

Another contrast between French and American attitudes toward risk was illustrated at the French offices of RPR. A French supervisor needed his American superior's approval on a purchase order. The American's French was only rudimentary, so he was unable to understand the contract and told his subordinate to sign off on it instead. This was extremely uncomfortable for the Frenchman, who was used to his previous boss (a Frenchwoman) having sole signature responsibility on all paperwork. His principal reason for being unwilling to sign the contract was fear of being blamed if anything went wrong, so they worked out a compromise solution in which they both signed the document. The American's management principle of empowering employees was respected, while the French subordinate's need to spread the risk was also satisfied. It was a nice blending of their styles.

Compensation policies in the two countries illustrate this bias for or against risk taking. Often in the United States, one's annual fixed salary is only a part of the overall financial package one receives, which includes bonuses, stock options, and other performance-related rewards. In France the fixed salary is usually all one gets, with the performance of the company, the department, or the individual being a minor factor in determining compensation, if it enters into the calculation at all.

Système D and Ethics. French institutions tend to be composed of Byzantine bureaucracies and vast quantities of administrative red tape, which are at least partially responsible for another high-context French institution: *Système D.* The letter *D* usually stands for *débrouiller* or *se débrouiller*, although a coarser version is *se démerder* (to remove oneself from ambient manure). As we noted in chapter 5, *débrouiller* means to unfog, to disentangle, to sort out, or even to clear up. *Se débrouiller* refers to one's individual actions and one's ability to manage for oneself.

Système D in France refers to the unofficial and possibly unorthodox method for getting things done or turning things around. It is a process of using relationships, connections, specific people, or knowledge to get information and to make things happen. It usually implies bypassing a few rules or regulations, a technique that you as an outsider must learn if you want to survive the bureaucracy and function effectively in the French corporate world. Being able to use Système D to get out of difficulties is seen as a high-level skill in France, and the adjective *débrouillard(e)* is often used as a compliment. All this means there is a cheerful disregard for petty rules and regulations in France—though, of course, decisions about which ones are petty are left up to the individual.

Bureaucratic rules and regulations in France unnecessarily *compliquent l'existence* (complicate one's existence). Rather than direct confrontation with an implacable wall, the French often prefer a flanking maneuver. Recall the American woman whose French boyfriend assumed she had already agreed to marry him. He knew that residency requirements for foreigners to marry in France were so complex and so time-consuming that if they went through the proper channels, they would have at least five years to plan their wedding. Fortunately, the boyfriend's cousin was the mayor of a small village near his hometown, and she was able to declare the American as a resident of the village, which she most definitely was not, since they lived in a large city some three hours away. The couple was married by the cousin about six months later.

An incident in an international school in Paris illustrates this "end-run" approach to solving problems and overcoming obstacles. An American student describes a tug-of-war match:

It was the Americans against the French. Monsieur René got us all started, eight on each side. We pulled and pulled. But they looped their rope around a tree. We were trying to pull a tree down. We were *plus forts* [stronger], but they were *plus malins* [cleverer]. In school at home, the teacher would have said it wasn't fair. But Monsieur René said, *"C'était malin"* ["That was clever"]. (Wylie and Brière 1995, 95)

An American expat in France analyzed the two approaches. A system that is too complex or too inconvenient in the United States must be simplified. The goal is to promote process improvement and take the waste out of the system. In any case, the rules are usually respected. In a similar situation, the French reaction is to go around the problem using Système D. When faced with an obstacle, the French person typically looks for a way around it and seldom attacks the problem head-on.

Because of their tendency to obey rules or change them within the system, Americans in France are generally astounded when they observe Système D in action, especially when they don't recognize what it is. One American expat made brilliant use of Système D without even knowing it when he tried to get a visa at the last minute for his son's school trip abroad. After fruitlessly making the rounds of various local government offices, he finally got to the right place, where the clerk informed him that, for a number of reasons, it would be impossible to issue the visa right away.

Despite this initial rebuff, the American started to listen to and empathize with the clerk as she went on to vent about her work situation. As he was about to leave, she discreetly told him that she might be able to help. She looked around twice to make sure no one was watching, then pulled out an official piece of paper, stamped it twice, and signed it. That was that. Rules had been broken, but the son was able to leave with his classmates the following day. The clerk's willingness to work in Système D was a result of her feelings toward a man who had listened sympathetically to her troubles. That was the beginning of a relationship, so he was no longer a total stranger, an object of indifference.

From the American perspective, the French may appear at least cavalier if not actually unethical, but French ethics are simply more flexible and situational. They are based on the notion that the literal truth may be less important than some other vital need, such as family loyalty or maintaining a relationship. As discussed in chapter 15, the French are experts at dancing on the line that separates truth from lies. Dualism—"either it's right or it's wrong"—is not a characteristic pattern of French thought. Americans, who play things strictly by the book, are seen by the French as unnecessarily rigid, plodding, and unimaginative. Doing things exactly according to the rules is dull and conformist. It also makes life more difficult and tiresome than necessary.

As you might imagine, Système D is also a means of getting power in a French company. It is part of a whole process that makes you valuable to the organization and its members. It is part of an intricate social organizational web, a network of connections that allows a person to break through the resistance of the normal system and make things happen.

Business Negotiations. Negotiations can take place within a company, between departments or subsidiaries, or between two or more companies. Theoretically, when negotiating parties work for the same organization, they should be able to reach agreement more easily, since they share corporate culture and over-arching corporate goals. In any case, cultural values, assumptions, and beliefs underlie the ways in which people prepare for, approach, conduct, and conclude negotiations.

Regardless of where the negotiation takes place, language is also a vital component. If the working language is French, it is a good idea to have a highly competent and qualified interpreter if your level of French is less than fluent. In addition to impeccable language skills, an interpreter needs to be culturally savvy enough to decode high-context and nonverbal communication. Proper presentation, manners, and knowledge of protocol are essential for the interpreter as well as for the negotiators. If the negotiations are conducted in English, the French are likely to need even more time than usual for side conversations to ensure that they all understand the same thing, whether or not an interpreter is present.

The choice of negotiators in France takes into consideration elements beyond operational competence or knowledge of the issues. The level of formality and concern for proper behavior reach their pinnacle in an important negotiation. French negotiators must show—discreetly—that they come from the right social and educational background and have the authority to make the final decision. A negotiator who has to "check back with the home office" loses credibility.

When not working with familiar people, the French arrive at the negotiating table with the slight mistrust they bring to any initial encounter. Here as elsewhere, trust is not a given but must be earned by virtue of personality and performance.

As in most French business operations, risk is minimized when it cannot be eliminated. The French try to avoid being caught short and having to improvise on the fly. A good way to reduce risk is to be ready for any eventuality by being thoroughly prepared. The French feel that, armed with complete, detailed information, they can handle any situation that arises. And they will do this, like every other task, by using logic, logic, and logic. They expect their negotiating partners to be equally well versed on all elements that make up the context of the subject, including legal, financial, and environmental issues, and so on. The French lose respect for those who neglect this preparation.

Confrontations in French negotiations can become quite heated. Ideas, including those that seem unrelated to the topic, are expressed and debated, even if there is little chance of their being accepted. Recall that the French love a good discussion for its own sake, so they do not necessarily feel pressured to conclude an agreement if there are more people who want to express their opinions. Time is not of the essence. Also, by observing the reactions, proposals, background, and style of the other party, French negotiators gather a lot of high-context information about the other party's position and what it is likely to do next.

An example of this occurred during negotiations between the French and American partners of an established joint venture. The Americans had prepared a cooperative strategy in which all members of the negotiating team would defend the agreed-upon platform, presenting a united front—which they expected the French to do as well. But the French, as usual, preferred to engage in arguing and discussing conflicting viewpoints among themselves. For the Americans, the apparent lack of cohesion and the resulting confusion indicated that the French had not prepared and had no organized strategy. The Americans felt that "being prepared" meant having one single position to put forward, while French preparation was a question of getting all the information needed to cope with anything that might come up during the meeting. From the French perspective, the Americans were showing a lack of creative spirit, falling into lockstep behind one position without entertaining options.

An American businesswoman describes the French as "aggressively intelligent." They need to show you they are made of stern intellectual stuff, and they usually do this in a combative, in-your-face way. Paradoxically, they can also be charming while they're doing it.

The French usually begin a business negotiation by "setting the stage" with a series of general considerations and statements before getting down to the details. For example, they want to discuss the general business climate, economic trends, market conditions, competing companies, and industry sales figures before discussing the financial details of a proposal. The inclusion of considerable background information is important to the French because they like to know exactly where they stand at all times, and where they are going.

Americans, on the other hand, tend to get right to the business at hand, concentrating on the "bottom-line" details of how to reduce costs and increase profits from the deal under negotiation. Americans, who are used to adopting a pragmatic, hard-sell approach, can find the intellectual orientation of the French unsettling. Profits and market share are also important to the French, but the bottom-line approach will never be as popular in France as it is in American corporate settings. To be so focused on money and profits would be considered rude in a culture where panache, elegance, intellectual wit, and cleverness are held in high regard.

Finally, the French do not understand the notion of a level playing field. Whoever has a dominant position or knows any critical information would be foolish not to take advantage of it. When it comes to business ethics, French boundaries are not as clear cut or black-and-white as they usually are in the United States. Rather, French business ethics depend on the context and the people you are dealing with. This is a very important concept, as it might influence the outcome of the negotiation.

As a final point, keep in mind that French diplomats traditionally use their language as one of their most precise and useful tools, though English is now more widely employed in the international arena. French diplomacy has a long and glorious history, and negotiation has traditionally been regarded as an art form. At the same time, the French are also past masters in the art of realpolitik and rarely lose sight of their main chance. Once again, they are able to dance on the fine line that separates truth from lies, to navigate that treacherous terrain between *en principe* and *en réalité*.

Good or Fast? Can a job be done both quickly and well? Americans tend to think so, but the French generally see this as an either-or proposition. The best Bordeaux and Burgundy wines are at least thirty years old. Like a fine wine, good work takes time to develop and mature. A decent table wine can be drunk shortly after it is produced, but it can't possibly be expected to match the quality of a 1955 Château Margaux.

This attitude is partly responsible for the French lack of urgency that frustrates Americans. The French want to work well and produce something of high quality. And for them, this simply takes a certain amount of time and no less. Speeding up the process can be done only by cutting corners, and quality will inevitably suffer.

A French admin tried to explain this to her American boss, who had told her to have a report ready for the following day. "Tomorrow?! In France, nobody would ever ask you to have something ready tomorrow. Well, I can get it done that fast, but I'll have to sacrifice quality. My boss said, 'Why? You can be fast and do good work at the same time.' Okay, but this is not very French" (Bull Worldwide Information Systems 1992).

It can be helpful to establish what level of quality will be "good enough" for the task at hand. "Good enough" is not a French concept. From primary school on, students are expected to aim for perfection, even though achieving it is impossible. This training stays with them in the workplace, and submitting a project in an "unfinished" state really goes against the grain. Americans' greater need for action and speed, on the other hand, can allow them to get up and running with only a rough draft. It may be less frustrating all around if there is a mutual understanding, for example, that if accuracy is most important, the presentation need not be fully polished with elegant illustrations and animations, which could be added later.

The Customer Is Not Always Right. Americans are taught to be polite and friendly toward those they do not know: retail employees with shoppers, people waiting in line at the post office or the dry cleaner, or a stranger asking directions in the street. Perhaps this stems from the experience that virtually all Americans share of being strangers in a strange land, since their families came here from somewhere else. Or perhaps it is because, in a fluid society, you can never be sure whom you will be working with, or living across the street from tomorrow, so it's best to get along in general. Friendliness helps overcome feelings of uncertainty about others by establishing an immediate connection. In any case, Americans amaze and amuse the French with their politeness to strangers on the street, in shops, and in public places.

As many Americans have learned to their distress, being polite to strangers is not a virtue in France. Laurence Wylie notes that "France has the social arrangement of the *cercle,* in which you are responsible only to the people in your own *cercle* and are indifferent to people outside the *cercle*" (1981, 23). People outside your cercle—those you don't know, customers who are not regulars, for example—are treated with an impersonality that strikes Americans as glacially rude.

One American businesswoman with years of experience in France explained it this way: "Americans are shocked by what they see as poor customer service. But the issue is not how you define service, rather how you define a customer." To an American, a customer is anyone who walks in the door. Even if she does not make a purchase, she will be treated like an honored guest, because if she feels comfortable, she is likely to come back and make a purchase at another time. A store in California even announced its grand opening to local residents with a postcard addressed to "Valued Customer." It is impossible for a store in France that has not yet opened its doors to have customers at all, valued or otherwise. To a French person, a customer is a regular, someone with whom he has an established relationship—perhaps even someone whose father or grandfather was a regular in the shop when it belonged to his father or grandfather.

The difference is significant. One American woman went grocery shopping during a visit to the small town where her French husband had been raised, where they had lived early in their marriage, and where his family still lived.

> Many of the shopkeepers remembered me, and greeted me warmly, chatting about the latest local news. In some shops where I was not recognized, I was treated with the normal French shopkeeper's indifference. A couple of days later I made the rounds of shops again with my little niece, Agnès, then about two-and-a-half. Her proud introduction in each shop of her Tatie Diana from America gave the previously indifferent shopkeepers a vital piece of information: this is Agnès and Alexandre's aunt, who is therefore Pierre's wife and therefore Ebert and Pierrette's daughter-in-law and therefore Brigitte and Ninon's sister-in-law. Suddenly, they knew where my rightful place in their *cercle* was, and I mattered.

French shops generally do not have "satisfaction guaranteed or your money back" policies. If a product actually doesn't work, you can usually exchange it without too much fuss. On the other hand, try to return a purchase just because you've changed your mind and you will find yourself subjected to a third-degree interrogation before being told you need to make up your mind before buying something. Before you know it, you are dismissed like a naughty child, the package still in your hand.

The French shopkeeper or restaurant owner is a proud person and demands respect from clients. As an example, consider a possibly apocryphal tale about Jerry Lewis, the American comedian, who is much admired in France. He had invited a large group of friends to one of the finest restaurants in Paris. Having ordered a rare vintage wine, he produced a bottle of Coca-Cola and mixed them in a glass as a gag. Outraged by what he considered an insult to French culture and savoir-vivre, the restaurant owner promptly threw the entire party out on the sidewalk, preferring to lose a substantial amount of money for the sake of his honor and the reputation of his establishment. In the United States, the owner would probably have chosen to "grin and bear it," letting the profit soothe his wounded pride.

An American expat in France offered some words of wisdom concerning customer relations.

Forget what you've learned in the U.S. about "the customer is king." Learn to play the French game where you have to please the shop owner because he has what you need or want. He is the king you need to court. You're certainly not on a pedestal and you shouldn't take anything for granted. Above all, be polite. If you play the game right and are a little more subservient than in the U.S., you'll be treated very nicely and you'll enjoy it. If necessary and possible, challenge people to perform. For example, tell the plumber, "I have a problem that no one will ever be able to fix—no one!"

These different attitudes toward customer service and customer relations, as well as different concepts of who controls the relationship, have obvious implications in doing business across cultures. What is customer service, and how is the role of customer service representative defined? How are customers to be treated, complaints handled, and disputes resolved? If such matters are not addressed properly, the repercussions on the company's image and sales can be significant.

MANAGING PEOPLE

Questions Needing Answers

- What is good leadership?
- What is good management?
- What are the core competencies of managers and leaders?
- How are objectives set? Used? Measured?
- Will performance be appraised? By whom? How?
- How will we handle rewards, recognition, and motivation in general?
- How will short-term performance deficiencies be dealt with?
- Will feedback be given? How? To whom? When? Public or private? Positive, constructive, or negative?
- What is "high potential" in our organization?
- Who can be a manager?
- How are managers developed?
- How are nonmanagerial staff developed?
- Should talent be expected to take overseas assignments?
- What is the importance and impact of credentials, education, and experience?

Leadership, Hierarchy, and Management. The literal French translation of the word *leader* is *meneur,* but the cultural meaning of the word is at odds with the American notion of leadership. A meneur is a person who leads a rebellion, a prison revolt, or even a revolution on the barricades. In this sense, it would be more of a negative, even disturbing kind of leader. Another, more neutral translation would be *responsable.* As a noun, *un responsable* is someone who is in charge, who directs operations, but not necessarily someone who has to lead.

That explains why, when transposed in the social and political arenas, the English word *leader* is often used. The French tend to conceive of *leadership* in connection with political rather than business leadership. Political leadership, as well as political authority, must be earned and, beyond the necessary background qualifications, demands human qualities that inspire people to follow and commit. Political leaders may indeed have to prove themselves more than leaders in business, where education usually determines the ascribed level of leadership, at least initially.

French business leadership is not earned by one's actions in a position so much as by the fact that one has advanced to that position in the first place. Leadership is often related to social class and education (meaning a diploma from the right school, usually one of the grandes écoles) and is perceived as a logical extension of one's personal attributes. In other words, if an individual has the right pedigree, has been to the right school, and has made it to executive status, he or she logically has followers—although not always obedient followers—because of the position he or she has attained. Leadership, at least in the sense of having followers, is essentially a result of climbing the corporate hierarchy and the right educational grooming.

In the United States, leadership is more dynamic. As Edward Hall notes,

> Unlike many countries and cultures, where leadership is based on class (and other criteria) and is functional in all situations, leadership in the United States happens to be situational. Leadership does not carry over from situation A to B. (1992, 231)

In other words, depending on the context and the stakes, just about anyone can become a leader when his or her talents and personal qualities allow him or her to rise to a challenge and meet it head-on. Leadership usually means someone is at the vanguard and promotes unity while moving forward toward a well-crafted vision. This egalitarian concept also means that someone from a modest background can become a leader or even a hero. Social and educational backgrounds do not guarantee leadership ability and may be completely insignificant.

Leadership traits may be interpreted differently, and French leaders (at least by position) may not be recognized as such by outsiders. One of our American seminar participants remarked, "The French are followers, not leaders; they have a hard time making decisions. No one likes to be responsible, but everyone has to have a say." Another non-French employee echoes this person's words, "The French need to understand what the Mothership wants before being willing to take a position or offer help. They are very, very risk averse." Another American commented, "It is sometimes difficult to discern in France who has the final decision authority."

What these people—who have never worked or lived in France—may not be able to decipher is the way decisions are made and the way French subordinates operate, based on their positioning in the corporate pyramid. Fear of failure, and consequently fear of being reprimanded or punished (as French children often are at home or in school), is a very influential, pervasive French cultural factor. It is a stigma that, as the French say, sticks to peoples' skin (*leur colle à la peau*). The expression *"on n'a pas le droit à l'erreur"* ("you have no right to make a mistake") is a good illustration of this cultural influence. Making mistakes, especially serious ones, can be damaging to a French executive's career to a much greater extent than a mobile, go-getter American can imagine.

A French participant reports, "French people often explain why they were late or wrong whereas Americans care more about action plans and strategies to repair what is broken. Once a decision is made, Americans deploy the plan, whereas French people often spend more time questioning themselves to make sure it was the best decision, collecting additional elements in case there may be a better solution. French people are afraid of failure; that is why they need to explain why they fail when they do, and they must think several times about a decision before diving in."

And yet, things are not that clear-cut—black on one side and white on the other. This would be too simple. Another French participant shares his perception, "Americans are taught to be very respectful of the group and the management while French people are usually more inclined to have their own opinions and challenge what is brought by the management. French people often sound hysterical compared to U.S. counterparts." Another French person sums up the comparison pretty succinctly, "Americans say they don't like hierarchy but they respect it. French people like hierarchy but they don't respect it."

Remember, these are not absolutes, and the context as well as the personalities of and the relationship among the different actors need to be factored in. What we offer here are cultural elements and explanations that need to be contextualized based on the French-American environment, social or professional, that you are dealing with.

Are good managers born or made? Is management an art or a science? In France, especially at a fairly high level, relationships, personal touch, authority, and decision-making ability matter more than anything else. Accordingly, management is not considered a science but rather an art or a state of mind. In the United States, management is a science that can be taught and whose results can be measured objectively. Management tools and techniques can be mastered and, beyond that, learned on the job.

American managers do not necessarily have all the answers and their subordinates do not expect them to. Coaching and developing one's team are important management responsibilities, and most managers would have no problem acknowledging that a subordinate is better informed in a certain area and might ask in a meeting, "I'm not sure about that. Cynthia has been doing the research on it. Cynthia, can you fill us in?" Similarly, a vice president of a U.S. telecommunications company made a self-deprecating comment during a presentation about her career path: "When I got this job, I didn't know 75 percent of what I had to do." Such an admission from a French top-level manager would be the equivalent of giving the order to drop the guillotine blade. Since education plays such a crucial role in French society, high-level managers are often hired because of their educational brilliance, rather than their work or managerial track record alone. Their subordinates, therefore, expect them to know everything and to have all the answers, just like their teachers in school did. Confessing one's ignorance is usually perceived to be a sign of weakness, and it would most likely be associated with a loss of face or credibility.

French notions of hierarchy, again, play a role here as well. The boss is most emphatically not "one of the guys" and is not expected to get down in the trenches with everyone else. His or her role is usually to make the decisions and then send in the troops. A British journalist extends the metaphor:

> Bosses in France tend to be Napoleonic. Graduates, as a rule of one of the elite *grandes écoles*, are expected to be brilliant technical planners, equally adept at industry, finance and government. They can be vulnerable to surprise when troops below fail to respond to orders from on high. Stiff hierarchies in big firms discourage informal relations and reinforce a sense of "them" and "us." (*Economist* 1991, 64)

American companies often encourage empowerment for their employees, giving them greater control and responsibility in their jobs. The idea behind this popular practice is that employees who have real input regarding their jobs will be more satisfied and more motivated. Work becomes a richer experience for empowered employees, since they have greater possibility for learning and growth on the job. Employees sometimes complain that the concept is little more than window-dressing: "Yeah, we've been empowered to do what we're told!"

"Empowerment" is difficult to translate into French, both literally and culturally. *Autonomisation*, a translation developed by UNESCO, tends to be used in an administrative and governmental context rather than in business. *Délégation* may come close, but it usually implies that the task is transferred, not necessarily decision-making authority or control (via a signature). A French manager in the U.S. summed it up by saying, "Of course, we agree with the principle of empowerment, but you still need to retain a certain level of control." Another splendid example of one thing being true *en théorie* while the opposite happens *en réalité*!

In the U.S., an individual is empowered by having authorization and responsibility to make decisions and take action—which clearly means that she is accountable. Managers can ensure that the person understands his or her role by providing detailed and explicit information, and by responding to his or her questions and comments.

Many nonmanagerial French employees are not particularly interested in growing on the job, nor do they often get the chance. They may prefer *un petit boulot tranquille* (a peaceful little job) that allows them to earn enough money, is not too demanding, and leaves plenty of time for family, friends, and vacation. In addition, French business culture provides a formalized structure where everyone's career path is pretty much determined from day one, and the culture does not nurture employee development with the goal of making major upward or lateral moves. One French junior executive, a graduate of a second-tier business school, moved to the United States to get away from an excess of job security: "At age twenty-five, I could sit in my office and know exactly where I would be sitting when I retired and exactly what my job would be. It was a horrifying prospect."

Power sharing in France can threaten the status quo, since subordinates might eventually gain enough leverage to replace the manager. Some older middle managers are suspicious of talented and well-educated subordinates, seeing them as rivals. Protected in their little fiefdoms, French managers can sometimes develop the mentality of feudal lords or *petits chefs*, fearful of the peasants getting ideas above their station.

Given the French tendency not to promote personal growth on the job, French employees at American companies might react positively to development opportunities. A woman working as a janitor at Disneyland Paris, for example, was surprised and delighted to be asked to participate in the orientation and training of new employees. It is extremely unlikely that she would have been offered such a chance in a traditional French company.

Adapting to Different Management Practices. Young French mid- and lower-level managers adapt to certain American management practices quite well: more delegation of authority, more empowerment of subordinates, greater information flow, wider involvement in decision making, and greater respect for the individual. As a French RPR expat in the United States put it, "MBA versus MBC—management by authority versus management by collaboration."

A few American RPR expatriates have implemented these practices in France with a great deal of success at lower management levels. An American woman was sent to France as a coordinator of clinical studies. During her time there, she was promoted to a management position, supervising her former colleagues. After a few months, she wanted to know how she was doing and sent out a confidential questionnaire to her staff asking them to evaluate her. Initially, they were quite surprised, since they had never been asked to do such a thing before, but they responded once they recognized that their input could be useful, particularly for an expat without the usual landmarks to guide her.

A similar example is that of a typically American training technique, a manager assimilation exercise, that was introduced at RPR in France. It was designed to help a manager who had been on the job only a few months obtain critical feedback from her subordinates. Given the hierarchical nature of French organizations, this was no easy task and took careful mediation by a skilled facilitator.

Generally, information channels tend to be horizontal in France and vertical in the United States. The elitist French educational system encourages old-boy and-girl information networks. Since competition is intense, especially during the last years of high school and the first years of higher education, there is no natural reward for sharing information with your classmates. When French middle managers in the U.S. grasp the idea of sharing information and actually see its value in action, they can also adapt well to new ways of handling information. One American company in France successfully "deprograms" grandes écoles graduates as soon as they are hired. The new employees go through a two-week management training program designed to help them assimilate American management techniques.

Gaps: Generation and Other. There are marked differences between young French employees (20 to 35 or 40) and senior staff (40 to 45 and older). As one would expect, older staff members won't be as receptive as younger ones are to new management techniques and innovative ways of doing things. This is an important consideration when defining responsibilities across cultures and choosing people for expatriate assignments.

The generational divide is not as wide or as clear-cut in the United States, since Americans place a high value on newness and change. In addition, change may not be a matter of choice: in the American labor market, if you don't perform adequately, quickly adapting to new techniques and changes, you are usually quickly pushed aside with few scruples. French labor practices tend to be more tolerant of mediocre performance and more protective of senior workers, some of whom have become part of the furniture—*il fait partie des meubles*, as the French put it so well. "Encrusted" or obstreperous employees are sometimes "promoted" to positions where they can do minimal damage. The reassignment of Bishop Gaillot to the diocese of Partenia is a masterful example of the technique.

Other factors in a person's willingness to accept change and new ways of working include level of international experience, degree of openness to the world at large, job responsibility, social background, and level of education. Openness is particularly significant. Those who have never lived in another culture or never escaped the "expat bubble" have a mindset quite different from that of people whose international living and working experience has broadened their outlook. The effective intercultural manager needs to be skilled in bridging these differences or gaps in subordinates' backgrounds by meeting them where they are before leading them further on.

Merit, Mobility, and Appraisal Standards. Many American managers in France are frustrated by being unable to promote employees on the basis of their performance alone. While they can suggest promotions or pay raises for their subordinates, the decisions are ultimately made jointly with higher-level managers and even other departments, particularly human resources. Such decisions are based on a number of factors other than performance, many of which are inappropriate by American standards.

As said before, seniority and education, particularly graduating from the right school, are important factors in awarding promotions in France. A brilliant thirty-year-old employee who has made enormous contributions to the company in just a couple of years cannot move up to management or *cadre* (executive) status with people who are much older and have put in many more years with the company. He or she must spend a certain amount of time at a given level before being allowed to advance. In one case, an American RPR manager was unable to promote an excellent employee because of her poor academic record.

When he discussed the promotion with the human resources department, he was told that her outstanding job performance carried less weight than the fact that she had dropped out of college, which disqualified her from moving beyond a certain level.

As noted earlier, French teachers comment freely, publicly, and sometimes sarcastically on their students' work, particularly if it is not up to standard. Employee appraisal follows the same pattern: comments are usually negative to begin with, focusing on what was done wrong or needs to be improved. Managers do not concern themselves with employees' feelings of self-esteem, nor do they stress positive comments as a means of motivation. American-style praise such as "Terrific job!" or "Awesome report!" strikes the French as overkill. A French HR manager commented drily on the number of "excellent" evaluations in U.S. personnel files, "They all look so brilliant!" Conversely, *"Ce n'est pas trop mal"* ("It's not too bad") sounds none too encouraging to American ears, but in France it is fairly standard as positive feedback.

An Anglo-Canadian RPR expat noted that although employees on both sides of the Atlantic were evaluated on the same 1–5 scale (1 being excellent, 5 being poor), there were considerable discrepancies in the meaning of the various marks across cultures. A 3 in France is good and fairly common. In the United States and Canada, it is not unusual to see 1s on appraisal forms. A 2 is considered average, and a 3 is actually considered a poor rating.

Employee appraisal can be a potential bombshell. Employees who are evaluated according to the other culture's standards are likely to be confused and upset. A French manager in the United States who appraises his or her employees according to French standards will probably be seen as a slave driver and impossible to please. Similarly, an American manager giving American-style positive appraisals in France may be seen as hypocritical or undemanding.

Because of the hierarchical nature of the French workplace, 360-degree feedback (where employees are evaluated by peers and subordinates as well as supervisors) is unlikely to work well there. In a traditional French company, it is inconceivable that a subordinate would be asked to provide feedback about his or her supervisor. Most French employees would also be concerned that their evaluation might be used against them or have other negative consequences. Similarly, French university students in the United States are astounded to see that students' evaluations of their professors are sometimes printed in helpful booklets sold at the bookstore. American managers in France who wish to implement such upward evaluation techniques need to proceed with great caution. Much preparation and coaching will be needed for managers as well as employees. The French will want to know what they have to gain by taking the risk of participating. The results will need to be evaluated with cultural differences taken into account as well.

Pay differentials can also become a flash point in international mergers. In the case of the Daimler-Chrysler venture, a Bavarian professor of finance gave a succinct summary of European opinion when speaking of the discrepancy between CEO compensation packages at Chrysler (about $16 million) and Daimler (about $2 million) in 1997, which echoes the controversy around Henri Proglio's salary at EDF and VEOLIA: "The only ones who deserve such sums are entrepreneurs. No executive deserves that much money" (Steinmetz and White 1998, B1). The "pay for performance" justification is not acceptable in the European view, because the concept of performance is not the same. American executives are judged on shareholder return, so a CEO who improves an already healthy bottom line by laying off employees is rewarded. Such a thing is unconscionable in France, where *la performance* is more broadly defined and includes elements of social responsibility as well as financial well-being.

Labor market conditions also determine compensation policies in the United States, where employees are less likely to remain loyal to one company for their entire career. If another company offers two or three times as much money, one would be regarded as stupid not to accept it. Competition determines salary levels, and American companies, at least in theory, have to pay higher salaries to attract and retain talented people. Because the European labor market is very different, French managers often do not understand this, and French people tend to give weight to elements other than money in evaluating a job offer. A Frenchwoman in the U.S. was in fact offered twice her salary to move to another company but turned down the offer because she really enjoyed her job and got along so well with her coworkers. Some of her American colleagues were simply unable to understand her reasoning, saying they would jump at the chance to double their salaries.

Gender Relations. The number of French firms headed by women is statistically small, but such companies generally enjoy twice the average rates of profitability and growth. Not only do women bosses work harder, according to the authors of a recent study, but they are also more likely than their male counterparts to base their authority on competence and consensus rather than on position and power. They also tend to read the market better and anticipate its needs and evolution.

The percentage of women on the board of major companies in Norway is the highest in the world at 44.2 percent, up from 6 percent in 2001. (For more information, see *www.europeanwn.net*.) The change was the result of legislation in 2003 that required nearly 500 public companies, including 175 firms listed on the Oslo stock exchange, to increase the number of women on their boards to 40 percent, or face closure. The move was controversial, as is the whole concept of quotas, but the difference with other countries is dramatic:

France	10.5%
U.S.	15.2%
UK	12%

At the end of 2009, a bill was submitted in France that, if accepted, will require companies on the Paris stock exchange to ensure that female employees make up 50 percent of their board members by 2015. Many of those who formerly opposed quotas have now come out in favor of such a requirement.

Nonetheless, women at the highest levels of French business are still a rare sight. At any hierarchical level, though, a woman in business is generally treated as a woman above all. She will generally be seated first, doors will be opened for her, and male coworkers will notice and comment appreciatively on her appearance. Good-natured bantering between the sexes is considered normal. Chauvin, after all, was a Frenchman!

> A French manager recently transferred to his company's headquarters in Texas received a memo that his mandatory sexual harassment training would be taking place the following week. Grinning, he showed the document to some colleagues, saying, "Actually, I don't need any training. I already know how to do this very well!"

Sexual harassment is illegal in France, but the French legal definition is very narrow and refers only to sexual blackmail of a subordinate by a superior, the forcing of an employee (almost always female) to perform an act against her will as a condition of continued employment or promotion. Of course, this is also forbidden by American sexual harassment legislation, where it is known as quid pro quo, exchanging something for something.

The second type of sexual harassment defined by the Equal Employment Opportunity Commission and the U.S. courts is called the "hostile working environment." It is this aspect of the issue that often puzzles the French and can potentially lead to serious legal and financial consequences. The ramifications of differing cultural perceptions in this area are extremely important and wide-ranging, whether the employees involved are French people in the United States or Americans in France.

A hostile working environment refers to "sexual comments, physical touch-ing, or displays of objects that 'unreasonably interfere' with work performance or that create an 'intimidating, hostile, or offensive' work environment" (*Business & Legal Reports* 1996, 7). These may include

- displaying suggestive calendars, graffiti, sexual objects, and pictures and
- regular, persistent use of offensive language, jokes, suggestions of a sexual nature, gestures, or comments.

Examples of a hostile working environment cited in employee training programs include the following:

- A male employee puts up a pinup calendar at the office. The nude female pictures displayed on the wall make Rachel uncomfortable whenever she looks at them. The male employee ignores Rachel's requests to remove the calendar.
- Mark is embarrassed and offended when his female coworkers continuously talk about their sexual encounters, even though he has told them it offends him. (7)

Both of these examples could describe everyday life in a French workplace. No efforts have been made, either legally or in company policies, to regulate how people look at each other, the words they use with each other, the artwork and posters they put in their offices, or other things that are the basis of lawsuits in the United States. Witness the complete incomprehension with which the French followed the 1991 Clarence Thomas versus Anita Hill sexual harassment case. One Frenchwoman, Elisabeth Badinter (1995), said she could not understand why a woman would feel upset if a male colleague left an obscene drawing on her desk. "For me, the idea of leaving an obscene drawing on a female colleague's desk seems just silly. I think if it happened to me, I would just laugh because it is so clumsy and childish; not effective *séduction* at all."

Being an attractive woman, even a seductive one—in the French sense—is not seen as being incompatible with being competent, strong, and powerful. The American female co-owner of a French company notes, "Although it is still a more chauvinistic world in France, I found that once Frenchwomen have a position of authority, they don't have a problem going out and claiming their rights" (Quibell 1995, 8). Another American woman manager agrees:

The Frenchman's approach is more traditional than that of the American businessman. It is more chauvinistic, but in a positive way. When I'm [in France], I don't feel inferior but I am aware that I am a woman. (8)

In France, as one RPR female expatriate reported, an older, paternalistic male manager might well use affectionate terms such as *ma petite fille* or *ma petite fleur* (my little girl or my little flower) with a younger female subordinate. Such comments in the United States would be considered demeaning and derogatory. An American woman in this situation would most likely complain to the HR department, and a lawsuit would not be out of the question.

To avoid giving offense in this way, many American organizations aim to neutralize or prevent conflict by simply forbidding any reference to sex or gender in the workplace. An American woman who posted a photo from *Life* magazine showing the back view of some naked French rugby players was quickly asked to take it down by the HR manager. French expatriates—both male and female—perceive such a neutral environment as antiseptic and mechanized. For them, the affective side of relationships, the element that humanizes and binds people together, has been removed.

Because sexual harassment is such an explosive issue in the United States, it is important that French and American employees understand how gender relations operate in both cultures. An employee without such an understanding in either country is a loose cannon.

EIGHTEEN

Professional Guidelines

GUIDELINES FOR DEVELOPING
RELATIONSHIPS AND BUILDING TRUST

It is difficult to overstate the importance of building a solid relationship with your business colleagues. Of course, this is true in any culture, but there are particular challenges for those doing business across French and American cultures. In the U.S., business tends to drive the relationship. In practice, this means that the preliminary relationship-building phases are often rushed or skipped by Americans eager to save time and money by getting right down to business. They may be frustrated to find that they haven't saved time or money at all and seem to be running into brick walls as they try to get things accomplished and meet their goals.

In France, the relationship tends to drive the business. With a good relationship, many of the French *"C'est impossible!"* objections simply dissolve but, without one, it may be virtually impossible to get the business off the ground or get a response to a question, urgent or not.

These differences and distinctions are especially important for American managers to understand when involved in an organizational development scenario where selling changes and new ways of doing things to French colleagues is essential to the success of an assignment.

Over the years, our seminar participants have done a lot of reflection and discussion around concepts of trust, commitment and promise, and the best ways to build relationships across French and American cultures. We offer some of them here, not as a step-by-step formula to follow, but rather as a starting point for your own thinking and creativity.

These are the responses we received when participants addressed the following questions: "What is trust and how is it earned? To what extent do we value commitments or promises?"

Question 1: What is trust?
- Believing what the person says is accurate and true
- Not misleading someone: mean and do what you say; honor commitments
- Having confidence in the unseen/unproven
- U.S.: I trust you until you screw me!—default mode is to trust others quickly, assuming they are trustworthy until they show they are not, including those suggested as trustworthy by those we trust already
- France: show me first!—default mode is to trust only when a person is known and has demonstrated trustworthiness
    - First spend time together, second meet small commitments, third meet large commitments—tendency to test even those suggested as trustworthy by others we trust already
    - Notion of trust more implicit in French culture—embedded in the concept of knowing someone; "I know him," may also mean "I trust him."

Question 2: How will we establish trust—or lose it?
- Trust takes time to earn and is easily lost
- Start with common goal
    - Do we share assumptions/understanding of the situation?
    - Both parties have a vested interest: joint success versus individual failure
- Basis for trust
    - Respect for skills, expertise, competence
    - Information on previous success
- First/initial trust is different from long-term trust: needs to be maintained after being earned/proven
- Earn trust by:
    - Doing what you say you will do; following through
    - Showing respect through shared experience
    - Availability, consistency, knowledge/skills/expertise

- Sharing success
- Proposing and discussing options; compromising or showing consideration for other positions
- Being helpful: available/present to assist others
- Learning from, improving from mistakes
- Personal/professional meeting → build trust → relationship
- Don't be "used car salesmen" (don't exaggerate, don't try to sell what you've got if it's not what the person needs or wants)
- French: by being "*digne de confiance*" (worthy of trust)

Out of these reflections emerged some guidelines for building trust across French and American cultures:

- Recognize that building trust takes time; even in the U.S., it's not just a given
- Americans assume someone is trustworthy unless proven otherwise
- French need to build trust and often use intermediaries (e.g., new French employee expected to be introduced in the office)
- Americans need to take time and explain in order to earn French trust
- French need to recognize American desire for timeliness and structure
- It is helpful to have social activities and time allowed to socialize at work—water cooler or lunch discussions, even evening and weekend activities

Question 3: To what extent do we value commitments or promises?
- Commitment versus promise: what is the cultural meaning of words?
  - Promise is serious, personal
  - Commitment is contractual, group-related

France:
- Tend to prefer promise to individual rather than commitment to goal or task
- Sense of honor is important to French; if you don't keep promises, you lose your honor—more serious, more emotional, more personal
- Commitment after cautious risk analysis and management plan
  - "I have to be convinced I need to do it, and have to believe in it"
  - I have to believe I am not "cornered" by committing to something, that I still have autonomy
  - Personal connection—higher probability of delivery

United States:

- Commit more rapidly with higher degree of risk due to tolerance/forgiveness for mistakes
- May hear "I'll do my best" vis-à-vis target date to mean person is not committed and will look for an excuse not to deliver

Understanding and Managing Commitments and Promises

Consider and discuss together:

- What happens if a commitment is not met?
- Is commitment given just to please or get someone off my back?
- What is the value of a written versus a verbal commitment?
- Is commitment conditional if someone must rely on others' actions to deliver?
- Value of three-way communication—clarifying assumptions and understanding among all concerned
  Americans need to:
- Substantiate the need for commitments (the "why" behind a commitment)
- Listen more to the French "whys"
- Recognize French need for flexibility on commitments, especially time commitments
  French need to:
- Be open and willing to ask why a commitment is needed
- Recognize American understanding that commitment means action and on-time task completion

GUIDELINES FOR AMERICAN MANAGERS IN FRANCE

- Learn the language, learn the language, learn the language. Just learn it! The importance of speaking French cannot be overstated. It will open doors for you, build credibility, and get you through initial rounds of observation much more rapidly. Since you might need to break through an initial barrier of mistrust—assuming you know few, if any, of the people you are going to be working with—making an effort to learn and speak the language will help you get started on the right foot.
- Some expatriates come to France with an exaggerated sense of their own importance or hide their insecurities behind an "I know everything; everything should be given to me" attitude. Neither will be endearing to the French. A little humility and a healthy respect for the host culture will go

a long way in neutralizing this problem. For example, even if you don't speak much or any French, don't start right off in English. Begin with a brief disclaimer in French, such as *"Pardon, je ne parle pas bien le français"* ("Sorry, I don't speak French well"), or with a polite *"Parlez-vous anglais?"* ("Do you speak English?") Avoiding the appearance of arrogance will forestall the French from striking back by speaking extremely rapid and slangy French just to make your life miserable. And, yes, there are French people who enjoy doing just that.

- If you must speak English with your French colleagues, adapt your language to their level of understanding. Speak simply but not simplemindedly. Keep in mind that most French people learn British English in school and may be more used to British accents and expressions. Use standard American English, and, if possible, play down any strong regional accent you might have if it seems to be causing comprehension problems. Speak more slowly and speak "French English" with your colleagues, which means occasionally using French expressions in English (e.g., French people don't "make" a decision or an appointment; they "take" them). Avoid colloquial American expressions, slang, and jargon unless you are in a situation where it is appropriate or where you can teach it to your colleagues.

- Using a foreign language—even English—may play an important role in your colleagues' communication patterns, and they may not understand as well as you think they do. The French will rarely openly admit that they don't understand; it would cause them a loss of face. This can result in serious misunderstandings that you discover only later. Pay attention to your colleagues' facial expressions, as French people tend to use strong nonverbal cues when confused, lost, or experiencing difficulty. Some typical gestures and expressions include the infamous Gallic shrug, grimaces, and various kinds of smiles.

- Don't be afraid to rephrase your sentences and get feedback about your listeners' understanding of the discussion by asking open-ended questions. Build in some extra time in your meeting plans so you can use this communication technique as often as needed.

- Learn to appreciate the French joie de vivre. Show you can mix work efficiency with an enjoyment of life, allowing for more quality time in the workplace. Enjoy the French tradition of long vacations and appreciate French food, social life, and the many other little pleasures that make a difference. Ask yourself these questions: Are you in France only to work? Is work the single most important thing in your life? What other interests does France offer you a special opportunity to pursue? The French find the workaholic American difficult to understand and often difficult to work with.

- Upon arrival, spend a lot of time building rapport with your French colleagues. Put your personal convictions on hold and learn how things work and how people interact in the French environment. Give yourself the luxury of not setting quantifiable objectives or goals to achieve during this period.

  According to one French RPR manager, this observation and adaptation period should last about three months, an idea inconceivable for a new manager arriving from the United States. Don't panic—the French universe has enough staying power to avoid collapse in a few short months. Bureaucracy can be your friend in this case, since it will sustain the course of the business while you observe and adjust. Train your senses to use subjective criteria—the emotional well-being of your department, the quality of conversation you have with people—to measure your progress.

- Become skilled at observing people and the way they interact. Postpone judgment until you understand the situation, the people, and their motives. Work relationships in France have a higher degree of affect or feeling than in the United States. Don't let the emotional content of French interactions disturb you. Harmony is not critical to achieving your goals.

- Watch for Système D in action. At first, you might think it's not very different from the way you do things back home—just calling good friends when you need help. Once you have collided with French bureaucracy, however, try to avoid making a negative judgment. You may in time learn to see Système D differently and perhaps not view it as unethical as it seemed at first. But remember that favors are usually person-related and depend on the quality of the relationship. Système D can be used only with people in your *cercle*.

- Ties between business and government are very close in France. Relations between the two are collegial rather than adversarial, as is often the case in the United States. It is not unusual to find a major private-sector company managed by graduates of the same grande école with considerable public-sector experience. Their background in *l'Administration* (civil service) allows them to build particularly effective old-boy networks of power and influence, which can be used to advantage in their new roles.

- Competence and performance are not the only considerations for being a successful manager in France. Your personal background, seniority, education, and other intangible elements, such as your personal network of information sources, might play at least an equally important role. This may seem terribly hierarchical and class-oriented if you come from a society that in principle values egalitarianism, and you may have trouble integrating these elements into your personal way of reasoning. However, they are definitely part of French culture and should not be overlooked.

- The American cowboy management style—"Ready, aim, fire!" (or worse, "Ready, fire, aim!" as in Rorer's "directionally correct" philosophy)—is virtually guaranteed to irritate and alienate the French. It will cause a lot of damage, and you will rapidly lose credibility and support.

- Be patient in dealing with the French thinking process and appreciate its advantages; also note its limitations. Look for ways to combine the French desire for analysis and "thinking things through to the end" and the U.S. imperative for action. Blend the strengths of both cultures, leading French theory to practice and ensuring that American actions are based on solid reasoning. Keep in mind that the French need to understand before they act: they debate, argue, and contradict if necessary. From debate comes clarification, rephrasing, and understanding. The French usually argue with the position and not the person, so try not to take things personally. You may even begin to enjoy the bite and challenge of French-style discussions and find American politeness a bit dull by comparison.

- Time-management patterns vary across cultures. The French do not share the American sense of urgency to accomplish tasks. Therefore, you need to establish deadlines that everyone can realistically meet and feel comfortable with. It will definitely take more time to get things done in France than in the United States, so it is essential to allow for this in project planning and management.

- The word *accountable* does not translate directly into French, which says a lot about the culture and the willingness or unwillingness of French people to shoulder responsibility. The only approximate translation is, in fact, *respons-able* (responsible). A French manager will rarely admit to making a mistake, and French people do not accept blame well, especially when it comes from a foreign manager in a public session. *"Les gens n'aiment pas passer pour des cons"* ("People do not like to look like jackasses") is a very common popular expression. Therefore, don't embarrass employees by making them lose face in front of their colleagues. If things are not going well with someone, see the person privately and fix the problem between the two of you. In public, talk honestly, but generally, about things that are not working well without naming the people involved or the person in charge. The high-context French will have already figured out who the guilty parties are.

- French appraisal standards are rigorous. Evaluating people according to American standards will undermine your credibility as a manager and create discrepancies with other teams or departments. Learn first about local practices and seek advice from your French or American peers if necessary.

GUIDELINES FOR FRENCH MANAGERS IN THE UNITED STATES

- Relationships develop differently in the United States, where friendship is more situational, depending on where you live and work and not so much on with whom you went to school or with whom you grew up. Keeping this in mind will help ease some of your frustration when interacting with Americans on a social basis—when things seem, through French filters, to be going too fast or to be going nowhere (you get invited right away because you're French and exotic, but then you may never see your hosts again).
- Understand that you need to observe certain explicit rules in a professional environment (i.e., where the affective side of relationships plays a lesser role). These include the infamous "political correctness" and more sensitive ways of addressing women. Jokes and comments that raise no eyebrows in France—about women's driving or men's cooking, for example—would most likely be considered derogatory, condescending, and definitely inappropriate. "When in doubt, *don't*" is a rule of thumb that will keep you out of trouble.
- Work is a central and psychologically important aspect of an American's identity; other areas, including the family, are often secondary to work. This is sometimes hard for a French person to believe, but discussion of the matter with American colleagues should convince you. In a fast-moving, action-oriented society, work shapes a person's identity to a greater extent than in a relationship-oriented society like France.

  Consequently, American employees identify with their company to a greater extent than French employees do, even though the Americans change companies more easily. The concept of "corporate identity" resonates with American sensibilities. The social role of the corporation in the United States might include tuition reimbursement, health insurance, child care, personal counseling through employee assistance programs, and so on. In many companies mission statements are posted or are added to employee handbooks and company documents. While mission statements might appear too directive to you, they are important elements in the American workplace. Take them seriously.

- Learn to communicate the American way, and do not play the information retention game. A good flow of information, both vertically and horizontally, will benefit everyone, and you will receive much more useful information in return.
- American teamwork and empowerment practices involve delegating significant decision-making power and responsibility to subordinates. The typical American management style might be described as "hands-off," implying a limited amount of control from the manager. Saying that someone is a "micromanager" (keeping everyone on a tight leash and unwilling to delegate) is not a compliment in the United States.
- Be a good team player. Take time to build a relationship with every member of the team, and explain where you are coming from in terms of your own reasoning and knowledge. People in one department of a company, be it headquarters or a subsidiary, know very little about what is happening overseas. Help them understand French cultural and professional realities. This disclosure will likely include personal details about your private life, which is quite common in the United States, and is an important part of building relationships.
- When intercultural misunderstandings occur, take care of the problems one by one and coach people individually if necessary. Give them the keys they need to understand the situation, especially from the French perspective, keeping in mind that Americans learn by doing. Stick to practical applications rather than abstract theories.
- Be ready for additional questions when new procedures are introduced. American employees don't mind change, but they are less accepting of authority than the French and readily question new practices that do not seem to be efficient.
- Try incorporating American management techniques that work well and with which you are comfortable in order to find the best compromise between your management practices and those of your host country.
- Americans like—and expect—informal feedback on how they are doing. Offer your subordinates more feedback than you normally would, and reinforce what they are doing well rather than continually pointing out problems. In the United States, positive feedback is an important management technique that builds self-esteem and enables Americans to grow on the job. This concept is quite foreign in France, but in the U.S. it is a key to good performance and enjoyable workplace relationships. It is also important in retaining employees, as people switch jobs and companies quite easily in

the more open American labor market. When you do have to give critical feedback, stress the positive before the negative. Stressing the negative first, or exclusively, will have damaging repercussions and ultimately lead to a loss of respect. An attitude such as "I only want to hear about problems; don't bother me when things are going well" is simply suicidal for a French manager in the United States.

- Familiarize yourself with American appraisal standards, and do not penalize your team by evaluating its members the traditional French way. American appraisals rely on hard and measurable facts and criteria. The appraisal is therefore less subjective than in France. The result may be substantially the same, but you reach your conclusions differently. Maintain personnel files continuously and be ready to document and back up appraisals and personnel decisions—your subordinates will likely do the same. These are especially important if dismissal becomes necessary. Undocumented disciplinary actions can lead to lawsuits. As they say in the United States: create a paper trail.

- Système D and power networks might not work as well in the United States as they do in France. Even though people use their relationships to get things done, organizations tend to be less political. Knowing the right person in the right place might help you open doors, but only occasionally will it be instrumental in getting the contract, accomplishing the task, or solving the problem. Most of the time, you will have to prove your case, and technical competence and sound argument are your best allies. This is particularly true when dealing with the U.S. government and other official agencies, since ties between the corporate world and the administration are far looser and less congenial than they are in France. In fact, the relationship might be adversarial.

NINETEEN

How to Succeed in an Expatriate Assignment: Insights and Guidelines

Key ingredients for successful expatriation and expatriate management are hard to quantify: openness, humility, a good sense of humor, the ability to look at all sides of different peoples and cultures and choose the best in them, flexibility and willingness to compromise, the desire for learning and adventure, a fascination with new ways and different cultures, the ability to cope with ambiguity, an understanding that "my way" is not always "the best way," a willingness to grow and change, and the self-awareness that "I'm not the same any more, even though I will never become 100 percent French or 100 percent American."

Candidates for successful expatriation, therefore, need an additional set of skills and competencies, which may even take precedence over professional competence. Research has shown that operational and functional mastery at home often plays only a minor role in determining the success of an overseas assignment. The personal qualities listed above can make or break an expatriation experience. In fact, the person who is most operationally competent in the home country may be the worst person to send abroad, since he or she may be unable to adapt to new ways of doing things. Candidates for expatriation and their families should have a desire to live abroad and be generally excited and positive about their new adventure.

Because experienced expatriates are a gold mine of information and resources, most of the material in this final chapter comes from our interviews with French and American personnel at RPR. Members of any culture should find much useful information here.

CULTURAL INSIGHTS

For many reasons, French international assignees seem to adapt more easily to the United States than do American assignees to France. Important elements mentioned by RPR expatriates include the following.

Everyday life in the United States is generally seen as more convenient and pleasant than in France. Longer shopping hours, easy friendliness with neighbors, the "customer is always right" attitude, and specialized customer service (home delivery, for example) contrast agreeably with the daily hassles of French life. French expatriates generally enjoy better housing conditions and a lower cost of living, especially if you compare Paris to rural Collegeville, Pennsylvania. However, single American people enjoy Paris' exciting cultural life to the extent that some have even made the decision to live there permanently after their first five-year assignment.

Virtually all French people learn some English in school, and it is a necessity once they cross French borders. Therefore, they usually know at least some English when they arrive in the United States and may be quite fluent. The French language is much more of a barrier for American expatriates. Foreign languages are not an important part of American education. In addition, Americans feel they can always get by in English and often don't see the need to make an effort to learn French.

The French worldview makes it easier for French expats to adapt to a different reality. They travel internationally early on, learn about other cultures, and have a good idea of where France fits in the global political and geographical arena. France is also a much smaller country—a little smaller than Texas—while the size of the United States makes it more comparable to Europe as a whole than to a single European country. French expatriates know things will be different in the U.S., so they are usually aware they can't manage in the workplace as they do at home. They are expecting a significant amount of change and know they will have to adjust to people who might not be familiar with French management practices.

Coming from the "American empire," in an Anglo-Canadian expatriate's words, Americans are less prepared for this adjustment than the French are.

Their education is narrower and more specialized, and through the filters of the media and sports, they constantly receive images of a world "Made in the U.S.A." The World Series actually includes only baseball teams from the United States and Canada, and the New Orleans Saints were considered the 2010 "world" champions of football in a contest involving only American teams. The American media also reflect and reinforce the limited importance of world affairs for most Americans: a broadcast entitled *World News Tonight* frequently includes mostly domestic news. Therefore, Americans often expect things to be more or less the same wherever they go and think their foolproof management practices will work everywhere, since they've proven successful at home. They are taken aback when faced with a different reality.

American management practices give more room for personal development and initiative than those of the French. It is therefore easier for French people to adapt to more employee-oriented management practices than it is for Americans to adjust to more confining and restrictive French conventions. French employees in the United States are often pleased to find less hoarding of information than in France, less emphasis on hierarchy, less rigidity and formality, more empowerment, and more "trying to make employees into minimanagers," in an American expatriate manager's words. Americans are usually faced with the reverse in France, depending on the kind of people they work with, manage, or report to.

French communication patterns and context are confusing for Americans, who are used to more direct ways of expressing themselves and of receiving information. If they do not speak French, they can hardly make sense of the French context and miss many nuances and subtleties that are part of typical nonverbal communication patterns. A lot of information is carried out in nonverbal ways (*non-dits*, or "unspoken"), and the power networks and politics in French corporate settings make it even harder for Americans to adjust. Often, they do not have the keys or frames of reference necessary to decipher all of this coded information, which places them at a disadvantage. Also, they do not realize the importance of building strong relationships based on shared experiences and do not value investing the time needed for such an activity. All of this usually accounts for longer periods of adaptation for American expatriates in France.

Learning the language is vital for American expatriates to succeed in France. Above all, it is a mark of respect toward the people and the culture. According to virtually all American RPR expatriates, it is the only way to become fully integrated and accepted. It is worth making the investment right at the beginning, even though you might struggle for a few months or years. This point cannot be overemphasized.

CULTURAL GUIDELINES

- The expatriate experience might not be as easy as you think. You need to be a strong individual with a solid sense of who you are and an understanding of your capabilities and limitations. If not, do not accept the assignment.
- Expatriation is a three-pronged challenge. You must perform your job functions. You must learn not just a new language but also new ways of thinking—and get the work done at the same time. In addition, your family will need more attention and support than at home.
- The first few months will be very tiring. You will be facing many new situations as well as learning to think and work in a foreign language. This is very demanding intellectually and is very fatiguing.
- Pack an "arrival-shock adjustment bag" and *keep it with you*. In addition to essential paperwork, medication, and other indispensables, have each family member include at least one little thing that can make a hotel room or new apartment feel more like home. An American sitcom character named Mary Richards always had a large wooden *M* hanging in her kitchen. When she moved, she triumphantly hung her *M* in her new kitchen. Figure out what your *M* is and take it with you.
- It is okay to make some sacrifices. Some of your favorite foods or other products may simply be unavailable. On the other hand, you are certainly not trying to achieve martyrdom. If there are certain things that mean "home" to you, and if they can be fairly easily packed or acquired, then by all means continue to use them in your new life.
- Do not try to impose your own culture on the host country. If this is your objective, you would do well to stay home. You are the one who must adapt to the local people and practices. If you cannot be flexible, you will lose in the end and miss many of the benefits of your overseas experience. This doesn't mean you should forget who you are or try to become someone else. It means you have to look at yourself, your job, and your situation in a different light.
- Although terminology such as "host country" and "host-country nationals" is common, try to avoid developing a host/guest mentality about your assignment. Your experience will be more successful and enriching if you participate on an equal footing, as much as possible, in everything that happens around you. You can do this more easily if you avoid casting your colleagues and yourself in canned "host" and "guest" roles.
- Learn the language, immerse yourself in the other culture, respect people for what and who they are, and honor their traditions and customs. Where

appropriate, play down social or professional distance and be part of the team regardless of your hierarchical position.

- Don't get stuck in your own ways, your own limitations. Be open-minded, fair in your judgment, accepting of people, and remember there is usually no right and wrong way of doing things. There are only different ways that need to be understood through communication and dialogue. What is right in one culture might prove wrong or silly in another.

- Do not reduce host-country nationals to stereotypes. Generalizations about people can be useful as a starting point for learning about a culture but should never be the stopping point. Give your colleagues the right to make a mistake and avoid rushing to judgment. Step back, reflect, and try to understand them in their own cultural framework. Your cultural filters and habits might be influencing your reaction.

- Try to see the positive in each of the cultures and blend them synergistically into a hybrid form of management that is neither French nor American but a cocreation of both. In the process, realize that you might need to do some bridging or mediating, opening up both parties to other ways of thinking or behaving. As often as possible, try to find an approach that combines the strengths of both cultures, leading to a more inclusive and contextual solution that all members of your team can own and internalize.

- Share stories and traditions from your culture. Sharing your own culture and traditions helps, no matter where you are. It broadens people's minds and gives them a chance to get to know you in a safe and nonintrusive way. For example, French administrative assistants were pleased when Administrative Professionals' Day was introduced in one French office by an American expatriate. Thanksgiving is another tradition to share. Similarly, French expatriates in the United States could introduce the *galette des rois* (king cake: a cake with a bean or tiny figure hidden inside) by offering a *galette* and a social drink to celebrate Epiphany and the beginning of the year. Check your company's alcohol policy first, though; most American companies forbid alcohol consumption on the premises or even off-site during working hours. Be careful that your cultural traditions do not conflict with those of your host country. Check them out with your local colleagues ahead of time. Before the French knew much about Halloween, an American woman living there organized a Halloween party on October 31st for her French and American colleagues. The French guests were shocked and upset with the humorous American paper skeletons and ghost decorations. The next day, November 1st, is All Saints' Day in France and is marked by solemn prayer and remembrance of the dead. Families traditionally spend part of the day at the local cemetery, cleaning the tombs and graves of their relatives and bringing chrysanthemums. The back-to-back occurrence of the disparate events related to death did not sit well with the French.

- Don't overreact to your new surroundings by becoming a cartoon caricature of your nationality. Conversely, do not try to go "native." It won't work, and the local people will not appreciate it.
- Expect differences and take it as a happy surprise when you find similarities. If you expect similarities, encountering differences can be very painful. To prepare yourself, try repeating the mantra of one successful American expatriate: "It's not right, it's not wrong: it's just different."

A final word: it may sound simplistic, but the initial stage of the intercultural experience—culture shock, if you will—is much more manageable if you view it as a game, a challenge, or an adventure rather than a difficult personal or professional experience. And once you start to figure things out, it becomes enjoyable. Remember also that there are many roads leading to success. When you find the right one, it may not always look like what you expected.

APPENDIX A

The French School System

THE FRENCH CURRICULUM

Age	France	United States
Ecole Maternelle		
3–4	Petite Section (PS)	Preschool
4–5	Moyenne Section (MS)	Prekindergarten
5–6	Grande Section (GS)	Kindergarten
Ecole Primaire		
6–7	11ème = Cours Préparatoire (CP)	1st Grade
7–8	10ème = Cours Elémentaire 1 (CE1)	2nd Grade
8–9	9ème = Cours Elémentaire 2 (CE2)	3rd Grade
9–10	8ème = Cours Moyen 1 (CM1)	4th Grade
10–11	7ème = Cours Moyen 2 (CM2)	5th Grade
Collège		
11–12	6ème = Cycle d'Observation	6th Grade
12–13	5ème = Cycle d'Approfondissement	7th Grade
13–14	4ème = Cycle d'Approfondissement	8th Grade
14–15	3ème = Cycle d'Orientation	9th Grade
Lycée		
15–16	2nde (Seconde)	10th Grade
16–17	1ère (Première)	11th Grade
17–18	T (Terminale)	12th Grade

Source: French embassy in the United States

L'ECOLE MATERNELLE

In light of the French child-rearing practices described in chapter 6, "With the Family," a study of the philosophy of French nursery schools may prove enlightening.

> The Ecole Maternelle is divided into three sections. Its aim is the intellectual development of the child through encouragement of different kinds of activities adjusted to the child's individual needs. The child learns to discover the world around him or her, to make things, to understand and use his or her body, to use language and numbers, and to develop logical thinking, imagination, and creativity. The child learns how to live in society and how to become autonomous. Games play an important pedagogical role, but this does not preclude the importance of rigor and effort. In the last year of Maternelle, activities are geared toward preparing the children for elementary school. The child becomes familiar with the written word. The desire to read and write is developed and the rudiments of both are taught. (Fabre, Whitbeck, and White-Lesieur 1995, 166)

L'ECOLE PRIMAIRE (PRIMARY SCHOOL): COURS PRÉPARATOIRE TO COURS MOYEN 2

Primary school begins at age six, with the *Cours Préparatoire* (CP), followed by *Cours Elementaire* (CE) 1 and 2, and *Cours Moyen* (CM) 1 and 2. These correspond, respectively, to the American first through fifth grades.

> An elementary school education is to ensure the acquisition of the basic tools of knowledge: oral and written expression, reading, and arithmetic. It stimulates the development of the intelligence, artistic sensibility, manual and physical skills, and sporting abilities. It provides a grounding in the plastic and musical arts, and, in conjunction with the family, undertakes the child's moral and civil education. (167)

LE COLLÈGE (MIDDLE SCHOOL): SIXIÈME TO TROISIÈME

French parents look carefully at their child's options for middle school, since graduation from a good *collège* can help a student get into a good *lycée*, improving his or her chances for entry into one of the *grandes écoles*. Of course, not all children are academically inclined, nor do all parents dream of a grande école for their children. But if one is to reach the top levels in French society, preparation starts early.

Children are assigned to middle schools based primarily on where they live, then on which elementary school they attended. Beyond this, a child may be authorized to attend a different (read, better) school if a brother or sister already attended that school, or if the child wants to study a foreign language not offered by the school originally assigned.

Middle school required subjects are French, mathematics, foreign language, history, geography, economics, civics (6ème only), physics (4ème and 3ème only), biology and geology, technology or manual and technical education, art, and physical education. In 4ème and 3ème at least one additional subject is added: a second or third foreign language, Latin, Greek, or industrial technology. The choice of electives plays an important role in the student's chances for admission into a good lycée.

In both the 5ème and 3ème, choices are made about each student's future studies. Recommendations are made by a council composed of the principal, all teachers of a given class, student and parent delegates, an educational adviser, and a guidance counselor. Generally, one of the following three options is recommended:

1. that the student continue his or her studies in either the "cycle long" (regular studies), leading to the first year of lycée, or in the "cycle court" (shortened studies), leading to vocational studies at an L.E.P. (*Lycée d'Enseignement Professionel*, or professional school) at the end of 5ème;
2. that after the age of 16, when school is no longer compulsory, the student enter the working world; or
3. that the student *redouble* (repeat) the year.

The student and his or her family, teachers, and administrators all have input on decisions regarding the child's future. Parents can appeal decisions with which they do not agree. Another cut occurs at the end of 4ème, when qualified students can continue to 3ème, where they follow either an academic or technological track. Those who do not fulfill the requirements to continue in this way are assigned to vocational training; first to a *classe de 3ème d'insertion*, followed by preparation for a C.A.P., (*Certificat d'Aptitude Professionelle*) that takes two years, or the B.E.P., (*Brevet d'Etudes Professionelles*) that takes three years.

Trade guilds dating back to the Middle Ages supervise and administer apprenticeships and other training programs in certain crafts. Membership in these organizations, particularly at the higher levels, is very prestigious, and a family whose ranks include a Master Guildsman is justly proud. Attainment of this rank usually involves years of working under master craftspeople in various regions of the country. This was the original *Tour de France*.

LE LYCÉE: SECONDE TO TERMINALE AND "LE BAC"

In their first year of lycée, all students study the same core curriculum of mathematics, French, history and geography, first foreign language, physics and chemistry, biology and geology, and physical education. Mandatory and optional electives are added, depending on the student's abilities and interests. The total student hours in *seconde* are twenty-nine to thirty-two per week, not including a substantial amount of homework.

Preparation for the rigorous *baccalauréat* exam begins in earnest in *première*. At the end of 2nde, students choose which type of *bac* exam to work toward, which in essence determines their curriculum for the last two years of high school and most likely their choice of undergraduate study. The most important academic options are the general sections: *littéraire* (Bac L), *scientifique* (Bac S), and *économique et social* (Bac ES). Each of these broad categories is divided into profiles that further focus the student's studies.

Terminale, the final year of secondary school, is notoriously demanding as students prepare for the bac. Families make every effort to support a child aiming for the bac. They may provide extra help at home or pay for additional tutoring or whatever else might give their child an edge. It is a comprehensive, all-or-nothing exam. Students who do not pass on the first try may retake the exam, but you cannot pass some parts and fail others, although individual subject grades are weighted according to their importance in the student's bac selection.

Regardless of the section and profile chosen, all students working toward the Bac L, S, or ES study philosophy in their final year of high school. This reflects the importance French culture places on abstract reasoning, logic, and ideas for their own sake. Students in their final year of secondary school are expected to provide cogent, well-reasoned essays (spelling and grammar definitely count) in response to such questions as "Can we consider nonviolence another form of violence?" "Do ethical problems have perfect solutions?" and "How can we determine the gravity of a mistake?"

Contrast this with exam questions from an American university Philosophy 101 exam: "What was Nietzsche's worldview?" "What was Sartre's view on morality?" and "What is Kant's 'imperative category'?" For the French, the study of philosophy is vital to a person's intellectual and moral development. The author of a study guide for the bac philosophy paper notes, "Philosophy leads you to continuously question your own ready-made ideas, not in order to systematically destroy them, but to make you understand why you think that way" (Marcus 1994, 18).

Major reforms of the structure and philosophy of the bac were instituted in 1992. A huge range of options now exists, and the changes are so numerous and so far-reaching that regular meetings among parents, teachers, and administrators are more important than ever. A child's progress is reviewed on a regular basis and corrections and adjustments are made as necessary. Parents can also request meetings with their child's teachers, the *censeur* (vice principal), or the *proviseur* (principal).

While French students specialize much earlier than their American counterparts, the quality of the general education they receive is extremely high. A French literary scholar, for example, has a solid grasp of a wide range of scientific disciplines, while a French engineer can carry on an intelligent conversation about philosophy. Since students who pass the bac already have a thorough grounding in a wide range of subjects, they do not need to acquire "general ed" at the university level; they move directly into courses in their major field of study.

GRADE EQUIVALENCIES BETWEEN FRANCE AND THE U.S.

France	U.S.
19–20	A+
17–18	A
16	A-
15	B+
13–14	B
12	B-
11	C+
10	C
9	C-
7–8	D+
6	D
5	D-
0–4	F

In general, school grades in France are lower than in the United States. Even though a child's work may be excellent, French teachers might not want to give the child the impression that she has reached her maximum potential; by French standards, there is (almost) always room for improvement and French parents, upon hearing their child's grade, will often stress the fact that there is indeed room for improvement: *Tu peux mieux faire, non?* (You can do better, no?)

A grade of A+ or even A++ has no reason for existence in the French system; it would mean, in a French literature class, that the student is greater than Baudelaire or Alexandre Dumas—*du jamais vu à un si jeune âge* (never seen at such a young age).

The passing grade is 10, and it often means the student is safe. Getting 10 as an average grade on the bac means the student passes. He or she doesn't get any honors but can continue on to university studies.

The French math program, at all levels of the curriculum and especially in high school, is extremely demanding and is far more theoretical and less practical in orientation than normal or advanced placement math programs in U.S. high schools. Remember that abilities in math determine a lot of what the French student will be able to choose in terms of career options. Doors that close very late in the U.S., for instance, when a student chooses his or her major, may close early on in France, around the age of fourteen or fifteen, when it is time to decide what section of a lycée to enroll in.

These comments are offered as general guidelines, knowing that the philosophy of the grading system and the meaning of the grades are hardly comparable between the two countries.

Nuts and Bolts of Social Etiquette in France

BUSINESS ENTERTAINING AND DINING ETIQUETTE

For a business lunch or dinner in a restaurant, the person who does the inviting pays the bill as discreetly as possible—you might excuse yourself for a moment to slip your credit card to the waiter and sign the receipt so that nothing suggesting payment is ever brought to the table. Note that tip (*service compris;* usually around 15 percent) and the sales tax are included in the bill.

A French meal is very structured and sequentially organized. Follow the pace and try to eat at least a little of everything, even if you don't like it. When going out for a social meal with friends, don't ever work out each person's share on a paper napkin or with a calculator on the table. One person or couple may pay the entire check with the understanding that someone else will pick up the tab the next time. Even if it's clear someone else is paying, it is polite to object by saying something like, "No, no, I'll get it!" until you are definitively overruled. Alternatively, the bill may be divided evenly by the number of diners. If one member of the group is being treated—a birthday or farewell dinner, for example—the others in the party will share the cost among themselves. And never ask for a doggy bag, your friends or colleagues may worry that you are penniless or starving.

Don't put your hands under the table or your elbows on the table, and keep your left hand on the table while you eat. French people cut and eat their meat with the fork in the left hand and the knife in the right without switching cutlery from hand to hand. French table manners are sometimes difficult for Americans, but don't worry too much about using utensils "continental style." Neatness, elegance, and conversation skills are more important than which hand holds the knife.

Coffee is never drunk with a meal but comes afterward, which means a waiter in a restaurant will never offer you coffee with your meal, and you will never see a coffee cup next to your plate on the table; it comes at the end with the coffee. If you're not drinking wine, a bottle of water is always available: *eau minérale ou gazeuse*, mineral or sparkling water. Always use the bigger glass for water.

Cheese is considered a real course, but it is not always served in restaurants. When it is, it is sometimes offered in lieu of a dessert, meaning you may have a choice of cheese or dessert (or both if you're still hungry). If you like it, take two or three kinds, mild ones preferably. When presented with a full cheese to cut from, be careful to cut your portion off so that the shape of the large piece of cheese is maintained. A round, flat cheese such as a camembert is cut into slices like a pie. In fact, what Americans recognize as a pie chart is a *camembert* chart in France.

HOST AND GUEST EXPECTATIONS

If you are a guest in someone's home, it's a good idea to bring something for the hostess; she is the queen of the house (*la maîtresse de maison*). Flowers or plants are always appreciated. The number, color, and type of flowers have very specific meanings. One dozen *pink* roses are a safe choice to thank your hostess. Never give chrysanthemums under any circumstances; they are for funerals and grave sites only. Bring gifts for the children if you know them: American candies like Jelly Bellies, T-shirts with the name of your town or state (but not company, except entertainment companies like Disney), or the latest children's and teenagers' gadgets from the United States.

It's a good idea to make some effort at the language and to ask questions about it. Despite their reputation of being intolerant with non-Francophone tourists, in social settings French people who know you are usually delighted to encourage you—and especially to correct you!

Do not "make yourself at home" or "help yourself." French hosts do not normally show guests around the house. Do not wander around if you need something—ask for it and don't follow the person who goes into another room to get it for you. Closed doors in a private home mean no admittance, except for the toilet (*les toilettes, les W.C.*), which may be in a separate room from the bathroom, so be precise when you ask for directions. Do not use the English word *bathroom* because it is confusing for the French. A bathroom (*salle de bains*) is a room where you wash yourself or take a bath. To be on the safe side, use the word *toilettes*. It is also a good idea to knock on the door of the toilet before you open it.

Depending on the occasion and the setting, you may not hear a "go ahead and sit where you like." Your hostess will have spent time and effort organizing the seating plan so that interesting juxtapositions are made. As guests are called to the table, stand back a bit and wait to be placed. Take advantage of your hostess' thoughtfulness by getting to know the dining companions she has chosen for you.

A French hostess does not expect her guests to lend a hand in the kitchen or with setting or clearing the table. The kitchen is her private area, so don't just wander in there. If you are asked to help out, consider it a sign of admittance into the family. Tell your host or hostess ahead of time if you have a problem with a specific food—a violent allergy is acceptable. People will understand your problem and it is always better than not at least sampling the food.

Accept wine in your glass but be aware that a good host keeps his or her guest's glass full, so adjust your sips accordingly. If you object to alcohol or prefer not to drink, allude to liver problems and be prepared for solicitous offers of various liver-friendly mineral waters.

TOPICS OF CONVERSATION

Avoid money and religion at all costs. They are very private topics. Talk about politics only if you are an expert or need an explanation about a specific event—you can always ask questions and expect a lively exchange of ideas.

Beware of violating or invading the privacy of your French host when talking about family and other personal matters. Safe conversation topics are life in the United States compared with France, any kind of information related to the business setting, sports, food, historical and cultural topics, and personal experiences traveling abroad and in France. French people like to talk about their or their parents' roots, as those in large cities often relocate for study or work purposes. Other good topics are typically American art forms (e.g., jazz or patchwork quilts), important American creative and performing artists, or American historical and literary sites. Know your own country and its culture—the French will generally have lots of questions.

Your conversational skills will mark you as a cultivated or uncultivated person, so keep informed on current events, literary and art news, and so on. Be prepared to discuss these things intelligently, or at least be able to ask intelligent questions.

Knowing a little French history helps, since it is so important to the French. If you need a detailed explanation of any monument, battle, invasion, or French victory or defeat, people will usually come to your rescue. Acknowledge their help gratefully and ask follow-up questions.

There is a big difference between asking for information or exchanging ideas about a certain topic and bluntly passing judgment on it. Important differences exist, for example, between diversity *à la française* and *à l'américaine*, as reflected in French labor laws and American affirmative action practices. Telling French people categorically that they should manage their diversity issues in the American way reflects a lack of knowledge of and respect for your hosts' culture. An open discussion, comparing and contrasting American and French situations and practices, is a much better way to go about a conversation. Similarly, if your French friends start talking enthusiastically about the thirty-five-hour workweek, listen to what they have to say. You are certainly entitled to disagree with them and to express your views, but a comment like "Europeans already get too much time off" is not a good way to get a dialogue going.

BUSINESS DRESS

How you dress mostly depends on the purpose of your meeting or presentation. It may be more formal the first day of your visit and casual the other days, going from a business suit to a more creative ensemble. Err on the side of formality to begin with. You can always dress more casually later.

A skirt and top or dress is fine for a woman. Frenchwomen do not generally wear stockings or pantyhose in the summer. A dark blue suit might be more appropriate for a board meeting or a meeting with important people. Pants are also accepted if they fit with the rest of the attire. Men should wear a business suit initially and, depending on circumstances, take a more casual outfit for later, for example, a blazer and trousers.

There is generally no "dress-down" practice in France, but men may take off their ties, depending on the setting. Things are changing, though, and depending on the industry and geographic location, you may see your French colleagues in jeans or similarly casual outfits on a routine basis. In some trendy professions like advertising and public relations, or in certain departments like programming, dress can be quite original.

French people do not always consider it important to wear something different every day of the week. Clothing is relatively expensive and they prefer a small number of quality items to many cheaper ones. Don't be surprised to see someone wear the same outfit two days in a row.

FINAL ADVICE

Although the French have a smaller spatial bubble than Americans, they don't like someone touching them unless they know that person well. Don't put your hand on someone's arm or shoulder and don't do any friendly backslapping or shoulder punching.

Rushing things and neglecting the human side of a deal or project won't get you far in France. Be patient and learn to appreciate the small wonders that French life has to offer. Quality of time as a whole (what the French call *qualité de vie*), and not only quality of work time, is of great importance. Doing something you enjoy is a French way of living.

Don't be overenthusiastic and use superlatives like "great," "wonderful," or "terrific." They are not popular in France and sound insincere. An overly positive or rosy outlook might strike the French as arrogant or hypocritical. *"Un chat est un chat"* ("A cat is a cat"), the French say, meaning "call a spade a spade" in English, and the French do not sugarcoat or mince words.

Avoid the aggressive, hard-sell approach. The French will not be impressed when you tell them that your American know-how is just what they need to get them out of the mess they are in. They might not agree that they are in a mess at all. The typical American self-confident, "sell yourself" approach strikes the French as arrogant and abrasive.

The French generally like people with personality, those who do not simply follow the herd and are able to "bring some water to the mill." The French sometimes regard consistency as boring, and being boring is one of the worst sins.

Finally, acknowledge the cultural importance of food and wine, and understand the primary purpose of a French meal: to get to know each other and enjoy a good conversation. A three-hour business lunch is the French equivalent of a two-day ropes adventure team-building program, even if you do not discuss business. You will survive (and possibly even enjoy) the experience and may learn some important information about your French counterparts, either in a business or a social setting.

Sojourning: Start with an Empty Suitcase

Traveling or living abroad can be a life-changing enlightenment or a confirmation of your very worst fears and prejudices.

When you arrive in a new country, you bring along not just a ratty backpack or designer luggage but also something called "cultural baggage"—your own set of assumptions, values, beliefs, and certainties. Although they take up no space in your suitcase, they can be a heavy burden, slowing you down as you explore new territories. But don't worry. If you can't lighten them up before arrival, they will probably become less cumbersome during your trip through the process of increasing cultural self-awareness prompted by the mirroring of the other culture.

However you choose to journey, whatever your sojourn's length, you stand to gain the most by trying to empty the cultural baggage from your mental suitcase. See not only what you expected to see; also be open to anything and everything that comes your way. All experiences can be enriching; often the experience is its own reward. On the other hand, when everything around you is going to hell in a hand basket, remind yourself that—assuming you live through it—this will make a heck of a story to tell the folks back home.

The best advice usually comes from those who have gone before you and have returned changed in some fundamental ways. We have gathered here some of the best quotations from all kinds of sojourners—famous, infamous, and unknown.

Au revoir et bon voyage!

The tourist takes his culture with him; the traveler leaves his behind.

—Anonymous

A broad, wholesome, charitable view of men and things cannot be acquired by vegetating in one little corner of the world all one's lifetime.

—Mark Twain

Everywhere I've been I've found wisdom. In every country I've visited I've found caring and friendship. In the people of every culture I've known I've found humor. And every experience was unique.

—Anonymous

Why do the wrong people travel, travel, travel
While the right people stay at home?
What compulsion compels them
And who the hell tells them
To drag their cans to Zanzibar
Instead of staying quietly in Omaha?

—Noël Coward

Charlie? Well, he's been all over fifteen countries. He's brought back half of them in paintings, sculptures and the like. You know something, young fella? I don't think he talked to a single human being in any of those countries. He just looked at things.

—Jed Leland on Charles Foster Kane, *Citizen Kane*

To travel is to discover that everyone is wrong about other countries.

—Aldous Huxley

To feel at home, stay at home. A foreign country is not designed to make you comfortable. It's designed to make its own people comfortable.

—Clifton Fadiman

There are some things one can only achieve by a deliberate leap in the opposite direction. One has to go abroad in order to find the home one has lost.

—Franz Kafka

I imagine that if we should meet we would stand clear in the gaze of each other.

—Anonymous

Greetings! I am pleased
To see that we are different.
May we together become greater
Than the sum of both of us.

—Vulcan Greeting, *Star Trek*

In America, everything goes and nothing matters. While in Europe, nothing goes and everything matters.

—Philip Roth

Europe has what we do not have yet, a sense of the mysterious and inexorable limits of life, a sense, in a word, of tragedy. And we [Americans] have what they sorely need: a sense of life's possibilities.

—James Baldwin

I grew up in Iowa and I knew what to do with butter: you put it on roastin' ears, pancakes, and popcorn. Then I went to France and saw a Frenchman put butter on radishes. I waited for the Cosmic Revenge—for the Eiffel Tower to topple, the Seine to sizzle, or the grape to wither on the vine. But that Frenchman put butter on his radishes, and the Gallic universe continued unperturbed. I realized then something I hadn't learned in five years of language study: not only was speaking in French different from speaking in English, but buttering in French was different from buttering in English. And that was the beginning of real cross-cultural understanding.

—Genelle Morain

J'ai deux amours: mon pays et Paris! I have two loves: my country and Paris!

—Josephine Baker

Lunch kills half of Paris, supper the other half.

—Montesquieu

Good Americans, when they die, go to Paris.

—Thomas Gold Appleton

Everything ends this way in France—everything. Weddings, christenings, duels, burials, swindlings, diplomatic affairs—everything is a pretext for a good dinner.

—Jean Anouilh

In the United States there is more space where nobody is than where anybody is. That's what makes America what it is.

—Gertrude Stein

Whoever wants to know the hearts and minds of America had better learn baseball.

—Jacques Barzun

"Take it easy, darling," he would say. "We've got to be absorbed into these customs. We're still too tough to be ingested quickly, but we've got to try and soften ourselves. We've got to yield."

—From *The Enemy in the Blanket* by Anthony Burgess

I really don't know what happens next—one so seldom does.

—E. M. Forster

Homesickness is . . . absolutely nothing. Fifty percent of the people in the world are homesick all the time. . . . You don't really long for another country. You long for something in yourself that you don't have, or haven't been able to find.

—John Cheever

And yet, there is only
One great thing,
The only thing:
To live to see in huts and on journeys
The great day that dawns,
And the light that fills the world!

—Inuit poem

So the journey is over and I am back again where I started, richer by much experience and poorer by many exploded convictions, many perished certainties. For convictions and certainties are too often the concomitants of ignorance. Those who like to feel they are always right and who attach a high importance to their own opinions should stay at home. When one is traveling, convictions are mislaid as easily as spectacles; but unlike spectacles, they are not easily replaced.

—Aldous Huxley

New Country

I have already moved to another country.
Already think in a new language.
Borders crossed and boundaries now much expanded.
I have caught a glimpse of how big life is
and how much bigger I could be.
Capacity threshold so much larger than I realized.
How to translate this to the motherland?
I loved there authentically.
Still do.
But I think in a new tongue now
and must claim on this new land the life that is truly mine.

—Monica Pohlmann

REFERENCES

Algan, Yann and Pierre Cahuc. 2007. *La société de défiance : Comment le modèle social français s'autodétruit?* Paris: Rue d'Ulm.

Amado, Gilles, Claude Faucheux, and André Laurent. 1989. *Changement Organisationnel et Réalités Culturelles–Contrastes Franco-Américains.* Paris: Centre HEC-ISA.

André, Christophe. 2006. *Imparfaits, libres et heureux: Pratiques de l'estime de soi.* Paris: Editions Odile Jacob.

———. 2009. *Les états d'âme : Un apprentissage de la sérénité.* Paris: Editions Odile Jacob.

Ardagh, John. 1981. *The New France: A Society in Transition 1945–1977.* Pelican Books.

Asselin, Gilles. 1994. "Work: Its Meaning and Centrality among French and American Workers." Master's thesis, University of Wisconsin-Oshkosh.

Axtell, Roger E. 1994. *The Do's and Taboos of International Trade: A Small Business Primer.* New York: John Wiley & Sons.

Badinter, Elisabeth. 1995. "The Women/Men Relationship in France and the U.S." Lecture attended by the authors. New York University.

Barzini, Luigi. 1983. *The Europeans.* London: Penguin Group.

Baumard, Maryline. 2009. "Les étudiants français toujours aussi nuls en anglais." *Le Monde,* 25 August.

Baumard, Maryline. 2010. Ecole : l'échec du modèle français d'égalité des chances. *Le Monde,* 12 February. www.lemonde.fr/societe/article/2010/02/11/ecole-l-echec-du-modele-francais-d-egalite-des-chances_1304257_3224.html

Browning, E. S., and Michael J. McCarthy. 1991. "Coke Reassigns Aggressive Head of French Unit." *Wall Street Journal,* 13 February.

Bull Worldwide Information Systems. 1992. *Cultural Diversity: At the Heart of Bull*. Yarmouth, ME: Intercultural Press. Videocassette.

Business & Legal Reports. 1996. *Pocket Guide to Preventing Sexual Harassment*. Booklet.

Carroll, Raymonde. 1987. *Cultural Misunderstandings: The French-American Experience*. Translated by Carol Volk. Chicago: University of Chicago Press.

Carter, Charla. 1996. "On the Cutting Edge." *France Magazine*, Fall, 34.

Chevalier, Francois and Mansuy, Anne. 2009. *Une photographie du marché du travail en 2008: Résultats de l'enquête Emploi*. INSEE. www.insee.fr/fr/themes/document.asp?ref_id=ip1272

Croze, Aurélie, and Gilbert Croze. 2008. *Les 12 lois incontournables du marché américain: Réussir aux Etats-Unis*. Paris: Gaulino.

Dale, Reginald. 1998. "In a French Airport, a Pointed Lesson." *International Herald Tribune*, 9 January.

de Beauvoir, Simone. 1949. *Le deuxième sexe*. Paris: Editions Gallimard.

de Chikoff, Irina. 2000. "Les Basques réclament leur département." *France-Amérique* 1471, 19 août–1er septembre.

de Gramont, Sanche. 1969. *The French: Portrait of a People*. New York: Bantam Books.

Dicks, Dianne, ed. 1995. *Breaking Convention with Intercultural Romances*. Freedom, CA: Crossing Press.

Economist. 1998. "How Racist Is France?" 18 July, 43.

———. 1995. "France's Bathroom Blues." 29 November, 56.

———. 1991. "A Question of Culture." 7 December, 64.

Fabre, Kathryn, Tara Whitbeck, and Carolyn White-Lesieur, eds. 1995. *AAWE Guide to Education*. 4th ed. Paris: AAWE.

Faulkner, William. 1994. In *Novels 1942–1954: Requiem for a Nun*, edited by Joseph Blotner and Noel Polk. New York: Library Classics of the United States.

Ferry, Luc. 1995. "Descartes, père fondateur de la science moderne?" *Le Point*, 3 June, 59.

France 2 Website (www.france2.fr.). 1998. "Resultats pour le baccalaureat." 14 July. No longer accessible.

———. 1998. "The World Cup Victory." 13 July. No longer accessible.

Giroud, Françoise, and Bernard-Henri Lévy. 1993. *Les hommes et les femmes*. Paris: Le Grand Livre du Mois.

Grearson, Jessie C., and Laureen B. Smith, eds. 1995. *Swaying: Essays on Intercultural Love*. Iowa City: University of Iowa Press.

Guillet, Alexandra. 2009. "Education—Dictée: Naux Enphan Son Nulle!" TF1 website, January 29. http://lci.tf1.fr/france/societe/2009-01/dictee-nos-enfants-sont-nuls-4888894.html

Hall, Edward. T. 1992. *An Anthropology of Everyday Life*. New York: Anchor Doubleday.

Hall, Edward T., and Mildred Reed Hall. 1990. *Understanding Cultural Differences: Germans, French, and Americans*. Yarmouth, ME: Intercultural Press.

Hermary-Vieille, Catherine, and Michelle Sarde. 1997. *Le Salon de Conversation*. Paris: Editions Jean-Claude Lattès.

Hill, Richard. 1994. *Euromanagers and Martians: The Business Cultures of Europe's Trading Nations*. Brussels: Europublications.

―――. 1992. *We Europeans*. Brussels: Europublications.

Hohenadel, Kristin. 1998. "In an Old House in Paris." *Los Angeles Times*, 18 January.

Isambert. 1906. "Letters Patent Establishing the French Academy in 1635." Recueil général des anciennes lois françaises. In *Readings in European History*, vol. 2, edited by J. H. Robinson, 180–83. Boston: Ginn.

Jenkins-Ghiglione, Margaret, Janis Takahashi-Kaas, and Sallie Wise-Chaballier, eds. 2006. *Guide to Education in France: A Comprehensive Guide to Educating English Speaking Children in France*. Seventh edition. Paris: AAWE.

Kohls, L. Robert. 1988. *The Values Americans Live By*. Duncanville, TX: Adult Learning Systems.

Kuisel, Richard. 1997. *Seducing the French: The Dilemma of Americanization*. Berkeley: University of California Press.

Lacorne, Denis. 1998. "Multicultural Identities: France and the United States." Paper presented at the Institute of French Studies Colloquium. La Maison Française, New York University, 11 November.

Lavin, Douglas. 1996. "European Consumers Decide High-Tech Is a Low Priority." *Wall Street Journal*, 27 December.

Lelord, François, and Christophe André. 1999. *L'estime de soi: S'aimer pour mieux vivre avec les autres*. Paris: Editions Odile Jacob.

Lutz, Natalie. 2010. *French and American Perceptions of Arrogance in the Other: A comparison of French and American values and implicit norms*. VDM Verlag Dr. Müller.

Marcus, Elena. 1994. "Doing It the French Way." *Educational Vision* 2, no. 2, 18.

Marnham, Patrick. 1994. *Crime and the Académie Française: Dispatches from Paris*. Harmondsworth, UK: Penguin Books.

Maurin, Eric. 2009. *La Peur du Déclassement. Une sociologie des récessions*. Seuil.

McGoldrick, M., J. Giordano and N. Garcia-Preto. 2005. *Ethnicity and Family Therapy*. Third Edition. New York: Guilford Press.

Mercil, Michael C. 1984. "How to Learn About a New Culture." In *Planning and Conducting Re-Entry/Transition Workshops*, edited by Youth for Understanding.

Moran, Robert T., Harris, Philip R. and Moran Sarah V. 2007. *Managing Cultural Differences, Seventh Edition: Global Leadership Strategies for the 21st Century*. Butterworth-Heinemann.

Nadeau, Jean-Benoît, and Julie Barlow. 2006. *The Story of French*. New York: St. Martin's Griffin.

Orleman, Paul. 1992. "The Global Corporation: Managing across Cultures." Master's thesis, University of Pennsylvania, Philadelphia.

Orleman, Paul, and Jeff Cohen. 1995. "What Has RPR Learned and What Actions Has RPR Taken to Manage Cultural Differences." Report, The Pennsylvania State University, Collegeville.

Peyrefitte, Alain. 1976. The Trouble with France. New York: New York University Press.

Peyrefitte, Alain. 2005. La société de confiance : Essais sur les origines du développement. Odile Jacob.

Quibell, Allyson. 1995. "Les Femmes: Doing Business in France." France Today, October/November, 8.

TF1 website. 2009. Travail dominical—Les députés adoptent le texte. July 15. http://tf1.lci.fr/infos/france/politique/0,,4472058,00-apres-la-bataille-parlementaire-le-vote-.html

TF1 website. 2009. Toulouse—"Le professeur désobéissant sera puni." July 24. http://tf1.lci.fr/infos/france/societe/0,,4496635,00-le-professeur-desobeissant-sera-puni-.html

TF1 website. 2009. DSK présente ses excuses à tout le monde. October 20. http://tf1.lci.fr/infos/monde/institutions/0,,4130741,00-dsk-presente-ses-excuses-a-tout-le-monde-.html

TF1 website. 2010. "Voile intégral : à Sarkozy et au gouvernement le dernier mot." January 30. http://lci.tf1.fr/politique/2010-01/voile-integral-a-sarkozy-et-au-gouvernement-le-dernier-mot-5664845.html

TF1 website. 2010. La pire récession depuis l'après guerre. Video. February 12. http://videos.tf1.fr/jt-we/la-pire-recession-depuis-l-apres-guerre-5690957.html

Revel, Jean-François. 1995. "Descartes, c'est la France, hélas!" *Le Point*, 3 June, 63.

Rifkind, Hugo. 2008. "Supersize . . . moi? How the French learnt to love McDonald's." *The Times*, August 18.

Romano, Dugan. 2008. *Intercultural Marriage: Promises and Pitfalls*. Third edition. Boston, MA: Nicholas Brealey/Intercultural Press.

Rosenblatt, Roger. 1988. "American Best: Variety, Optimism, Bounty, Talent: An Accounting." *Time*, Special issue, 16 June, 24–25.

Rosenblum, Mort. 1988. *Mission to Civilize: The French Way*. New York: Anchor Press Doubleday.

Simons, George. 1996. Electronic conversation with George Simons, 16 November.

Steinmetz, Greg, and Gregory L. White. 1998. "Chrysler Pay Draws Fire Overseas." *Wall Street Journal*, 26 May.

Stewart, Edward C., and Milton J. Bennett. 1991. *American Cultural Patterns: A Cross-Cultural Perspective*. Rev. ed. Yarmouth, ME: Intercultural Press.

Valente, Judith. 1994. "The Land of Cuisine Besieged by 'Le Big Mac.'" *Wall Street Journal*, 25 May.

Van Eeckhout, Laetitia. 2009. Relance du CV anonyme, outil de lutte contre la discrimination à l'embauche. Le Monde. 4 November. www.lemonde .fr/societe/article/2009/11/03/relance-du-cv-anonyme-outil-de-lutte-contre-la-discrimination-a-l-embauche_1261942_3224.html

Virard, Marie-Paule. 2006. L'autorité en crise. *Enjeux*. March.

Vitiello-Yewell, Joëlle, and Claire Nacher. 1998. *La Vie aux Etats-Unis*. Paris: Editions Solar.

Wallace, Tim. 1999. Electronic conversation with Tim Wallace, 27 September.

Weisman, Kathie. 2006. "For some French designers, business is better the American way." *International Herald Tribune*, October 5.

Wolf, Martin. 2005. *Why Globalization Works*. 2nd ed. New Haven, CT: Yale University Press.

Wylie, Laurence. 1981. "The Civilization Course." In *Société et culture de la France contemporaine*, edited by Georges Santoni. Albany: State University of New York Press.

Wylie, Laurence, and Jean-François Brière. 1995. *Les Français*. Second edition. Englewood Cliffs, NJ: Prentice-Hall.

ADDITIONAL READINGS

Alston, Jon, Melanie Hawthorne, and Sylvie Saillet. 2003. *A Practical Guide to French Business*. New York: Writers Club Press.

Althen, Gary. 2002. *American Ways: A Guide for Foreigners in the United States*, Second edition. Yarmouth, ME: Intercultural Press.

Archdeacon, Thomas J. 1983. *Becoming American: An Ethnic History*. New York: The Free Press.

Ardagh, John. 1990. *France Today*. Harmondsworth, UK: Penguin Books.

———. 1999. *France in the New Century: Portrait of a Changing Society*. Harmondsworth, UK: Penguin Books.

Asitimbay, Diane. 2009. What's Up, America? A Foreigner's Guide to Understanding Americans. Second Edition. Culture Link Press.

Austin, Clyde N. 1994. *Cross-Cultural Re-Entry: A Book of Readings*. Abilene, TX: Abilene Christian University.

Behr, Edward. 1998. *Une Amérique qui fait peur*. Paris: Editions Plon.

Bernstein, Richard. 1990. *Fragile Glory: A Portrait of France and the French*. New York: Alfred A. Knopf.

Blonsky, Marshall. 1992. *American Mythologies*. New York: Oxford University Press.

Blow, Robert, ed. 1990. *Abroad in America: Literary Discoveries of the New World from the Past 500 Years*. New York: Continuum.

Boorstein, Daniel. 1995. *Histoire des Américains*. Paris: Editions Robert Laffont.

Brierley, William, Colin Gordon, Collin Randelsome, Kevin Bruton, and Peter King. 1993. *Business Cultures in Europe*. Oxford: Butterworth Heinemann.

Brillat-Savarin, Jean-Anthelme. 1988. *The Philosopher in the Kitchen*. Harmondsworth, UK: Penguin Books.

Butler, Jill. 1994. *Paintbrush in Paris: The Artistic Adventures of an American Cat in Paris*. New York: Workman.

Camber Porter, Melinda. 1993. *Through Parisian Eyes: Reflections on Contemporary French Arts and Culture*. New York: Da Capo Press.

Carles, Emilie. 1992. *A Life of Her Own: The Transformation of a Countrywoman in Twentieth-Century France*. New York: Penguin Books.

Clarke, Stephen. 2004. *A Year in the Merde*. New York: Bloomsbury.

Cogan, Charles. 2003 *French Negotiating Behavior: Dealing with La Grande Nation*. Washington D.C.: U.S. Institute of Peace Press.

Corbett, James. 1994. *Through French Windows*. Ann Arbor, MI: University of Michigan Press.

Corbin, Alain. 1988. *The Foul and the Fragrant: Odor and the French Social Imagination*. Translated by Mirian L. Kochan. Cambridge, MA: Harvard University Press.

Crossman, Sylvie, and Edouard Fenwick. 1990. *California: Le Nouvel Age*. Paris: Editions du Seuil.

Darnton, Robert. 1990. *The Kiss of Lamourette: Reflections in Cultural History*. London: Faber and Faber.

Descartes, René. 1986. *A Discourse on Method: Meditations and Principles*. London: J. M. Dent and Sons.

———. 1934. *Discours de la Méthode*. Paris: Librairie Larousse.

de Tissot, Olivier and Roger Blachon. 1996. *Le Livre de Tous les Français*. Paris: Gallimard.

DeVita, Philip R., and James D. Armstrong, eds. 2010. *Distant Mirrors: America as a Foreign Culture*. Fourth Edition. Belmont, CA: Wadsworth Publishing Company.

d'Iribarne, Phillipe. 1989. *La Logique de l'Honneur*. Paris: Editions du Seuil.

Fenby, Jonathan. 2010. *France on the Brink: A Great Civilization Faces a New Century*. New York: Arcade Publishing.

Fraser, Matthew. 1994. "How France Grooms Its Elite." *The Globe and Mail*, 13 June.

Gannon, Martin J. 1994. *Understanding Global Cultures: Metaphorical Journeys through 17 Cultures*. Thousand Oaks, CA: Sage.

Garreau, Joel. 1989. *The Nine Nations of North America*. New York: Avon Books.

Gauthey, Franck. 1989–1990. "Universalisme et Particularismes dans les Approches du Management." *Intercultures* 8: 81–90.

Gay, William C. 1996. *Living in the U.S.A.* 5th ed. Yarmouth, ME: Intercultural Press.

Gillan, Maria M., Jennifer Gillan, and Marna M. Gillan, eds. 1994. *Unsettling America: An Anthology of Contemporary Multicultural Poetry.* Harmondsworth, UK: Penguin Books.

Goodstein, L. D. 1981. "Commentary: Do American Theories Apply Abroad?" *Organizational Dynamics*, 49–62.

Gopnik, Adam. 1996. "The First Frenchman." *New Yorker*, 7 October, 44–53.

———. 1996. "The Virtual Bishop." *New Yorker*, 18 March, 59–63.

———. 2001. *Paris to the Moon.* New York: Random House Trade Paperbacks.

Griffin, Rene. 2004. *Descartes* (Collector's Library Essential Thinkers). Barnes & Noble.

Grizell, R. 1992. *A White House in Gascony: Escape to the Old French South.* London: Victor Gollancz.

Gruère, Jean-Pierre. 1990. "Réflexions d'un Français sur l'application de méthodes pédagogiques américaines dans un contexte 'latin.'" *Intercultures* 11: 13–20.

Hall, Edward T. 1983. *The Dance of Life: The Other Dimension of Time.* New York: Anchor Books/Doubleday.

———. 1976. *Beyond Culture.* Reprint, New York: Anchor Books/Doubleday, 1981.

———. 1966. *The Hidden Dimension.* Reprint, New York: Anchor Books/Doubleday, 1982.

———. 1959. *The Silent Language.* Reprint, New York: Anchor Books/Doubleday, 1981.

Hoffman, Eva. 1989. *Lost in Translation: Life in a New Language.* New York: E. P. Dutton.

Hofstede, Geert. 1997. *Culture's Consequences: International Differences in Work-Related Values.* Newbury Park: Sage Publications.

———. 1980. "Motivation, Leadership, and Organization: Do American Theories Apply Abroad?" *Organizational Dynamics*: 42–63.

Jarvis, John. 1995. "Euro Disneyland Paris Cultural Research Project." Research Report no. 2. Pittsburgh: Robert Morris College, 16 August.

Jeambar, Denis. 1994. "Hommes politiques: où s'arrête leur vie privée." *Le Point.* 5 novembre, 36–44.

Kalb, Rosalind, and Penelope Welch. 2007. *Moving Your Family Overseas.* National Book Network.

Kaplan, Alice. 1994. *French Lessons: A Memoir*. Chicago: University of Chicago Press.

Kaspi, André. 2002. Les Américains. Tome 1 : Naissance et essor des Etats-Unis, 1607–1945. Paris: Seuil.

Kaspi, André. 2008. Les Américains. Tome 2 : Les Etats-Unis de 1945 à nos jours. Paris: Seuil.

Kedward, Rod. 2006. *France and the French: A Modern History*. Woodstock NY: The Overlook Press.

Kenna, Peggy, and Sondra Lacy. 1994. *Business France: A Practical Guide to Understanding French Business Culture*. Lincolnwood, IL: Passport Books.

Kohls, L. Robert. 1996. *Survival Kit for Overseas Living: For Americans Planning to Live and Work Abroad*. Third edition. Yarmouth, ME: Intercultural Press.

Koning, Hans. 1995. "A French Mirror." *Atlantic Monthly*. December, 95–106.

Lallée-Hognon, Isabelle. 1995. "L'expatriation, une affaire de famille." *L'Expansion*, 4–17 septembre, 117–19.

Lamont, Michèle. *Money, Morals & Manners*. 1992. Chicago: University of Chicago Press.

Laporte, B. 1995. "Point de vue américain: Les charmes pervers de la solidarité." *Le Point*, 28 January, 47–48.

Lasch, Christopher. 1979. *The Culture of Narcissism: American Life in an Age of Diminishing Expectations*. New York: Warner Books.

Lewis, Tom J., and Robert E. Jungman, eds. 1986. *On Being Foreign: Culture Shock in Short Fiction*. Yarmouth, ME: Intercultural Press.

Lilla, Mark, ed. 1994. *New French Thought*. Princeton, NJ: Princeton University Press.

Lindenfield, Jacqueline. 2000. *The French in the United States: An Ethnographic Study*. Westport, CT: Bergin & Garvvey.

Luce, Louise F. 1991. *The French-Speaking World: An Anthology of Cross-Cultural Perspectves*. Lincolnwood, IL: NTC.

Mermet, Gérard. 2009. *Francoscopie, 2010*. Paris: Larousse.

Midda, Sara. 2008. *Sara Midda's South of France: A Sketchbook*. New York: Workman Publishing.

Miller, Stuart. 1996. *Understanding Europeans*. Second Edition. Avalon Travel Pub.

Mooney, C. 1997. "Food for Thought: In France, Cafés Return Philosophy to Its Popular Roots." *The Chronicle of Higher Education*, 14 March, B2.

Nadeau, Jean-Benoît. 2004. *Les Français ont aussi un accent*. Paris: Editions Payot & Rivages.

Nadeau, Jean-Benoît, and Julie Barlow. 2003. *Sixty Million Frenchmen Can't Be Wrong: Why We Love France but Not the French*. Naperville, IL: Sourcebooks.

Nevers, Guy. 1992. *Les Français vus par les Français*. Paris: Bernard Barrault & Eugenie.

O'Hara-Deveraux, Mary, and Robert Johanson. 1994. *Globalwork: Bridging Distance, Culture and Time*. San Francisco: Jossey-Bass.

Ollivier, Debra. 2009. *What French Women Know: About Love, Sex, and Other Matters of the Heart and Mind*. New York: G.P. Putnam's Sons.

Pascoe, Robin. 1993. *Culture Shock! Successful Living Abroad: A Wife's Guide*. Portland, OR: Graphic Arts Center Publishing Company.

Pérec, Georges, and Robert Bober. 1994. *Récits d'Ellis Island: Histoires d'errance et d'espoir*. INA—Institut National de l'Audiovisuel.

Peyrefitte, Roger. 1968. *Les Américains*. Paris: Flammarion.

Platt, Polly. 2003. *French or Foe?* Third Edition. London: Culture Crossings.

Robinson, Danielle. 2005. Customs & Etiquette Of France (Simple Guides Customs and Etiquette). Bravo Ltd.

Schifres, Alain. 1993. *Les Hexagons*. Paris: Editions Robert Laffont.

Stanger, Ted. 2003. *Sacrés Français! Un Américain nous regarde*. Paris: Michalon.

———. 2004. *Sacrés Américains! Nous les Yankees, on est comme ça*. Paris: Michalon.

———. 2005. *Sacrés Français, le roman!* Paris: Michalon.

Steele, Ross. 2004. *The French Way*: Aspects of Behaviors, Attitudes and Customs of the French. McGraw-Hill.

Stehli, J. S. 1994. "L'Amérique et le sexe." *Le Point*, 12 octobre, 22–23.

———. 1992. "Les Américains." *Le Point*, 31 octobre.

Storti, Craig. 2007. *The Art of Crossing Cultures*. Boston, MA: Intercultural Press.

Taylor, Sally Adamson. 2008. *Culture Shock! France*. Third Edition. Marshall Cavendish Corporation

Timoney, Charles. 2007. *Pardon My French: Unleash Your Inner Gaul*. Harmondsworth, UK: Penguin Books.

Todorov, Tzvetan. 1992. *Nous et les Autres. La réflexion française sur la diversité humaine*. Paris: Editions du Seuil.

Varro, Gabrielle. 1988. *The Transplanted Woman: A Study of French-American Marriages in France*. New York: Praeger.

Vigarello, Georges. 1987. *Le Propre et le Sale: L'hygiène du corps depuis le Moyen Age*. Paris: Editions du Seuil.

Wanning, Esther. 2008. *Culture Shock! U.S.A.* Second Edition. Marshall Cavendish Corporation.

Weber, Eugen. 1992. *My France: Politics, Culture, Myth.* Cambridge, MA: The Belknap Press of Harvard University Press.

Wilson, Margaret D. 1969. *The Essential Descartes.* New York: Mentor.

Winter, Jane. 1995. Culture Shock! U.S.A.—The South. Graphic Arts Center Publishing Company.

Wylie, Laurence. 1977. *Beaux Gestes: A Guide to French Body Talk.* Cambridge, MA: The Undergraduate Press.

Zeldin, Theodore. 1997. *The French.* The Harvill Press.

INDEX